RESEARCH IN GLACIAL, GLACIO-FLUVIAL, AND GLACIO-LACUSTRINE SYSTEMS

Proceedings of the

6th Guelph Symposium on Geomorphology, 1980

Edited by

R. DAVIDSON-ARNOTT

W. NICKLING

B. D. FAHEY

GEO BOOKS NORWICH 1982

in association with

GEOMORPHOLOGY SYMPOSIUM

University of Guelph

PREVIOUS BOOKS IN THIS SERIES

No 1.   Research Methods in Geomorphology,
         1969 *Out of print*

No 2.   Research Methods in Peistocene
         Geomorphology, 1971
         0 902246 17 8

No 3.   Research in Polar and Alpine
         Geomorphology, 1973
         0 902246 22 4

No 4.   Mass Wasting, 1976
         0 902246 58 5

No 5.   Research in Fluvial Systems, 1978
         0 86094 013 6

Information about the Guelph series of Symposia
in Geomorphology may be obtained from

'Geomorphology Symposium'
Department of Geography
University of Guelph
GUELPH, Ontario, Canada

Copies of these volumes may be obtained from
the sole publishers:

Geo Books (Geo Abstracts Ltd)
Regency House
34 Duke Street
Norwich NR3 3AP
England

Contents

Foreword   iii

Part 1   Glacial erosion and deposition

✗1   Subglacial processes and the development of   1
      glacial bedforms
      G.S. BOULTON

2   A till hummock (proto-drumlin) at the ice   33
      glacier bed interface
      J. MENZIES

3   The formation of glacial flutings in east-central   49
      Alberta
      NORMAN JONES

4   Contemporary push moraine formation in the Yoho   71
      Valley, BC
      R.J. ROGERSON & M.J. BATTERSON

Part 2   Glacio-fluvial sedimentation and processes

5   Subglacial fluvial erosion: a major source of   93
      stratified drift, Malaspina Glacier, Alaska
      THOMAS C. GUSTAVSON & JON C. BOOTHROYD

6   Depositional processes in the development of   117
      eskers in Manitoba
      SUSAN RINGROSE

7   Bed form diagrams and the interpretation of   139
      eskers
      HOUSTON C. SAUNDERSON

8   The hydraulic geometry of the lower portion of   151
      the Sunwapta River valley train, Jasper National
      Park, Alberta
      RANDY J. RICE

9   Derivation of a summary facies sequence based   175
      on Markov chain analysis of the Caledon outwash:
      a Pleistocene braided glacial fluvial deposit
      J.Z. FRASER

Part 3 Glacio-Lacustrine and marine sedimentation

10 Comparison of sedimentation regimes in four   203
    glacier-fed lakes of western Alberta
    NORMAN D. SMITH, MARK A. VENOL
    & STEPHEN K. KENNEDY

11 Site location and instrumentation aspects of a   239
    study of sedimentation processes in a proglacial
    lake in southeastern British Columbia, Canada
    FRANK H. WEIRICH

12 Glacio-Lacustrine sedimentation on low slope   261
    prograding delta
    D.A. LECKIE & S.B. McCANN

13 Coarse grained facies of glacio-marine deposits 279
    near Ottowa, Canada
    RICHARD J. CHEEL & BRIAN R. RUST

14 Nearshore deposits of the Champlain Sea, near   293
    Ottawa, Canada
    M. HAYWARD & H.M. FRENCH

Appendix   317

Foreword

In 1969 the Department of Geography at the University of Guelph hosted the first in a series of symposia in geomorphology designed to promote the dissemination of information on a selected topic through the presentation of papers, and through informal discussion. We are happy to announce the publication of the sixth symposium in the series, held at Guelph in May 1980, and hope that it will generate as much discussion and interest as its predecessors.

The basic theme for the sixth symposium was that of research in glacial, glacio-fluvial, and glacio-lacustrine/ marine systems. It was kept purposefully broad in order to provide an opportunity for earth scientists from backgrounds incorporating both geography and geology to discuss their common research goals. A total of sixteen papers were delivered during the two-day event, although only fourteen appear in the proceedings. The remainder were not presented by the authors for publication, but abstracts are provided in the Appendix.

The symposium was divided into three sessions, and these form the basis for the organization of the Proceedings. Part I deals with the topic of glacial erosion and deposition. The opening paper by Geoffrey Boulton from the University of East Anglia sets the theme for the three subsequent papers in this section by discussing erosion and deposition at the glacier bed from theoretical considerations coupled with field observations. The early stages in the formation of drumlins is investigated by John Menzies (Brock University), and Norman Jones (University of Alberta) discusses the origin and morphology of streamlined drumlins and flutings in east-central Alberta. R.J. Rogerson and M. Batterson (Memorial University of Newfoundland) close this section with their paper on end moraine formation in the Yoho Valley, British Columbia.

Part II on glacio-fluvial sedimentation and processes opens with a contribution on esker deposition and development in Manitoba by Susan Ringrose (Department of Energy and Mines, Manitoba). The general topic of esker formation is continued in Houston Saunderson's (Wilfred Laurier University) paper on the hydraulic interpretation of eskers in which he discusses the results of flume experiments. Randy Rice (Amoco Canada Petroleum Ltd., Alberta) investigates the hydraulic geometry of the Sunwapta River valley train, Jasper National Park, Alberta, and the section ends with John Fraser's (Ontario Geological Survey) study of the Caledon outwash in southern Ontario, using Markov chain analysis.

The last section in the proceedings focusses on the two related topics of glacio-lacustrine and glacio-marine sedimentation. Norman Smith (University of Illinois, Chicago Circle) sets the scene by reviewing recent work in the glacio-lacustrine sedimentation field, and Frank Weirich (University of Toronto) describes the sedimentation process in a pro-

glacial lake in the Canadian Rockies, with particular
emphasis being given to the instrumentation. Dale Leckie
and Brian McCann (McMaster University) discuss the development of a model of glacio-lacustrine sedimentation in a
recessional valley glacier environment in southern Newfoundland; the sources of glacio-lacustrine and glacio-fluvial
sedimentation associated with the Malaspina Glacier in
Alaska is the topic of Thomas Gustavson's (University of
Texas, Austin) and Jon Boothroyd's (University of Rhode
Island) paper. The proceedings conclude with two related
papers, one by Richard Cheel and Brian Rust on coarse grained
facies of glacio-marine deposits near Ottawa, and the other
by M. Hayward and Hugh French on nearshore deposits of the
Champlain Sea in the same area.

Many people contributed to the success of the symposium
and the preparation of the proceedings. In particular we
would like to thank Carol Bromley of the School of Part Time
Studies and Continuing Education for her assistance on the
logistics side, and Dr. Howard Clark, Vice-President
(Academic) for officially welcoming the participants to the
University.

Barry D. Fahey
Robin Davidson-Arnott
Bill Nickling
Symposium Organizers

PART 1

GLACIAL EROSION
AND
DEPOSITION

1 Subglacial processes and the development of glacial bedforms

G.S. Boulton

ABSTRACT

Studies beneath modern glaciers reveal three sets of glacial
(sensu stricto) depositional processes:
*   a) Falling of debris or debris-rich ice from the glacier*
       onto the floors of subglacial cavities.
*   b) Lodgement of debris in traction over the bed.*
*   c) Deformation of subglacial sediments.*

All three processes have the capacity to develop stream-
lined subglacial landforms. Process a) may fill subglacial
cavities on the lee of bedrock crags to produce streamlined
'tails'. Process b) may produce streamlined drumlin forms
as a result of differential lodgement as a glacier flows over
obstacles on its bed. Process c) may produce mobile drumlin
forms around relatively slowly deforming nuclei in an in-
homogeneous deforming sediment, or a static drumlin around
a stationary obstacle, or a static residual drumlin where
surrounding material has flowed away from a more resistant
mass.

Processes b) and c) in particular have a strong tendency
to produce forms with typical drumlin asymmetry, a steep
stoss side and a shallow lee side, whilst process a) may help
to produce rock-cored drumlins or crags and tails.

All processes may be combined, and the probability that
'drumlins' are polygenetic requires that internal structures,
in addition to surface forms, must be studied to understand
their origin.

Ice sheet models, one of an ancient ice sheet and one of
West Greenland, are utilised to understand how sediment and
landform production by ice sheets may vary spatially. It is
concluded that the precise location of most forms is deter-
mined by the properties of the glacier bed, but that glacier
variables play an important role in determining their larger
scale distribution. Glacier properties are almost invariably
conducive to production of these streamlined landforms in the
marginal area, although under appropriate bed conditions they
may be produced deep beneath the glacier. These conclusions
have considerable implications for the reconstruction of
Pleistocene ice sheet conditions.

*G.S. Boulton, School of Environmental Sciences, University of East
   Anglia, Norwich, England.

1

INTRODUCTION

Of the earth's major sedimentary environments, the subglacial environment is the one in which it is most difficult to describe with confidence the processes which occur there. Because of its unique inaccessibility to direct or remote study it has been necessary to support the few direct observations of subglacial processes by inferences drawn from the nature of ancient landforms and sediments to an extent unknown in other fields. However, although the study of ancient features tells us what a process theory must explain, it has not been able to tell us what the fundamental processes are. Since the time of Forbes and Chamberlin the few opportunities of penetrating just a little way beneath a glacier have yielded invaluable observations about subglacial environments which have enabled such geomorphologists as Matthes and Demorest to give a plausible structure to their explanations of erosional landforms.

The last two decades have allowed an even deeper penetration into the subglacial environment, often under controlled conditions which have facilitated experimentation. Nonetheless despite several deep boreholes through ice sheets and ice caps, which sadly have yielded little useful information to the glacial geologist, this deeper explanation still only penetrates a few tens, or at most a few hundreds of metres below the surface.

To what extent are conclusions about subglacial processes drawn from such relatively shallow depths applicable to subglacial sites which are thousands of metres below an ice sheet surface? The only major difference between the two situations which could be of significance in influencing sedimentary processes is that of mean hydrostatic pressure. However in no theory of subglacial processes is this parameter alone considered to be important. Effective stresses, shear stresses, and stress deviators are important in subglacial theories, but none are simply proportional to hydrostatic pressure. Maximum values of these parameters are attained under relatively small ice thicknesses, and indeed, where cavities develop, even beneath ice thicknesses of a few metres, stress concentrations are produced which give equivalent values and which can thus be examined by well-designed field experiments.

Rigsby's (1958) important experiments demonstrated that the rheological properties of ice were unaffected by changing hydrostatic pressures. Nye's (1952) calculation of the ice thickness necessary to generate a sufficiently high deviatoric stress in the side of a crevasse to cause significant plastic flow and to produce crevasse closure, has often been misunderstood as demonstrating that ice becomes 'more plastic' below a certain depth. This is quite wrong. If the deviatoric stresses are sufficiently high, we expect crystallographically similar ice to deform similarly, no matter what its depth, under similar temperatures.

Another criticism of subglacial observations is that the manner of observation disturbs the sub-glacial environment so as to make the observations unrepresentative. However this is a problem common to many non-trivial field experiments in earth science, which must be overcome by judicious experimental design.

A more severe criticism in my view is that there are a relatively small number of subglacial observations, biased naturally towards glaciers flowing over rock beds where access to natural cavities can be gained. However we now have at least ten detailed series of observations of subglacial sites. There are many common features to these observations and surprises are becoming fewer, suggesting that the principal outlines of subglacial processes can be defined.

I believe that the proper actualistic approach to the explanation of glacial sediments and landforms is to generate theories on the basis of these observations, theories which may be refined or invalidated by the extent to which they are able to anticipate further subglacial observations, or account for the products of subglacial processes.

There are now well-developed theories based on such observational data which attempt to assess quantitatively the conditions under which erosion of lithified bedrock or deposition of till upon it will occur, the rate at which erosion will occur, and the forms that will develop under different glacial conditions as bedrock hummocks are progressively eroded. In this article I wish to investigate the ways in which streamlined subglacial landforms might develop as a result of sedimentational processes which are currently known to occur. Thus I shall not refer to theories of sediment and landform genesis based on inferences from ancient, particularly Pleistocene, evidence.

THE KNOWN PROCESSES OF SUBGLACIAL DEPOSITION

Three major processes of subglacial deposition are currently known to occur in which water is not the dominant agent of deposition. These are:-
  i) Falling of debris from the glacier sole onto the floors of subglacial cavities.
  ii) Lodgement proper, where the tractive force imposed by the moving glacier is inadequate to maintain in motion debris or debris-rich ice against the frictional resistance offered by the glacier bed.
  iii) Deformation of subglacial sediment beneath the glacier, which may accumulate locally because of some change in subglacial conditions.

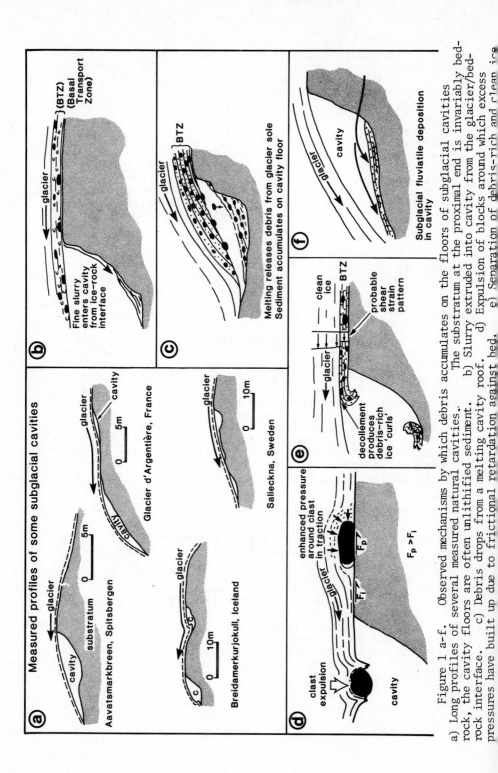

Figure 1 a-f. Observed mechanisms by which debris accumulates on the floors of subglacial cavities
a) Long profiles of several measured natural cavities.. The substratum at the proximal end is invariably bedrock, the cavity floors are often unlithified sediment.   b) Slurry extruded into cavity from the glacier/bed-
rock interface.   c) Debris drops from a melting cavity roof.   d) Expulsion of blocks around which excess
pressures have built up due to frictional retardation against bed.   e) Separation of debris-rich and clean ice

4

i) Falling of debris or debris-rich ice from the glacier sole into underlying cavities

Subglacial cavities are known to occur where glaciers flow over irregular bedrock surfaces. If the sliding velocity of a glacier is high, its thickness small, and the aspect ratio (a/λ, where a is amplitude of bedrock -umps and λ is the length parallel to glacier flow) is high, large cavities in the lee of these -umps may result (Figure 1). For instance, Vivian (1976) describes cavities up to 20 m in length in the lee of obstacles of λ = 50 m, a = 10 m, and where ice sliding velocity is 1-3 cm/hour, and ice thickness is 100 m.

In both temperate and cold-based glaciers it is normal to find glacially-eroded rock debris in the basal transport zone. In temperate glaciers there is net melting at the glacier sole and temperatures in cavities have been measured which are high enough to allow strong melting in the basal ice forming the cavity roof (Vivian, 1976). Melted-out debris may thus simply fall directly from the glacier sole onto thefloor of a cavity (Figure 1c). If melted-out debris exists beneath the glacier sole where there is no cavity, and this debris is maintained in motion by the drag force transmitted from the overlying ice, debris may be introduced into a cavity from its up-glacier extremity (e.g. Boulton, 1970; and Figure 1b).

The force transmitted to the basal ice by a clast in traction retarded relative to the ice by the fact that rock/rock friction is greater than rock/ice friction (Figure 1d), leads to locally enhanced hydrostatic pressures on the up-glacier side of the clast. When such a clast moves above a cavity there is a net force on the clast tending to extrude it into the cavity (Peterson, 1970; Vivian, 1976). I see no reason why this mechanism, unlike the first, should not also occur in the cavities which occur beneath cold-based glaciers, although it has not been described from them.

The process of production of 'till curls' (Peterson, 1970) whereby basal debris-rich ice peals away from over-lying ice at the point of decollement in cavities, and frequently falls as debris-rich masses onto cavity floors, may also be explained by a similar pressure release mechanism (Figure 1e).

Thus there are several processes whereby sediment derived directly from the glacier sole may accumulate on the floors of subglacial cavities, and, of course, subglacial fluvial activity commonly deposits sediment in such places (Figure 1f).

ii) Lodgement

Clasts transported in the basal transport zone of a glacier frequently come into contact with the glacier bed (the so-called sub-zone of traction, Boulton, 1975). The frictional coefficient between these clasts and the bed is greater than

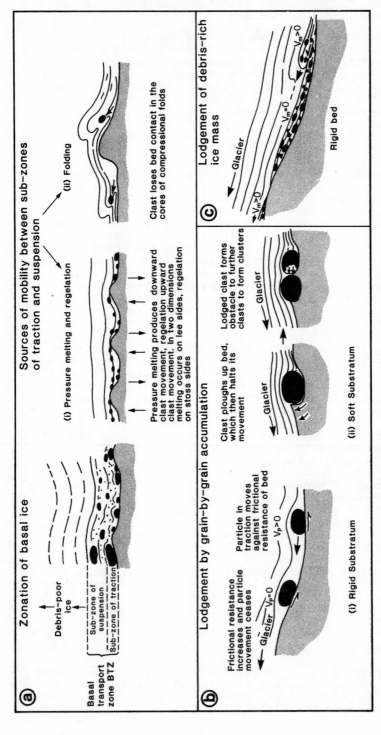

Figure 2 a-c. The lodgement process

a) Distinctions between debris in traction over the bed and debris in suspension above it in the basal transport zone. This zone is characterised because of the ease of transition between traction and suspension by the mechanisms of pressure melting/regelation and flow folding.
b) Grain by grain lodgement on rigid and soft substrata.   c) Lodgement of debris-rich masses.

that between ice and the bed, and thus the clasts are retarded relative to the surrounding basal ice (Boulton et al., 1979). These clasts in traction over the glacier bed abrade and erode it. It has been suggested that deposition by *lodgement* occurs when the frictional drag exerted by the bed on these clasts is sufficient to inhibit further movement of the clasts (Boulton, 1975) and experimental evidence has been adduced to suggest that this is so.

Debris-rich masses of basal ice have also been observed to have come to rest beneath a sharp decollement below relatively clean overlying ice (Boulton, 1970; 1975).

These processes (Figure 2) appear to correspond well with Chamberlin's (1895) concept of lodgement.

It has also been suggested (Boulton, 1975) that lodgement will occur when the following critical conditions are satisfied:-

$$\left[B\ell(\mu NS)^n + \frac{\mu NSCK}{L} \right] \frac{1}{V_i} > 1 \tag{1}$$

where B and n are constants in Glen's flow law for ice, μ is a clast/bed coefficient of friction, N is the effective normal pressure at the glacier/bed interface, S is a clast-shape factor, ℓ the clast diameter, V_i the basal ice velocity, C gives the pressure dependence of the freezing point for ice, K is the thermal conductivity of clasts and L is the latent heat of ice. Provided that these conditions are satisfied, and with constant values of μ, S and ℓ, and assuming a constant rate of supply of debris, the rate of lodgement L_R should be:-

$$L_R \propto \left(\frac{aN^n + bN}{V_i} \right) \tag{2}$$

where a and b are constants.

iii) Deformation of subglacial sediments

The possibility of widespread shear deformation of subglacial sediments has long been inferred from the evidence of Pleistocene glacial sediments (e.g. Slater, 1926; MacClintock and Dreimanis, 1964). Frontal pushing by glaciers is a well-known phenomenon (e.g. Gripp, 1929) and localised, relatively small scale deformation is well-known in the formation of flutes (Hoppe and Schytt, 1953; Paul and Evans, 1974; Boulton, 1976). Direct evidence has recently been presented of a mechanism of shear deformation of subglacial sediments (Boulton, 1979) which thus complements the evidence from Pleistocene sediments. It has been further argued from a consideration of the controls on this deformation process, that this is likely to be an important and widespread process where glaciers rest on extensive areas of unlithified sediments, and may thus have been of great potential importance for the large Pleistocene ice sheets of Europe and North America (Boulton and Jones, 1979). It seems reasonable to suppose that the rate of deformation of subglacial sediments D* will be given by:-

$$D^* = f\left(\frac{a}{C'}, \frac{b}{N\phi}, cV_i \right) \tag{3}$$

where C' is the sediment cohesion, ϕ its angle of internal friction, and a, b and c are constants. It is extremely unlikely that the discharge of deforming subglacial sediments along a line of glacier flow can be maintained constant for any great distance because of changes in mineralogy and granulometry of sediments (effecting ϕ and C'), and changes in effective pressure (N) and ice velocity. In a two-dimensional case, such changes will lead to zones of extension where the sediment becomes weaker or V_i larger and zones of compression where the sediment becomes stronger or V_i smaller. The zones of extension will be zones of net erosion, and the zones of compression, zones of net deposition (Figure 3). Thus, this process will lead to differential deposition rates on the glacier bed. Longitudinal extensional or compressive strains in subglacial sediment are more likely to result from variations in sediment strength than longitudinal strains in the overlying glacier as the former show much greater magnitudes of change than the latter.

DEVELOPMENT OF STREAMLINED LANDFORMS

In the previous section we have seen how the three principal known processes of subglacial deposition lead to differential rates of accumulation. In this section we discuss how these may lead, in each case, to the development of streamlined landforms.

A) Streamlined landforms from subglacial cavities

It is well known that cavities which develop in the lee of bedrock hummocks have streamlined forms (Theakstone, 1967; 1979; Boulton, 1979; Vivian, 1976). If such cavities fill up with sediment falling from the glacier sole above the cavity, a streamlined 'tail' will develop behind a bedrock 'crag'.

Figure 4 shows a cavity near the margin of the glacier Salieckna in north western Sweden. The cavity has developed on the lee-side of a bedrock hummock. The floor of the cavity is made up of a ridge of sediment which in general reflects the three-dimensional form of the cavity, and is largely composed of till, although washed material is present on the flanks of this ridge. At the down-glacier point of cavity closure the glacier sole and the till are in close contact. Smoothing and grooving of the till surface were apparent in places, especially on the lateral flanks of the till mass, suggesting that the glacier, at some time, had been in contact with the till mass at these points (Figure 4). Over much of the upper surface of the till mass its loose and unconsolidated nature strongly suggest that much of this material had fallen from the glacier sole.

In several places the till surface was frozen, and in one place a frozen mass of till had adhered to the glacier sole, and seemed to have been 'plucked' away from the till mass by the moving glacier sole. This cavity was very close to the glacier margin, and certainly within range of seasonal

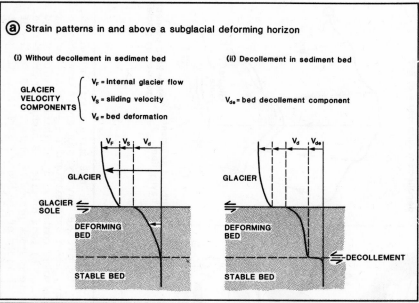

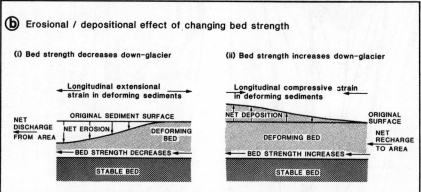

Figure 3a-b.   Patterns of subglacial bed deformation
a) Patterns of strain in basal ice and deforming bed when i) there is
   no major decollement surface in the bed, and ii) when such a
   decollement exists.
b) The erosional/depositional effects of changing the strength and
   therefore the rate of deformation of a subglacial deforming bed.
   The longitudinal strain in the bed is unlikely to be influenced by
   the very small longitudinal strain rates in the ice if the bed
   strength varies.   The scale of this process could be small (a few
   metres) or large (tens of kilometres).

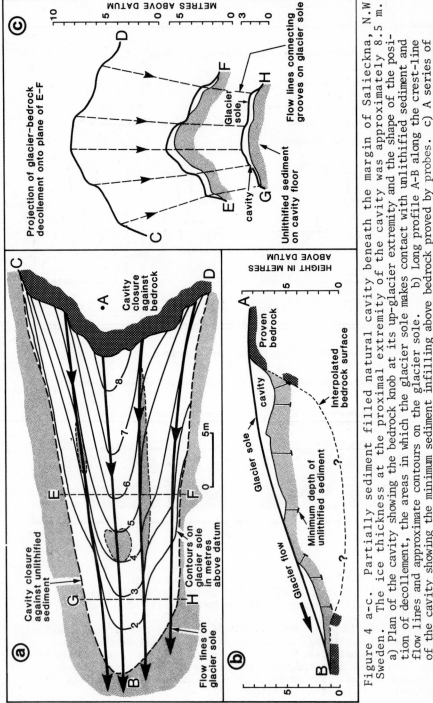

Figure 4 a-c. Partially sediment filled natural cavity beneath the margin of Salieckna, N.W. Sweden. The ice thickness at the proximal extremity of the cavity was approximately 8.5 m. a) Plan of the cavity showing the bedrock knob at its up-glacier extremity and the shape of the position of decollement, the areas in which the glacier sole makes contact with unlithified sediment and flow lines and approximate contours on the glacier sole. b) Long profile A-B along the crest-line of the cavity showing the minimum sediment infilling above bedrock proved by probes. c) A series of cross-profiles across the cavity. Profile C-D reflects the form of the bedrock surface at the point of decollement. Subsequent deformation of the glacier sole during flow is represented by E-F and G-H.

Figure 5. Smoothed and striated bedrock hummock beyond the retreating
margin of Salieckna in N.W. Sweden, with a till mass forming a
streamlined accumulation on its lee side. Ice movement was from
right to left. The hummock stands about 8 m above its surroundings.
Surrounding surfaces are almost entirely of bedrock. In this immediate area, substantial masses of till only occur where they have
been deposited in lee-side cavities. Elsewhere the bedrock surfaces
have been swept clear of till.

temperature fluctuations which might produce alternate
freezing and thawing of the till mass, and variable meltwater
activity. However, even cavities well beyond the range of
seasonal temperature fluctuations may suffer other seasonal
effects. Some glaciers show seasonal velocity changes and
in valley glaciers, subglacial water flow is certainly
seasonal. In such glaciers summer might be represented by
high ice velocities, thus enlarging the cavity and giving
more space for till falling from the glacier sole to accumulate. Meltwater activity will also be enhanced. In winter
ice velocities will tend to decrease, thus diminishing cavity
sizes. Till or fluviatile sediments deposited in an enlarged
summer cavity will be compressed into a smaller volume, producing consolidation and potentially complex small scale
glaciotectonic structures. Some of the attributes of so-
called 'lee-side till' (Hillefors, 1973) may be acquired.

The results of this process may be clearly seen beyond
the margin of Salieckna. Here, there are many areas where
bedrock surfaces have been generally smoothed and striated
by the glacier and swept clear of any subglacially deposited
till. However, many well-defined *roches moutonnées* have
considerable till 'tails' (Figure 5). These are streamlined forms, tapering in a down-glacial direction, whose

11

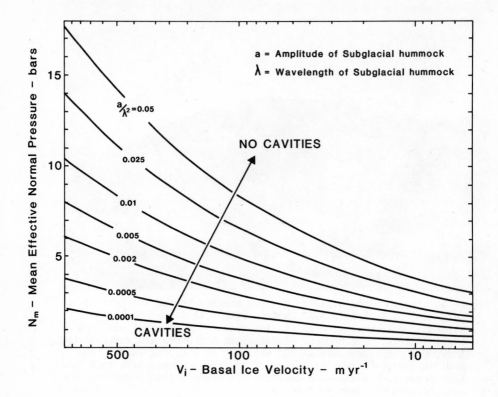

Figure 6. The conditions of effective normal pressure (ice pressure
   minus subglacial water pressure) and basal ice velocity under
   which subglacial lee-side cavities will tend to develop for
   different values of a/λ^2. For a given shape (a/λ) smaller hummocks are more likely to generate cavities. For a given size (λ),
   steeper hummocks are more likely to develop cavities.

transverse surface profiles reflect the transverse profile
of the rock masses in whose lee they stand. This together
with the similarity of the till to that found in subglacial
cavities, strongly suggests that the 'tails' have formed in
subglacial cavities.

   Mathematical analysis of the form of three dimensional
cavities is currently an intractable problem. However, it
is possible to assess the conditions under which they might
develop by analogy with two-dimensional surfaces of low
slope. We expect ice flowing over a two-dimensional hump
to produce a normal pressure fluctuation (ΔP), giving an
enhanced normal pressure on the up-glacier side and a reduced
normal pressure on the downglacier side. Lliboutry (1968)
estimates the magnitude of this fluctuation to be:-

$$\Delta P = (36\pi V_i \ a/\lambda^2)^{1/3} \qquad\qquad (4)$$

where a is the amplitude and λ the wavelength of bedrock
hummocks.

Cavities will open on the lee side of subglacial hummocks when:-

$$\Delta P > N_m \tag{5}$$

where N_m is the mean effective normal pressure on horizontal surfaces in the region of the hummock. Figure 6 shows the conditions of mean effective normal pressure and basal ice velocity which will allow cavities to develop in the lee of two-dimensional bedrock hummocks of given shape. The development of cavities and drift 'tails' deposited in them in the lee of bedrock 'crags' is clearly favoured by high basal ice velocities, low mean effective normal pressures and high values of aspect ration (a/λ).

It should be stressed that the effective normal pressure at the base of a glacier is only given by the ice pressure in cold glaciers where no water phase exists at the glacier/bed interface. Where a water phase does exist the mean effective normal pressure will be $\rho_i gh - p_w$ (where ρ_i is the density of ice, g the gravitational acceleration, h the glacier thickness and p_w the water pressure). Assessment of the water pressure where a glacier flows over a bedrock surface is extremely difficult (see Weertman, 1972).

B) Production of streamlined forms by lodgement

We expect the location and rate of lodgement to be dependent primarily upon ice velocity and effective pressure at the glacier/bed interface (equations 1 and 2). Over small areas of the bed, where the glacier is thick, we expect variations of ice velocity to be small. However, if there are obstacles to glacier flow on the bed, we expect large variations in normal pressure (equation 4).

Using equation (1) to establish if lodgement will occur, equation (2) for the non-dimensional lodgement rate and equation (4) for the distribution of normal presssure over a two-dimensional obstacle, it is possible to calculate the resultant distribution of lodgement till, and by assuming an arbitrary rate at one point to calculate the rate at which it will accumulate over the whole surface. Because of differential lodgement, the form of the surface will change progressively, so that we must use a Fourier expansion of equation 4, the terms of which must be changed at each computation step. Figure 7 shows the results of such calculations for different values of ice velocity and constant mean normal pressure. If ice velocities are small or effective pressures large, lodgement takes place over the whole surface with small differences between maximum and minimum lodgement rates, and the crest line of the nucleated depositional landform migrates up-glacier at a high angle. If ice velocities are large or effective pressures small, lodgement may not occur against the down-glacier side of the hummock, producing large differences in lodgement rate, and causing the crest line of the form to migrate up-glacier at a relatively low angle. Thus, the forms of original hummocks are changed by lodgement around them. I expect the depositional hummock to be streamlined, notwithstanding any irregularity in the nucleating obstacle.

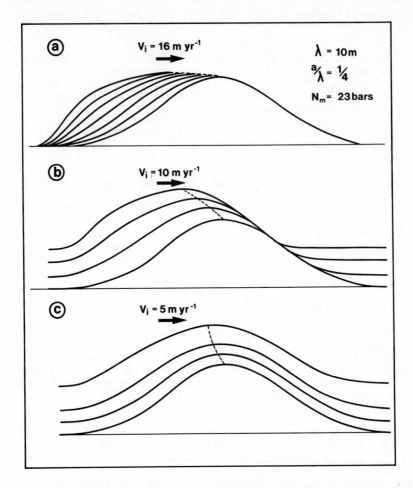

Figure 7 a-c.   Theoretical incremental patterns of lodgement around
an original obstacle of a/λ = $\frac{1}{4}$ (a = amplitude, λ = wavelength)
and λ = 10 m for constant mean effective pressure (N_m) and varying
ice velocities. The dashed line shows the way in which the crest
line migrates up-glacier more markedly with higher ice velocities
and the form becomes more asymmetric. A similar effect would be
produced by a decreasing mean effective normal pressure. Note the
similarity to an anti-dune in a water flow.

C) Production of streamlined landforms by subglacial sediment
deformation
    i) *Mobile bedforms*

Where homogeneous subglacial sediments deform above a smooth
plane of decollement the thickness of the deforming layer
can be expected to remain locally constant, and flow lines
within the sediment to parallel those in the basal ice.   In
this case effective pressures at the glacier/bed interface
and basal ice velocities can be expected to remain locally
constant.

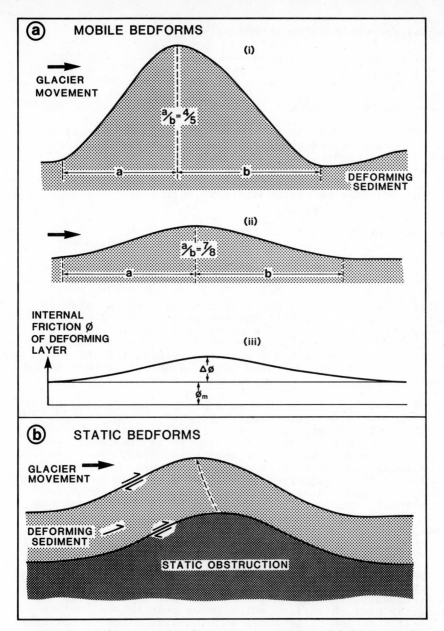

Figure 8 a-b. Bedforms produced by net accumulation of deforming sediment.
a) Mobile bedforms developing around a more slowly deforming mass
whose symmetrical variation in internal frictional resistance ($\Delta\phi$)
is shown in (iii). The resulant bedforms in (i) and (ii) are asymmetric, with a steeper stoss slope. The different shapes are produced by varying the dependence of accumulation rate on $\phi(N_m \pm \Delta P)$.
b) A static bedform produced by an irregularity on the decollement
surface over which the deforming bed is moving. The crest of the
static bedform occurs up-glacier of the crest of the underlying
obstacle (crest displacement shown by dashed line). The resultant form is also asymmetric with a steeper stoss slope.

Glacial erosion and deposition

If however an inhomogeneous subglacial sediment begins
to deform, we may expect the rate of deformation to vary in
accord with sediment strength (Figure 3), and the form of
the decollement beneath the deforming mass to be partially
controlled by inhomogeneities within the sediment.

Let us consider the simple two-dimensional case of a
mass of cohesionless-subglacial sediment deforming over a
smooth decollement plane. The angle of friction of the
sediments (ϕ) is constant, apart from in a zone where it
varies as shown in Figure 8a(iii). Let us suppose that the
rate of deformation of the sediment varies as:-

$$D* = K(\frac{1}{N\tan\phi})^n \qquad\qquad (5)$$

where K and n are constants
If we assume a steady state, the sediment discharge (Q_S)
due to deformation is:-

$$Q = D*t = \text{constant} \qquad\qquad (6)$$

where t is the thickness of the deforming sediment.

If we assume n = 1, and that N = constant, we predict
that the sediment bed will thicken in the zone of high ϕ.
However, this will produce a change in normal pressure at
the glacier bed interface given by equation (4). Thus we
recalculate values of t for changing values of N and ϕ.
The calculations are repeated until a stable distribution of
t values are achieved. The result is shown in Figure 8a.

This should not be taken as a precise description of
the form that a two-dimensional bed with a local inhomogeneity will take on, but as a qualitative estimate. It is
important in that the form of a drumlin is predicted, with
a steep stoss side and a more gentle lee side. The three-
dimensional problem is more complex, and will be dealt with
later, but it is suggested that local increases in the
strength of bed sediments will lead to streamlined three-
dimensional drumlin forms. The drumlin is not static, but
a mobile form, whose rate of movement is a product of the
strength of the constituent sediments.

ii) Static bedforms

If the plane of decollement over which sediment deforms is
irregular, the argument used above predicts the development
of stationary drumlin bed-forms. Take for instance, an
irregular bedrock surface which comes near to the surface so
as locally to penetrate above an otherwise planar decollement
(Figure 8b) beneath a homogeneous deforming sediment mass.
As an initial condition we expect the sediment surface to
reflect the form of the bedrock surface. This will produce
a normal pressure fluctuation over the bed undulation given
by equation (4). Using equations (5) and (6) we recalculate
t for changing values of N, and the calculations are repeated
until a stable bedform is achieved (Figure 8b). Thus we
produce an asymmetric bedform, which, if the disturbance
on the decollement plane is localised, I suggest will be a
three-dimensional drumlin form but fixed in position rather
than mobile.

iii) Residual bedforms

A third possible mode of production of drumlin forms by subglacial deformation can be envisaged. The strength variations
in subglacial sediments may be such that some parts of the
sediment deform whilst others do not. This may lead to the
isolation of relatively resistant sediment masses which may
thus form 'erosional drumlins' (c.f. Goldthwait, 1974). It
has been shown (Boulton, 1974; Morland & Boulton, 1975) that
the stresses generated within a subglacial hummock by ice
flow over its surface may be enough to cause failure within
the hummock. The steeper the sides of the hummock the
greater will be the internal stresses, and thus one would
expect that for a given ice velocity and mean effective
subglacial normal stress, that there would be a limit to
steepness of these sides for a hummock of specified size and
composition.

A series of analyses were undertaken of two-dimensional
forms with different aspect ratios (a/λ) and different
symmetries; one set being symmetrical sine curves, another
with an upglacier skewness and another with a down-glacier
skewness (Figure 9). The method follows that set out in
Morland and Boulton (1975). Values of ice velocity over the
bed and mean normal stresses are assumed. The distribution
of normal stress over the bedform is then computed using
Fourier transforms of equation (4). A conformal mapping of
the form is then produced using low order polynomials, a
time-consuming technique which is the principal barrier to
the more general use of this method. The magnitude and
direction of internal stresses is then determined analyti-
cally using a complex variable method and assuming isotropic
linear elastic behaviour on the part of the bed material.
This is probably not too severe a departure from reality for
most frictional sediments, but is unlikely to adequately
represent the behaviour of clay-rich sediments.

Figure 10a shows the distribution and magnitude of maximum shear stresses in one of the bed forms for the condition
in which $\Delta P = N_m$ on the steepest part of its downglacier
side. Figures 10b and d show the shear stresses along planes
of maximum shear in the surficial layers of sediment together
with the shear strength components along these planes for
distally and proximally-skewed humps respectively. In the
first case, the reduced normal pressure on the downglacier
side reduces sediment strength locally, whilst shear stresses
are locally enhanced. Failure on the downglacier side is
thus predicted, which would lead to progressive failure of
the whole slope and thereby a reduction in its angle
(Figure 10c). In the second case (Figure 10d), the lower
angle downglacier slope allows a higher effective normal
pressure which mobilises a higher frictional strength component. As shear stresses do not attain those values, no
failure occurs, and the hummock is stable.

The stability of the three basic shapes (B = symmetrical
form, C = up-glacier skewed, A = down-glacier skewed) was
computed for different values of a/λ, and under different

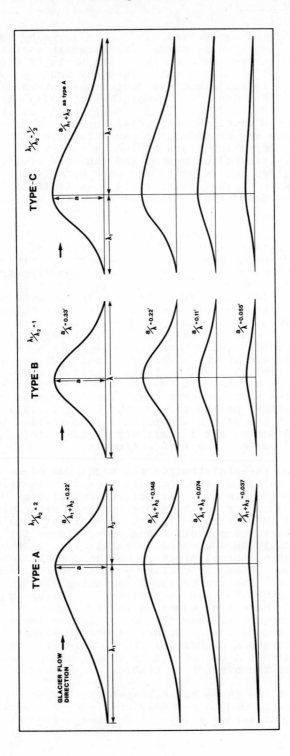

Figure 9. Shapes used to model the stability of different bedforms illustrated in figures 10 and 11. The three types A, B & C are used to illustrate the effects of different symmetries and aspect ratios.

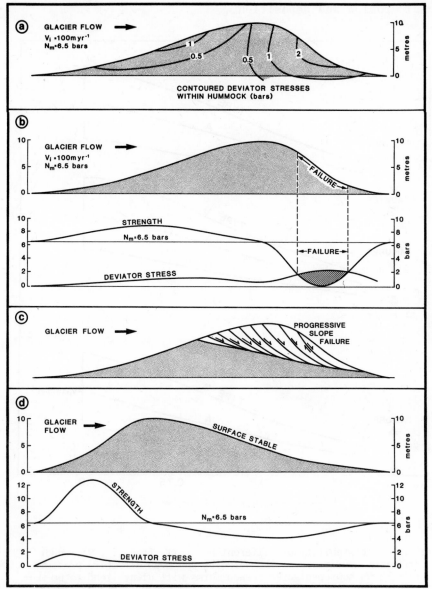

Figure 10 a-d.   The stability of bedforms of different shape and
the formation of 'erosional drumlins'.
a) The magnitude of stress deviators within a down-glacier
skewed sediment hummock under given conditions.
b) Stresses and sediment strength within the surface layer of
the sediment hummock. This stress/strength relationship indicates
failure on the down-glacier flank.
c) Schematic diagram showing how the situation in b) might
lead to progressive slope failure so reducing the lee slope
and changing the symmetry of the form.
d) An illustration of how an up-glacier skewed (drumlin-like) form
may be stable whilst a down-glacier skewed form of similar aspect
ratio (Fig. 10b) would be unstable under similar conditions.

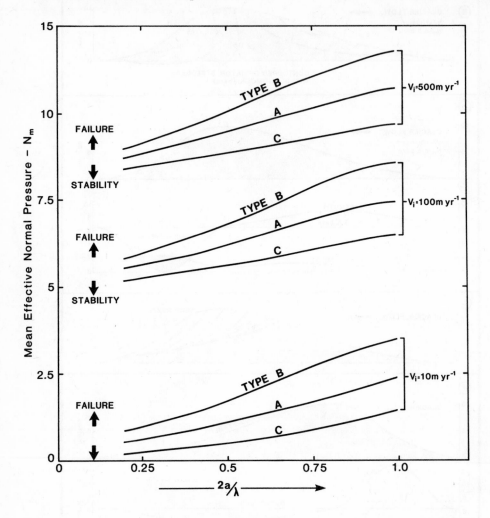

Figure 11.   The stability of different bed forms (see Fig. 9), under
             different conditions of ice velocity and mean effective pressure.
             This shows how up-glacier skewed forms will always tend to be more
             stable than symmetrical and down-glacier skewed forms of similar
             aspect ratio under similar conditions. Thus up-glacier skewed
             forms, the typical drumlin shape, will tend to predominate, other
             things being equal, although symmetrical and down-glacier skewed
             forms can be stable.

conditions of mean effective pressure (N_m) and basal ice
velocity (V_i) (Figure 11). Failure is more likely when a/λ
and V_i are large and when N_m is small. For any combination
of these three parameters, the most stable form, least prone
to progressive slope failure on its lee side, is shape C,
which shows up-glacier skewedness and which is most like the
typical drumlin in longitudinal form.

To summarise the conclusions:-

1) The results for symmetrical bedforms demonstrate that lee-sides are less stable than stoss-sides.

2) For a given aspect ratio, up-glacier skewed forms are the most stable, and down-glacier skewed forms the least stable.

3) Forms of large aspect ratio are less stable than forms of low aspect ratio.

4) The higher the ice velocity the lower the slope of the form on the threshold of stability.

5) The higher the mean local normal pressure, the greater will be the slope of the form on the threshold of stability.

Thus, for bedforms which develop as residuals after the removal of relatively easily deformable materials from around them, the most frequently developed form is likely to be one in which the stoss-side is steepest, though other forms are not ruled out.

The process of preferential failure of the lee-face of subglacial bedforms will also place a limit on the lee-face of the bedforms developed by the other mechanisms described in this article.

D) Interaction of different processes

The three processes discussed in this article all depend upon some irregularity on the glacier bed or inhomogeneity in the materials which compose it. Thus, it seems very likely that they could be frequently associated.

For instance, the lodgement process and the process of dumping into cavities may occur together around the same rock hummock, whilst post-depositional deformation may affect both. Thus, the simple modelling in this article in which all are considered separately may not be a good guide to the real world in which we expect complex interactions to take place. The modelling exercises merely represent attempts to demonstrate the plausibility of the thesis that these processes can produce streamlined landforms.

This exercise also suggests that all the processes considered here are capable of producing similar landforms, and that all have the potential to produce forms which would normally be described within the scope of the term 'drumlin' or 'rock drumlin'. These terms are generally used in a semi-descriptive semi-genetic sense to refer to streamlined drift hillocks, elongated in the direction of glacier movement and thought to originate subglacially. This study suggests the probability that they are polygenetic, that their morphology alone is not a reliable indicator of genesis but that their internal structure must also be considered.

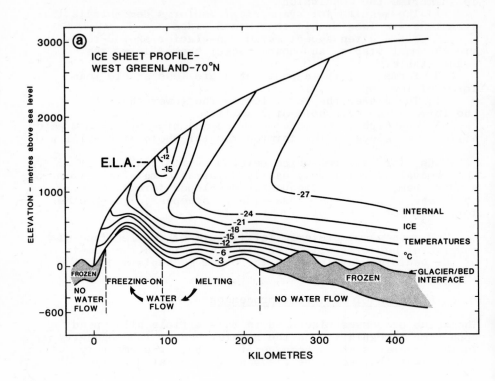

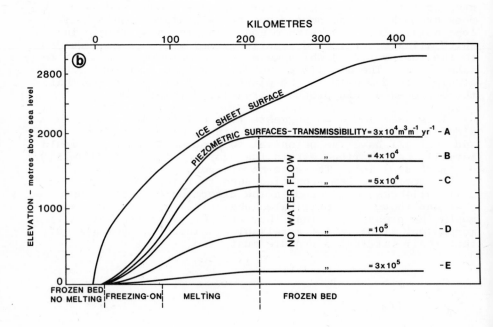

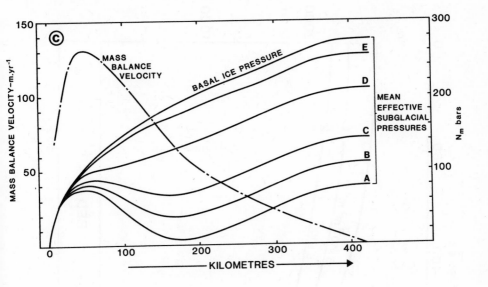

Figure 12 a-c (a + b opposite). Model of the West Greenland ice
  sheet at 70°N.
  a) Thermal regime and basal hydrological regimes.
  b) Piezometric surfaces for uniform subglacial beds (A-E) of given
  hydraulic transmissibility. The gradient is zero in areas of no
  water flow where there is neither subglacial water production nor
  recharge from other zones; it increases in the zone of melting,
  and decreases in the zone of freezing-on. The glacier bed has been
  flattened.
  c) Mean effective subglacial pressures for beds (A-E) of different
  transmissibility, and mass balance velocities.

LARGE SCALE PATTERNS

It has been argued that there are large scale spatial patterns
in glacial landforms which reflect spatial changes in processes beneath ice sheets (e.g. Vernon, 1966; Sugden, 1977;
Clayton and Moran, 1974). We should thus enquire whether
the processes discussed here are controlled by variables
which change systematically beneath the area of an ice sheet
or glacier.

All three processes are controlled both by the properties of the bed and the glacier. In all cases the

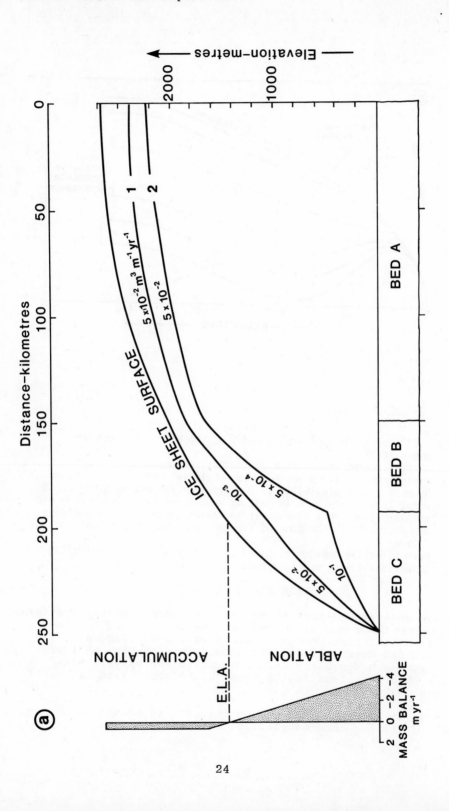

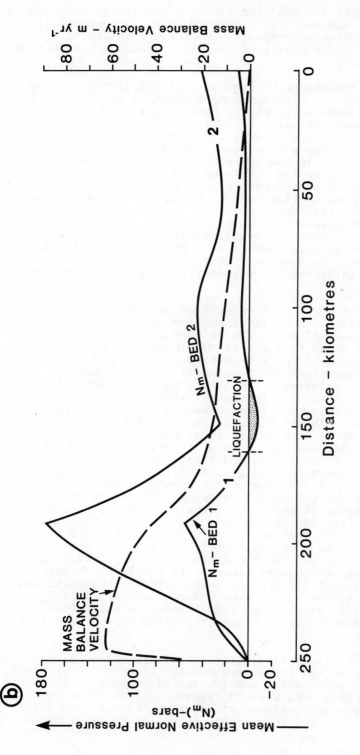

Figure 13 a-b (a opposite). Model of an ice sheet (a similar size to the Late Devensian British Ice Sheet) showing:
a) The piezometric surfaces (1-2) for beds in which hydraulic transmissibilities vary along a flow line, and for a given mass balance.
b) Mean effective normal pressures for beds 1 and 2 and mass balance velocities. In the case of bed 1 mean effective stresses are sub-zero at about 150 km, leading to liquefaction of the bed.

25

nucleating agent for the landform is a bed irregularity or
inhomogeneity and not, as in some theories, a property of
the glacier. Glacier properties do however determine if
a particular landform will be nucleated around a bed hummock
or inhomogeneity.

It seems reasonable to suppose that bed irregularities
will be widespread, although some subglacial materials may
nucleate landforms more readily than others. How then do
the glacial controls vary? In all three cases, the principal glacial controls are basal ice velocity and mean effective
pressure (N_m) at the glacier bed. For modern glaciers, it
is relatively easy to assess velocities, and they can be
predicted for former ice sheets by modelling. However,
estimations of N_m at the base of the glacier is much more
difficult. In much glaciological theory it is assumed that
N_m is zero, and that ice pressure is balanced by an equal
water pressure beneath a glacier (e.g. Nye, 1973). However,
this is not true where permeable subglacial beds allow
drainage to occur (e.g. Gow et al., 1968; Boulton, 1975)
and may not even be true over bedrock surfaces where joints,
cavities and intergranular permeability may play a similar
role.

In order to model what effective pressures might occur
beneath glaciers, a subglacial aquifer model has been
utilised. Figure 12 demonstrates such a model for a West
Greenland ice sheet transect at 70°N (Boulton, in press).
Thermal modelling of the ice sheet predicts central and
peripheral zones where the subglacial bed is frozen, and an
intermediate zone where it is at the melting point. In the
proximal part of this latter zone, basal ice is melting and
thus resultant meltwater flows outwards through subglacial
permeable beds. In the distal part, meltwater freezes to the
glacier sole so as to maintain it at the melting point. The
outer frozen bed zone begins when all meltwater has been
frozen. Beneath the frozen bed zones there is no water
flow and thus the piezometric surface in the sub-permafrost
beds is horizontal. In the melting zone there is a distally
increasing discharge, and if we assume relatively incom-
pressible subglacial sediments and a constant subglacial
transmissibility, the piezometric gradient must increase in
this zone to drive the increasing water discharge. Conversely
in the freezing-on zone meltwater is being lost and the
subglacial discharge thus diminishes distally, resulting in
a progressively decreasing piezometric gradient. Figure 12b
shows several possible gradients for uniform subglacial beds
of different transmissibilities. Resultant values of N_m
for these different beds and mass balance velocity (V_i) (the
true basal velocity will be less than this value) are plotted
in Figure 12c.

Plotted in Figure 14 are the velocity/pressure fields
in which some of the landform-producing processes will occur.
Simplified thresholds for deformation of horizontal subglacial beds have been assumed (Figure 14b) in which we
assume a subglacial sediment of cohesion (C) = 0, and angle
of friction (ϕ) = 40° in glaciers in which the basal shear

26

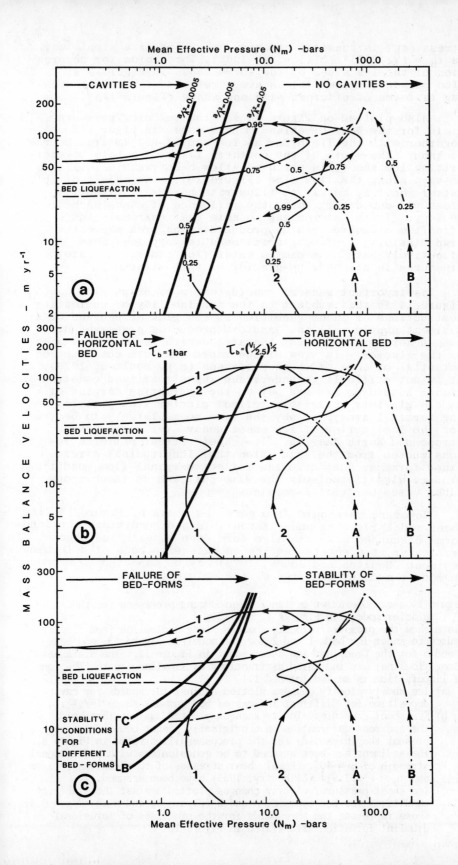

stress (τ_b) is constant at 1 bar, or varies in a simple way as $\tau_b = (V_i/2.5)^{\frac{1}{2}}$ (Lliboutry, 1965). Thresholds for deformation of the lee sides of the forms shown in Figure 9 are also marked (Figure 14c) as are thresholds for cavity opening in forms of diferent size and shape (Figure 14a).

Also plotted on Figure 14 are the velocity/pressure field for the West Greenland models shown in Figure 12 a & b together with the field for an ice cap of 250 km from source to snout (the width of the southern flank of a Late Devensian British ice sheet) in which we allow bed transmissibilities to vary along the flow line (Figure 13). The object of this latter model is merely to illustrate how basal effective pressures could vary under the influence of changing bedrock geology. It is interesting to note that extremely low effective pressures can be produced in an area where the transmissibility of subglacial beds is very low. This effectively acts as a dam to water flow and raises water pressures in all beds up-glacier of this stratum.

The important general conclusion to be drawn from Figure 14 is that subject to the availability of nucleating obstructions or inhomogeneities at the glacier bed and of a sediment supply, all the landform producing processes discussed here will at least operate beneath the marginal area of the glacier. In view of the rapid landform construction potential of some of these processes (e.g. Boulton, 1979), it is not difficult to understand why streamlined constructional landforms exposed beyond the retreating margins of modern glaciers invariably reflect glacier flow patterns in the terminal area, nor why the same seems largely to be true for the last period of ice sheet decay over north-west Europe and North America. Ice sheet retreat patterns reconstructed from the assumption that longitudinal stream-.lined forms such as drumlins reflect marginal flow conditions produce almost precisely the same patterns as isochronous lines based on frontal moraines.

However, we should also note, as shown by Figure 14 (ice sheet model 1), that under favourable bed conditions the landforms discussed here can also form deep beneath ice sheets. In particular, ice sheets resting on extensive beds of deforming sediment (Boulton and Jones, 1979) may be expected to produce them over much of the area of the deforming bed.

Figure 14 a-c. Operation of landform-producing processes for the glacier models in Figures 12 and 13.
Plots show the pressure/velocity changes along a flowline from glacier source to snout for beds 1 and 2 for the model in Figure 13, and beds A and B for the Greenland ice sheet model in Figure 12. The distances along flowlines are indicated as fractions of flowline length. The zone of liquefaction is marked for bed 1.
   a) Ice sheet/velocity changes plotted against thresholds for cavity deposition for different indices of bed hummock shape (a/λ^2).
   b) Ice sheet pressure/velocity changes plotted against thresholds for sediment deformation on an originally planar bed. These represent the thresholds for the processes illustrated in Figure 8. The sediment has been assumed to be cohesionless with a frictional strength of $\phi = 40°$. Basal shear stresses of τ_b = constant = 1 bar, and $\tau_b = (V_i/2.5)^{\frac{1}{2}}$ (Lliboutry, 1965) have been assumed.
   c) Ice sheet pressure/velocity changes plotted against the stability conditions for bed types C, A and B (Figure 9) and with $2a/\lambda = 0.415$. These represent the thresholds for the processes of 'erosional drumlin' formation illustrated in Figure 10.

ACKNOWLEDGEMENTS

I am grateful to Ken Cappell who developed some of the conformal mappings, to Professor Valter Schytt who made the visit to Salieckna possible and to the Natural Environment Research Council and the Royal Society who supported some of this work by generous grants.

REFERENCES CITED

Boulton, G.S. 1970, On the deposition of subglacial and melt-out tills at the margins of certain Svalbard glaciers. *Journal of Glaciology,* 9(56), 231-245.

Boulton, G.S. 1974, Processes and patterns of glacial erosion. in *Glacial geomorphology,* ed D.R. Coates, (New York State University), 41-87.

Boulton, G.S. 1975, Processes and patterns of subglacial submentation: a theoretical approach. in *Ice ages: ancient and modern,* ed Wright and Moseley, (Seel House Press), 7-42.

Boulton, G.S. 1976, The origin of glacially fluted surfaces - observations and theory. *Journal of Glaciology,* 17(76), 287-309.

Boulton, G.S. 1979, Processes of glacier erosion on different substrata. *Journal of Glaciology,* 22(88), 15-38.

Boulton, G.S. and A.S. Jones, 1979, Stability of temperate ice caps and ice sheets resting on beds of deformable sediment. *Journal of Glaciology,* 24(70), 29-43.

Boulton, G.S., Morris, E.M., Armstrong, A.A., and A. Thomas, 1979, Direct measurement of stress at the base of a glacier. *Journal of Glaciology,* 22(86), 3-24.

Chamberlin, T.C. 1895, Recent glacial studies in Greenland. *Geological Society of America Bulletin,* 6, 199-220.

Clayton, L. and S.R. Moran, 1974, A glacial process form model. in *Glacial geomorphology,* ed D.R. Coates, (New York State University, Binghamton).

Demorest, M. 1938, Ice flowage as revealed by glacial striae. *Journal of Geology,* 46, 700-725.

Forbes, J.D. 1859 *Occasional papers on the theory of glaciers,* (Black, Edinburgh).

Goldthwait, R.P. 1974, Till deposition versus glacial erosion. in *Research in polar and alpine geomorphology,* ed B.H. Fahey and R.D. Thompson, (Geo Abstracts, Norwich).

Gow, A.J., Ueda H.T., and D.E. Garfield, 1968, Antarctic ice sheet: preliminary results of first core hole to bedrock. *Science,* 161(3845), 1011-1013.

Gripp, K. 1929, Glaciologische und Geologische Ergebnisse der Hamburgischen Spitzbergen - Expedition 1927. *Naturwissenschaftlicher Verein in Hamburg: Abhandlungen aus dem Gebiet der Naturwissenschaften,* 22(2-4), 146-249.

Hillefors, A. 1973, The stratigraphy and genesis of stoss- and lee-side moraines. *Bulletin of the Geological Institute, Uppsola University,* 5, 139-154.

Hoppe, G. and V. Schytt, 1953, Some observations of fluted moraine surfaces. *Geografiska Annaler,* 35(2), 105-115.

Lliboutry, L. 1965, *Traité de glaciology, Vol 2,* (Masson et Cie., Paris).

Lliboutry, L. 1968, General theory of subglacial cavitation and the sliding of temperate glaciers. *Journal of Glaciology,* 1, 21-58.

Matthes, F.E. 1930, Geologic history of the Yosemite Valley. *United States Geological Survey Professional Paper,* 160.

McLintock, P. and A. Dreimanis, 1964, Reorientation of till fabric by overriding glacier in the St. Lawrence valley. *American Journal of Science,* 262(1), 133-142.

Morland, L.W. and G.S. Boulton, 1975, Stress in an elastic hump: the effects of glacier flow over elastic bedrock. *Proceedings of the Royal Society of London, A. 344,* 157-173.

Nye, J.F. 1952, The mechanics of glacier flow. *Journal of Glaciology,* 2, 82-91, 103-107 and 339-341.

Nye, J.F. 1973, Water at the bed of a glacier. *International Association of Scientific Hydrology, Publ. 95, Symposium on the Hydrology of Glaciers.*

Paul, M.A. and H. Evans, 1974, Observations on the internal structure and origin of some flutes in glaciofluvial sediments, Blomstrandbreen, north-west Spitsbergen. *Journal of Glaciology,* 13(69), 393-400.

Peterson, D.N. 1970, Glaciological investigations on the Casement Glacier, south-east Alaska. *Ohio State University, Institute of Polar Studies. Report,* 36.

Rigsby, G.P. 1958, *Journal of Glaciology,* 3, 273,

Slater, G. 1926, Glacial tectonics as reflected in disturbed drift deposits. *Proceedings of the Geologists Association,* 37(4), 392-400.

Sugden, D.E. 1977, Reconstruction of the morphology, dynamics and thermal characteristics of the Laurentide Ice Sheet at its maximum. *Arctic and Alpine Research,* 9, 21-47.

Theakstone, W.H. 1967, Basal sliding and movement near the margin of the glacier Osterdalsisen, Norway. *Journal of Glaciology*, 6(48), 805-816.

Vernon, P. 1966, Drumlins and Pleistocene ice flow over the Ards peninsula - Strangford Lough area, County Down, Ireland. *Journal of Glaciology*, 6, 401-409.

Vivian, R. 1970, Hydrologie et erosion sous-glaciaires. *Rèvue de Geographie Alpine*, 58, 241-246.

Vivian, R. 1976, *Les glaciers des Alpes occidentales*. (Imp. Allier, Grenoble).

Weertman J. 1972, General theory of water flow at the base of a glacier or ice sheet. *Reviews of Geophysics*, 10, 287-333.

2 A till hummock (proto-drumlin) at the ice glacier bed interface

J. Menzies

ABSTRACT

The initiation and subsequent development of drumlins is considered with regard to those drumlins lacking obvious rock or boulder cores, or bedrock knolls around which material has nucleated. The mechanics of glacial deposition to allow for localised points of agglomeration is discussed with reference to conditions in the subglacial environment.

When sufficient glacial detritus has agglomerated at localised points at the ice/glacier bed interface a state may be reached at which this agglomeration begins to act as an obstacle to the passage of the ice. It is at this point that the processes leading toward drumlin formation are initiated. Several mechanisms are suggested to account for the persistence of the material at the interface from which a till hummock (proto-drumlin) begins to be evolved. Marked geotechnical changes in the material occur such that the hummock persists and develops at the glacial interface. It is shown that, under specific ice velocities and thicknesses associated with varying detrital shear strengths, the size and growth of drumlins can be approximately predicted. Calculations reveal that drumlins will tend to form in zones close to and at some distance from the ice margin, with a less favoured area existing between.

INTRODUCTION

In order that drumlins remain at the ice/glacier bed interface it is necessary that the material comprising those drumlins that lack cores, be able to withstand the stresses imposed by the moving ice mass. As discussed elsewhere (Menzies, 1979a) the final dimensions of drumlins are inconsistent with most theories of drumlin formation. Rather an initiating phase of drumlin development is called for in which, most probably by an accretive process, a drumlin will increase in overall dimensions toward some upper limiting size critically defined by the interaction of ice velocities, pressures and the geotechnical nature of the drumlin material. If this initial premise of withstanding ice stresses is to be maintained then a lower limiting size for drumlin formation under varying ice and glacial material conditions should also exist.

---

* Department of Geography, Brock University, St. Catharines, Ontario, Canada

Glacial erosion and deposition

It is the objective of this paper to set out some approximate methods for defining these limiting drumlin dimensions. At this stage in our understanding of the complexities of the subglacial environment and of the mathematics needed to accurately define the conditions of stress and strain within a hummock of unconsolidated material, the results remain tentative and exploratory. As yet our total understanding of the stress forces acting at the base of an ice mass is meagre.

GEOTECHNICAL CHANGES IN SUBGLACIAL DEBRIS

Before discussing the mechanisms for till agglomeration at the base of an ice mass it is necessary to mention the geotechnical changes this material must be subject to if it is to survive in this subglacial position.

Subglacial debris is commonly observed as being of a slurry-like consistency when seen emerging from beneath an ice mass. If such material is to remain as a drumlin-like obstruction at the base of an ice mass then it must undergo rapid geotechnical changes, principally from low internal shear strength due to high porewater content to a much higher shear strength.

The means by which such transformations may occur are dependent upon either loss of porewater by dissipation or *in situ* porewater freezing. In the case of porewater dissipation, porewater within the material can be dissipated or expelled due to an increase in the total stress applied to the material thereby causing increased porewater pressure and thus porewater migration toward low pressure points within or beyond the stressed material. Porewater movement can also result from the effects of freezing front advancement into the material and expulsion from the front (McRoberts and Morgenstern, 1975).

The effect of *in situ* freezing has often been cited as a means of rapidly increasing the shear strength of subglacial debris and may, together with the latter instance of porewater expulsion, occur simultaneously (Menzies, 1979a; Baranowski, 1979).

TILL AGGLOMERATION

Before any of these transformations can take place it is necessary that sufficient material (till) agglomerate or nucleate at the bed of the glacier. Several mechanisms can be suggested to cause localised accumulations of debris in the subglacial position.

From Figure 1 the main mechanisms that lead to localised geotechnical changes are outlined. If porewater is dissipated from material either in traction or lodged at the glacier's sole and this dissipation of porewater is into permeable substrata or meltwater conduits, localised areas of higher strength material will be produced thereby creating nuclei

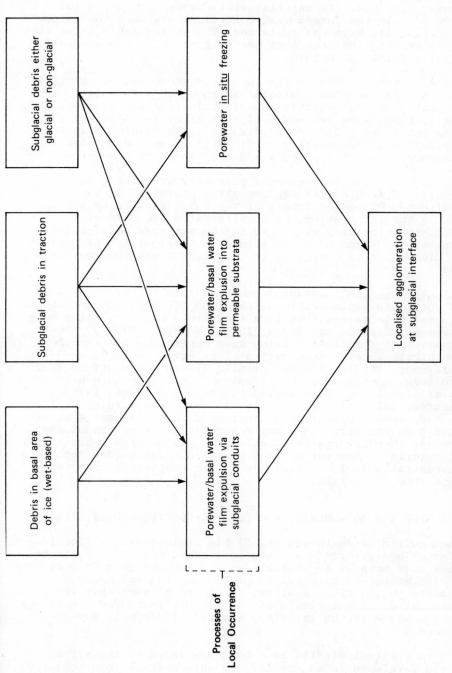

Figure 1. Possible mechanisms of till agglomeration at the ice/glacier bed interface.

or agglomerations around which other material may accrete.
If, alternatively, dissipation is over a widespread area of
the glacier bed, large scale lodgement of till and/or increased
consolidation of the material will ensue, with no nuclei
created. In the former case conditions are such that a proto-
drumlin (till hummock) is formed. The writer would argue that
it is in this instance that the triggering action needed for
drumlin formation occurs.

A further mechanism for localised accumulation exists if
a temperate, wet-based glacier slipping on a thin film of
meltwater or over distinct subglacial rills suddenly has this
lubricating layer removed. If this layer is effectively
dissipated, as indicated in Figure 1, the glacier will locally
'ground' and consequently debris will be melted-out and its
porewater also dissipated along the same pathways.

Finally, the influence of porewater freezing cannot be
ignored as a potential agglomerative process. As yet the
influence of freezing fronts at the subglacial interface is
little known. However, as an alternative to porewater
expulsion, freezing will lead to the required geotechnical
changes, in terms of shear strength of material, that cannot
be discounted if occurring in localised areas (Goodman *et al,*
1979).

Although the above processes may lead to the development
of localised agglomerations, the need for high concentrations
of available material in localised areas has also often been
stressed (Clayton and Moran, 1974; Menzies, 1979b). Past
theories of drumlin formation have mentioned, for example,
the highly local concentration of material in moraines
(Gravenor, 1953); however drumlin fields often extend over
too large an area for individual moraines to be a source for
material. It has been argued (Clayton and Moran, 1974;
Menzies, 1979b, Figure 5), that close to the margins of ice
masses where subpolar snout regions exist a 'hinge' area of
upward moving dirt lines may occur and stack on top of one
another thereby creating localised zones of high concentrations
of material. However other explanations are needed for local
concentrations of material within the subglacial zone far
back from the margin.

THE EFFECT OF AGGLOMERATION AT THE ICE-GLACIER BED INTERFACE

Once sufficient material (till) has agglomerated at the ice-
glacier bed interface a state is reached when this agglomerated mass acts as an obstacle past which the glacier must move.
If the amount of material is of too small a volume or if it
remains in too fluid a state, it can be assumed that the
material would not remain but be rapidly destroyed. With
this hummock at the interface a stress field will develop
across it.

Theoretical studies have been published on the stress
field developed in an elastic, two-dimensional, bedrock
hummock (Boulton, 1974,1979; Morland and Boulton, 1975).

Boulton (1974) has shown that plucking may or may not occur on the lee side of such a bedrock hummock depending on whether or not a lee-side cavity develops beneath the ice mass. The writer has attempted to utilise these theories in their application to a till hummock with certain assumptions being made that will be discussed later.

Stress Distribution within a Till Hummock

With a till hummock (proto-drumlin) acting as an obstruction at the ice/glacier bed interface a fluctuation in basal ice pressures occurs over this hummock thereby inducing a related pattern of stresses within the hummock. Following the work of Minell (1973) and Boulton (1974) it can be anticipated that the distribution of stresses within a two-dimensional till hummock will be of a pattern similar to that illustrated in Figure 2.

It can be noted from Figure 2 that although the distribution of stresses varies with cavitation and non-cavitation, at depth within the hummock a large zone of till remains almost totally unaffected by basal shear stresses due to stress dissipation within the material. This zone of till may constitute a 'core'. It can therefore be concluded that provided a till hummock is of sufficient initial size to allow stress dissipation no core of bedrock or previously frozen till is neccessary to allow till accretion to occur.

The Initial Size of a Till Hummock

In order to determine, at least in terms of orders of magnitude, what the initial size of a till hummock must be to survive at the subglacial interface under varying conditions of basal stress, ice velocity, and till shear strength, several equations used by Boulton (1974, p.67) have been adopted. The theoretical derivation of the equations used below has been developed by several workers (Nye, 1969, 1970; Boulton, 1974; Morland and Boulton, 1975). It can be shown that for any given hummock slope and basal ice velocity where no cavitation occurs the total normal pressure fluctuation across the obstruction is: $2\Delta P$ (Boulton, 1974, Figure 8). However in using till as the material composing the hummock several restrictive assumptions are made that deviate from the complex geotechnical nature of the sediment. It is felt by the writer that these assumptions must be drastically reduced in future work but serve at present to allow approximate calculations.

It is assumed, for the purposes of analysis, that the material of the hummock is isotropic and linearly elastic (cf. Radhakrishna and Klym, 1974; Milligan, 1976). A wavelength-to-amplitude ratio of 4/1 is assumed, and with wavelengths greater than 10 m it can be shown that:

$$\Delta P \approx \frac{10_\eta \, Vi}{\lambda} \quad \dots \dots \dots \dots (1)$$

where η is the viscosity of ice assumed to be 1 bar year, Vi is the basal velocity of the ice and λ the wavelength of the hummock.

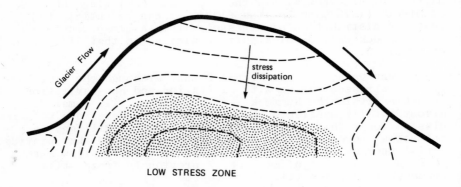

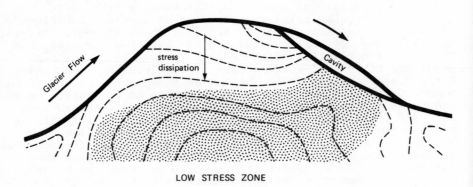

Figure 2. Theoretical distribution of stresses in till hummock.

It can also be shown that if:

$$\frac{\Delta P}{\rho gh} > 1 \quad . \quad . \quad . \quad . \quad . \quad . \quad . \quad . \quad . \quad . \quad . \quad (2)$$

then cavitation will occur in the lee of the hummock (Figure 2b) where ρgh is the normal pressure of the ice and where ρ is the density of glacier ice, g is the acceleration due to gravity and h the thickness of the glacier at that point.

Before going on to discuss the implications of these equations it is pertinent to mention that with the basal ice heavily charged with debris, values of viscosity (η) and density (ρ) of the glacier ice would be considerably different; but by how much still remains largely unanswered (Alkire and Andersland, 1973; comments by Drewry, Engelhardt and Meier, 1979, p.382).

Boulton (1974, p.64) has commented that 'if cavitation occurs, the maximum shear stress (at the surface of the hummock) will occur immediately up-glacier of the point of closure'. It therefore follows that erosion of the till will be initiated at this point on the till hummock tending toward a down-ice migration of the hummock crest (n.b. Boulton, 1979, p.25). Migration of the hummock crest in this manner leads toward the development of the 'classical' drumlin long profile.

PERSISTENCE OF A TILL HUMMOCK AT THE ICE/GLACIER BED INTERFACE

In order to estimate at what basal ice velocity and shear stress the till within the hummock will be eroded and the hummock begin to be destroyed three equations (after Boulton, 1974) were utilised.

Failure of the till was measured as a safety factor (F) given by:

$$F = \frac{\text{Till Shear Strength}}{\text{Basal Ice Shear Stress}} \quad . \quad . \quad . \quad . \quad . \quad . \quad (3)$$

The equations utilised on a bedrock hummock for conditions of cavitation and no cavitation are (Boulton, 1974, p.67):-

a) Cavitation
$$F = \frac{\tau}{\left(\dfrac{1.25\eta Vi}{\lambda} + 0.188\rho gh\right)} \quad . \quad . \quad . \quad . \quad . \quad . \quad (4)$$

b) No-Cavitation
$$F = \frac{\tau + \left(\rho gh - \dfrac{10\eta Vi}{\lambda}\right)\tan\theta}{\dfrac{3.13\eta Vi}{\lambda}} \quad . \quad . \quad . \quad . \quad . \quad . \quad (5)$$

where, τ applied to till hummocks, is the shear strength of the till and $\tan\theta$ is the angle of internal friction. It is further assumed that the till has a low permeability. This latter assumption would appear valid since on successful agglomeration porewater dissipation will have occurred with consequent consolidation and a marked reduction in the void ratio of the till.

Equations 4 and 5 were evaluated for a range of conditions to produce the graphs shown in Figures 3-5. In using these equations wavelengths of 10, 50 and 100 m were adopted, corresponding to hummock heights of 2.5, 12.5 and 25 m respectively. Values for basal ice velocity were taken as 3 m yr^{-1}, 30 m yr^{-1} and 300 m yr^{-1} (Paterson, 1969; Raymond, 1978). These values indicate the likely normal ranges of rates of glacier movement, although under 'surging' glaciers much higher rates are known to occur.

Till shear strengths vary considerably in practice from undrained, drained, peak and residual values of shear strength but for the purposes of this paper shear strengths of 0.75, 1.5 and 3.0 bars (1 bar = $100KNm^{-2}$) were used. From Boulton's work (1974) on bedrock hummocks it is assumed that when cavitation occurs the bedrock shear strength remains constant. However, although this assumption is adopted in this analysis, some change through continued dewatering might be expected to cause a slight increase in till shear strength even under circumstances of cavitation. A further problem in adopting values of shear strength for till is the possibility that till in traction at the ice/glacier bed interface may have reached a state after extensive interparticle dislocations and bond destruction where its ultimate shearing resistance on agglomeration is at a residual value (Terzaghi and Peck, 1967, p.121) such that the values of $\tau < 0.75$ bars may occur.

In considering values for the internal angle of friction a mean of $\tan\theta = 0.5$ was adopted. Values for till are found however to range from 6° to 40°, the former often being when till shear strength is at its residual level. Although the wide range in geotechnical parameters for till exists it can be argued that in terms of orders of magnitude this present analysis at least indicates the likely conditions affecting a till hummock at the subglacial interface.

Before discussing the values obtained from the graphs (Figures 3-5) it must be reiterated that, in using Nye's pressure law and its direct relationship with hummock geometry and the basal ice velocity, the results obtained are rough estimates and can be viewed only as qualitative descriptions of the anticipated behaviour of a till hummock at the ice/glacier bed interface.

Analysis of Graphs

At basal ice velocities of 3 m yr^{-1} it can be seen from Figure 3 that no failure will occur for $\lambda = 50$ and 100 m at an ice thickness <50 m for $\tau = 0.75$ bars. For $\tau = 1.5$ bars failure only occurs for $\lambda = 10$ m at ice thicknesses >20 m and for $\tau = 50$ and 100 m at ice thicknesses >100 m. At $\tau = 3$ bars failure begins in all hummocks at an ice thickness of between 100 to 300 m.

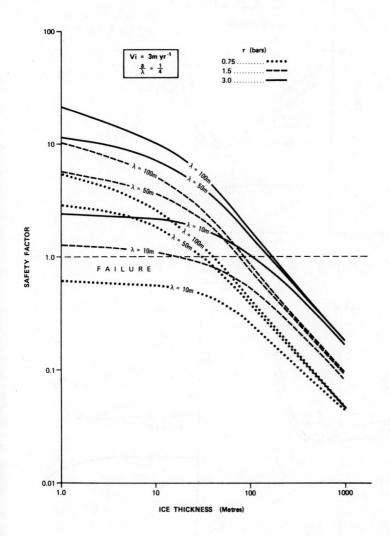

Figure 3. Safety factors for till hummocks of different
wavelength and constant geometry (a/λ = 1/4) for
different till shear strengths at basal ice velocity
= 3myr^{-1}. A safety factor of <1 indicates erosion
(failure) of till will occur.

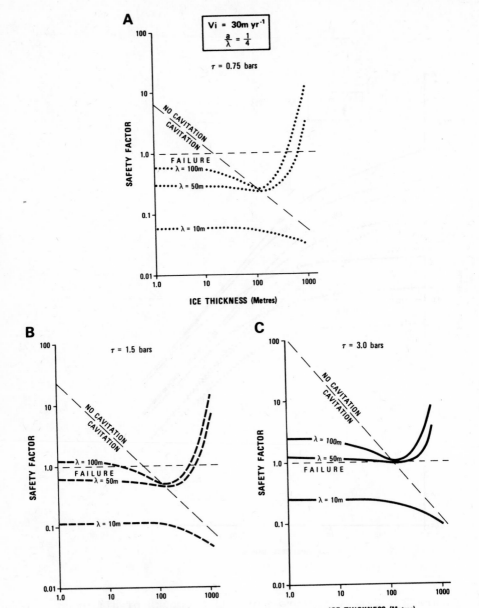

Figure 4. Safety factors for till hummocks (as in Figure 3) at basal ice velocity = 30myr^{-1}.

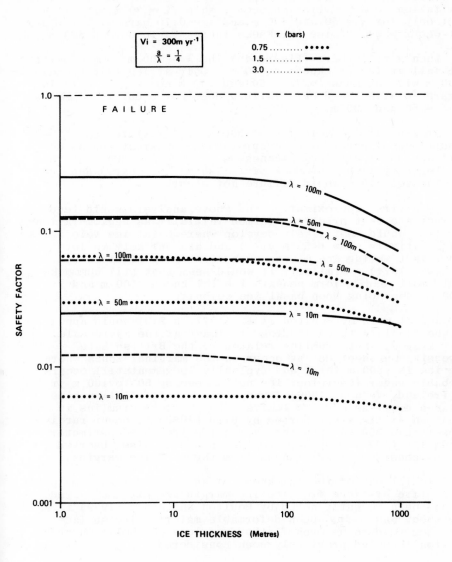

Figure 5. Safety factors for till hummocks (as in
Figure 3) at a basal ice velocity = 300myr^{-1}.

Glacial erosion and deposition

From Figure 4a the importance of the transition from cavitation to no cavitation occurs when Vi = 30 m yr^{-1} such that only for λ = 50 and 100 m and τ = 0.75 bars will failure not occur when the ice thickness increases to beyond 500 m.

When τ = 1.5 bars (Figure 4b) the λ = 100 m hummock will not fail at ice thicknesses <30 m. Only at ice thicknesses >600 m will hummocks of λ = 50 and 100 m no longer fail. In Figure 4c with τ = 3 bars failure does not occur in hummocks of λ = 50 and 100 m.

At a basal ice velocity of 300 m yr^{-1} failure, in conditions of cavitation, occurs at all shear strengths of till and under all ice thicknesses (Figure 5). Only at this ice velocity with a hummock of λ >420 m (τ = 3 bars) and ice thicknesses >10 m would failure not occur.

As a first approximation the above analysis would tend to indicate that drumlins, formed initially as agglomerations of till, would most likely develop where basal ice velocities are relatively slow (<50 m yr^{-1}) and are unlikely to form under fast moving ice masses such as surging glaciers (cf. Mathews, 1974). Similarly it would seem that till hummocks would most readily form beneath ice thickness <100 m and >400 m, depending upon basal ice velocity.

Recent work by Boulton et al (1977, p.243) would appear to substantiate these findings at least at the macroscale. They suggest that drumlins related to the British Late Devensian ice sheet do not occur in the marginal zones where the ice is <800 m thick and typically lodgement till occurs probably under ice velocities not exceeding 50 to 100 m yr^{-1}. In Ireland, Vernon (1966) found similar interrelationships between drumlins and ice limits. Furthermore drumlins in the Canadian Arctic are reported by Bird (1980) to occur rarely closer than 300 km from the Laurentide ice sheet perimeter. Lundqvist (1970) mapping drumlins in Sweden also observed fields considerable distances from the past ice margins.

Calculations of the thickness of an ice sheet at some point a specific distance from the ice margin are extremely crude. As has been recently noted by Boulton and Jones (1979) if an ice sheet was lying upon deformable material ice surface profiles tend to be much flatter and less parabolic in cross-section than had previously been considered.

Till of a much higher shear strength would, theoretically, under similar basal ice conditions form drumlins of much smaller dimensions than those formed with till of low shear strength. The influence of accretion build-up could in many instances invalidate this dimensional comparison but such observations on size have been made (Gravenor, 1974, p.52). Such morphological relationships may also help to account for the often reported dimensional changes observed both down-ice and laterally within a drumlin field (Smalley and Unwin, 1968; Crozier, 1975).

THE PROTO DRUMLIN - ITS ESTABLISHMENT

With the establishment of the till hummock at the ice/glacier bed interface the initial phase of drumlin formation is begun. It can be seen that with the presence of the till hummock at the interface porewater dissipation will continue within and from the till causing increased consolidation and rising shear strength. Thus with time the boundary conditions, as set out in equations 4 and 5, will change. The removal of the hummock by the ice will become less likely, provided no rapid variations in glaciological conditions occur. At this stage therefore drumlin development will continue uninterrupted.

ACKNOWLEDGEMENTS

I am grateful to Ian Smalley for his helpful discussions on drumlin formative processes and to Loris Gasparotto for his work on diagrams and to the typing staff of Brock University. This work was supported by an NSERC Grant (A6900).

REFERENCES CITED

Alkire, B.D. and O.B.Andersland, 1973, The effect of confining pressure on the mechanical properties of sand-ice materials. *Journal of Glaciology,* 12, 469–482

Baranowski, S. 1979, The origin of drumlins as an ice-rock interface problem (abstract). *Journal of Glaciology,* 23, 435–436

Bird, J.B. 1980, *The natural landscapes of Canada, 2nd edition,* (J. Wiley, Toronto), 260 pp.

Boulton, G.S. 1974, Processes and patterns of glacial erosion, in *Glacial geomorphology,* ed D.R.Coates, (State University of New York, Binghampton, N.Y.), 41–87

Boulton, G.S. 1979, Processes of glacier erosion on different substrata. *Journal of Glaciology,* 23, 15–38

Boulton, G.S. and A.S. Jones, 1979, Stability of temperate ice caps and ice sheets resting on beds of deformable sediment. *Journal of Glaciology,* 24, 29–44

Boulton, G.S., Jones, A.S., Clayton, K.M. and M.J.Kennings, 1977, A British ice-sheet model and patterns of glacial erosion and deposition in Britain. in *British Quaternary studies - recent advances,* ed F.W.Shotton, (Clarendon Press, Oxford), 231–246

Clayton, L. and S.R. Moran, 1974, A glacial process-form model. in *Glacial geomorphology,* ed D.R.Coates, (State University of New York, Binghampton, N.Y.), 89–119

Crozier, M.J., 1975, On the origin of the Peterborough drumlin field: testing the dilatancy theory. *Canadian Geographer,* 19, 181–195

Drewry, D.J. *et al.,* 1979, Comments made in general discussion. *Journal of Glaciology,* 23, 382

Goodman, D.J., King, G.C.P., Millar, D.H.M. and G. deQ. Robin, 1979, Pressure melting effects in basal ice of temperate glaciers: laboratory studies and field observations under Glacier d'Argentiere. *Journal of Glaciology*, 23, 259-272

Gravenor, C.P. 1953, The origin of drumlins. *American Journal of Science*, 251, 674-681

Gravenor, C.P. 1974, The Yarmouth drumlin field, Nova Scotia, Canada. *Journal of Glaciology*, 13, 45-54

Lundqvist, J. 1970, Studies of drumlin tracts in central Sweden. *Geogr. Lodz*, 24, 317-326

McRoberts, E.C. and N.R.Morgenstern, 1975, Porewater expulsion during freezing. *Canadian Geotechnical Journal*, 12, 130-141

Mathews, W.H. 1974, Surface profiles of the Laurentide ice sheet in its marginal areas. *Journal of Glaciology*, 13, 37-44

Menzies, J. 1979a, A review of the literature on the formation and location of drumlins. *Earth Science Reviews*, 14, 315-359

Menzies, J., 1979b, The mechanics of drumlin formation with particular reference to the change in pore-water content of the till. *Journal of Glaciology*, 22, 373-384

Milligan, V. 1976, Geotechnical aspects of glacial tills. in *Glacial till*, ed R.F.Legget, (Royal Society of Canada, Special Publication 12), 269-291

Minell, H. 1973, An investigation of drumlins in the Narvik area of Norway. *Bulletin Geological Institute, University of Uppsala*, 5, 133-138

Morland, L.W. and G.S.Boulton, 1975, Stress in an elastic hump: the effects of glacier flow over elastic bedrock. *Proceedings Royal Society, London*, 344A, 157-173

Nye, J. 1969, A calculation on the sliding of ice over a wavy surface using a Newtonian viscous approximation. *Proceedings Royal Society, London*, 311A, 445-467

Nye, J. 1970, Glacier sliding without cavitation in a linear viscous approximation. *Proceedings Royal Society, London*, 315A, 381-403

Paterson, W.S.B. 1969, *The physics of glaciers*, (Pergamon Press, Oxford), 250 pp.

Radhakrishna, H.S. and T.W.Klym, 1974, Geotechnical properties of a very dense glacial till. *Canadian Geotechnical Journal*, 11, 396-408

Raymond, C.F. 1978, The mechanics of glacier movement. in *Rockslides and avalanches, vol.1*, ed B. Voight, (Elsevier, New York), 793-833

Smalley, I.J. and D.J.Unwin, 1968, The formation and shape of drumlins and their distribution and orientation in drumlin fields. *Journal of Glaciology*, 7, 377-390

Terzaghi, J. and R.B. Peck, 1967, *Soil mechanics in engineering practice, 2nd edition*, (John Wiley, New York), 727 pp.

Vernon, P. 1966, Drumlins and Pleistocene ice flow over the Ards Peninsula/Strangford Lough area, Co. Down, Ireland. *Journal of Glaciology*, 6, 401-409

3 The formation of glacial flutings in east-central Alberta

Norman Jones

ABSTRACT

The Lac la Biche fluting and drumlin field originates at Lac la Biche, Alberta and extends southeastwards almost to North Battleford, Saskatchewan, a distance of approximately 390 km. The southeast orientation of the field is transverse to the regional north-east to south-west ice flow direction in Alberta. The Lac la Biche field appears to be a result of a late resurgence of the Wisconsin ice during deglaciation of this region, about 11 400 years ago. The purpose of this investigation is to determine the genesis of the glacial landforms in the Lac la Biche field.

Field investigations, including till fabric, texture and lithology, show ubiquitous glacial tectonic activity, implying that frozen-bed conditions and compressive ice flow probably ensued at some point during ice advance. The smooth, stream-lined appearance of drumlins and flutings indicates a trans-gression into wet-bed conditions and, possibly, extending flow. Initial frozen-bed conditions and compressive flow caused glacial thrusting and plucking of blocks of basal debris near the margin of the ice. The blocks lodge at the glacier bed and resist further movement. With continued advance thawed-bed conditions are encountered and deposition in a low pressure zone created in the lee of these obstacles occurs. Lateral transport of debris in the lee of the blocks was accomplished as a result of the presence of converging secondary flow cells, created by the basal pressure gradient. Till fabric analyses show a 'herring-bone' fabric pattern, supporting the existence of converging secondary flow.

Auger holes drilled through three flutings, numerous road cut examinations, and subsequent till textural and litho-logic analyses, show only one till is present in the stream-lined landforms, reducing the validity of any hypothesis which involves the addition of two or more till layers during consecutive ice advances. The complete formation of both the drumlins and flutings was found to have occurred during a single ice advance.

* Department of Geography, The University of Alberta,
  Edmonton, Alberta, T6G 2H4

INTRODUCTION

Explanations of glacial fluting formation are extremely
varied, but may be divided into two basic categories,
explanations of small-scale flutings, for example Hoppe and
Schytt (1953), Baranowski (1970), Morris and Morland (1976),
and explanations of large-scale flutings, for example Gravenor
and Meneley (1958), Shaw and Freschauf (1973), Aario (1977).
Hoppe and Schytt (1953) described the smaller type as being
not more than 1 m high, 4 m wide, and several hundred metres
in length. General figures for the large-scale flutings are:
height $\leq 25\,m$; width $\leq 100\,m$; and length $\leq 20\,km$ (Flint, 1971).

Small-scale flutings are generally considered to be
formed by the deposition of unfrozen, water-soaked debris in
a low pressure zone downstream of an obstacle (Dyson, 1952).
This obstacle may be a boulder, bedrock knob, block of frozen
till, frost heave, or any resistant block at the base of the
glacier. Although other hypotheses have been advanced this
basic mechanism has been widely accepted.

Explanations of the formation of large-scale flutings
remain much more controversial. In the past, this controversy
centred on the choice between erosional and depositional
theories. Recently, however, combined erosional/depositional
mechanisms for fluting development have been proposed,
beginning with Gravenor's (1953) modified erosional hypothesis. Gravenor's original hypothesis was followed by a
paper by Gravenor and Meneley (1958) on glacial fluting
development in Alberta in which they suggested the importance
of linear belts of high and low pressure beneath an ice
sheet. This paper, in conjunction with Allen's (1964, 1968)
work on secondary flow in fluvial processes, influenced Shaw
and Freschauf's (1973) kinematic discussion of glacial
fluting development through the action of alternating cells
of secondary flow in ice sheets (Figure 1). The secondary
flow proposed requires a transverse basal pressure differential. Aario (1977) proposed a similar mechanism for
glacial landform development in Finland.

A recent paper by Moran et al. (in press) has added an
important mechanism for fluting initiation. They postulate
streamlined landforms may be initiated through glacial
thrusting of basal material under compressive ice flow, and
particularly when three basic conditions occur: a frozen
bed; pre-existing planes of weakness (such as bedding or
jointing); and decreased shear strength in subglacial rock
or sediment (caused by locally elevated pore-water pressure).
If a block of frozen, basal debris is plucked by the ice,
and subsequently refreezes to the bed, a low pressure zone
will be created in its lee. Additional debris will be
transported to this low pressure zone from either side of
the block. Deposition through sub-glacial meltout will take
place with the advent of thawed-bed conditions.

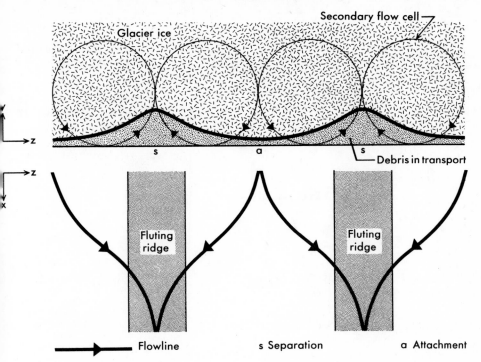

Figure 1. The formation of flutings in till by the relocation of debris in transport (after Shaw, 1980)

STUDY AREA

In order to test the above hypotheses, and discover other possible explanations for fluting development, a fluting field in east-central Alberta was investigated (Figure 2). The field extends from Lac la Biche, Alberta to North Battleford, Saskatchewan, a distance of approximately 390 km. A section approximately 80 km long, and from 15 km to 25 km wide near St. Paul, Alberta was chosen for the field investigations.

Flutings of two different sizes occur in the study area. Long, low flutings (~1 m high, up to 20 km long) are found southeast of St. Paul and northwest of the North Saskatchewan River, while short, high flutings (<5 m high, <5 km long) occur up- and down-ice of the section of longer flutings (Figure 3).

This fluting field, which shall be called the Lac la Biche field, is orientated in a northwest to southeast direction. This is transverse to the regional ice advance direction in Alberta, which was from northeast to southwest (Gravenor and Meneley, 1958). This transverse attitude probably indicates the Lac la Biche field was formed

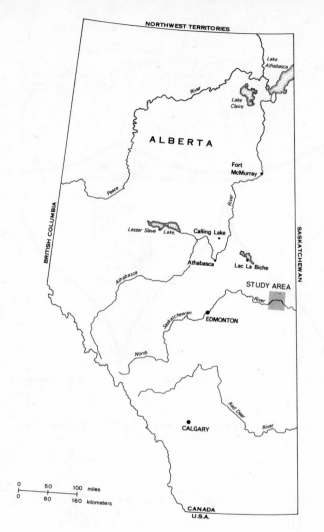

Figure 2. Location
of study area

Figure 3. Surficial
glacial deposits in
the study area

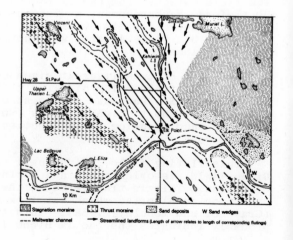

during a late Wisconsin re-advance. This re-advance may
have been channelled by large bodies of stagnant ice
associated with the down-wasting of the earlier main Wisconsin
ice. Stagnation moraine is found both southwest (Viking
moraine, Bretz, 1943), and northeast (Coteau moraine, Ellwood,
1960) of the Lac la Biche fluting field (Figures 3 and 4).
Ellwood (1960) noted the mobilization of the Lac la Biche ice
may have been caused by local high rates of snow accumulation
in the Athabasca area to the northwest. The narrowness of
the Lac la Biche field indicates constriction.

A second fluting field, the Cold Lake field, merges with
the Lac la Biche field northwest of St. Paul (Figure 4).
Deflection of fluting axes at the junction of the two fields
indicates that convergence of two ice streams probably
occurred (Figure 4), with subsequent movement of the combined ice mass to the southeast. The section of the Lac la
Biche fluting field studied in this paper was, therefore,
down-ice of the convergence.

Two large meltwater channels located on either side of
the Lac la Biche fluting field may indicate prolonged stable
positions of the margins of stagnant bodies of main Wisconsin
ice (Figure 3). The Moosehills meltwater channel (Ellwood,
1960), which contains Kehiwin Lake, defines a precise boundary
between the flutings and stagnation moraine to the northeast
(Figure 3).

Large deposits of aeolian sand, and the existence of sand
wedges approximately 1 m deep, found within the study area
(Figure 3) indicate a long, arid periglacial period ensued
prior to the Lac la Biche advance. The existence of permafrost from this periglacial period may have contributed to
widespread glaciotectonic activity during the later Lac la
Biche advance. This glaciotectonic activitiy is represented
by numerous thrust blocks which contain inverted stratigraphic sequences, and by faulted beds of fine to coarse
sands.

METHODOLOGY

National Topographic Series maps of scales 1:50 000 and
1:250 000 and aerial photographs of 1:63 360 and 1:80 000
scales were used to select and study the field area. The
aerial photographs were used as a more specific tool to
examine the relationships of glacial landforms in the area,
and the detailed characteristics of selected landforms and
landform suites. The large areas shown on the small-scale
photos (1:80 000) make them extremely useful for the former
purpose. The larger-scale photos (1:63 360) were used to
examine the detailed characteristics of individual landforms,
and for selecting potential sampling and fabric sites. The
locations of the selected sites are shown in Figure 5. Both
types of aerial photographs and personal photographs taken
during a low-level reconnaissance flights were used to map
glacial deposits (Figure 3). More detailed information
was obtained by ground reconnaissance and from earlier maps
of the area (Ellwood, 1960).

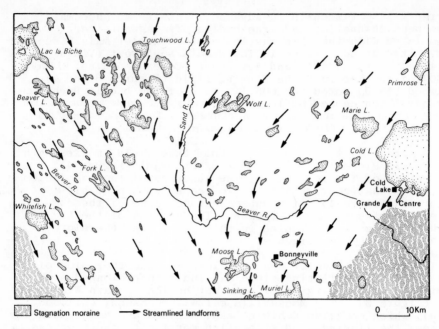

Figure 4. Zone of convergence of Lac la Biche and Cold Lake ice advances (from air photos and mosaics)

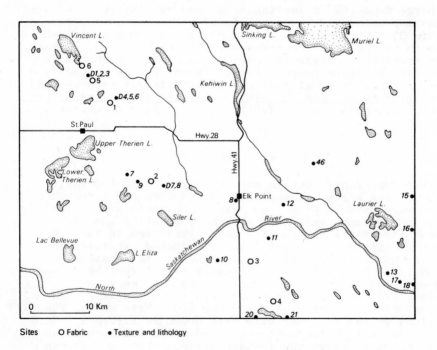

Figure 5. Location of sample sites

Roadcuts across three flutings were selected as sites for micro- and macrofabric analyses. Six sample sites were chosen at each roadcut, two at the ridge centre, one at the ridge top and one at its base, and two to each side. The side samples were taken at one-third and two-thirds of the distance from the crest to the adjacent trough.

Macrofabrics involve measurement of the long axis orientation and plunge of fifty pebbles. The pebble azimuths were plotted on two-dimensional rose diagrams (Figure 6), and contour diagrams of the combined azimuth and plunge data were plotted by computer (Corbató, 1966).

Horizontal and vertical thin sections were cut from impregnated blocks taken from each macrofabric site. The horizontal section was used to determine grain long axis azimuths, while the vertically cut section, which was cut parallel to the general direction of ice flow, was used to determine grain long axis plunge angles. One hundred axis measurements were made on each slide. This microfabric azimuth and plunge data were plotted in $10°$ classes on separate two-dimensional diagrams (Figure 7).

The macrofabric data were analyzed statistically using the methods of Steinmetz (1962). The vector mean (V), and the vector strength (R) of each fabric sample were calculated. Strong unidirectional pebble orientations yield large values of R, while dispersed orientations yield small R values. An estimate of precision coefficient (K), which is dependent on the R value, was also calculated for each distribution.

The macrofabric data were also analyzed using a Fisher-Watson analysis of directional data on a sphere (Fara and Scheidegger, 1963). The eigenvalues and eigenvectors of each three-dimensional contour diagram were calculated. Any preferred inclination of the principal plane of the enscribed ellipse, and whether a girdle or bipolar distribution pattern was apparent, were also determined. The macrofabric statistical data are given in Table 1.

The microfabric azimuthal data were analyzed statistically by comparing the distribution of grain azimuths to a von Mises distribution (Harvey and Ferguson, 1976). The von Mises distribution shows how well a set of data is distributed about the sample's vector mean. A chi-square value for each sample is obtained from the difference between the estimated von Mises distribution and the observed distribution. If the sample's chi-square value is less than the significant chi-square value, in this case 24.99 with 15 degrees of freedom and a 95% confidence level, the sample is said to satisfactorily fit the von Mises distribution, and, thus, the calculated mean accurately defines the sample trend.

The microfabric plunge data were tested for preferred up- or down-ice plunge by using a significance of proportion test outlined by Bruning and Kintz (1968). The number of grains dipping up-ice was compared to the number of grains dipping down-ice, and the resultant significance level

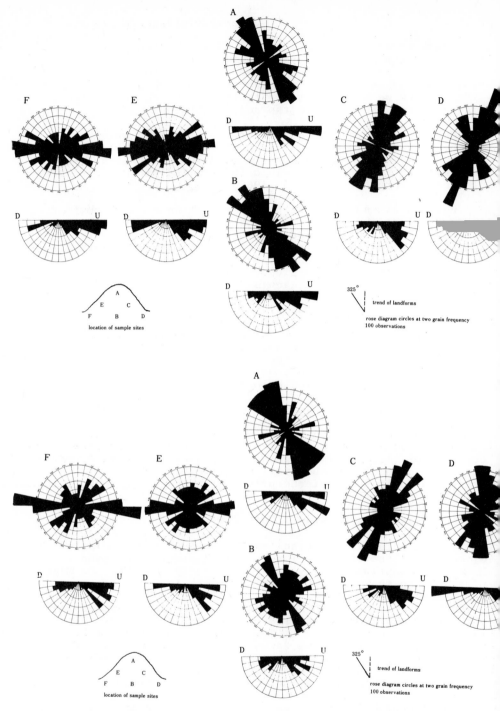

Figure 6. Two-dimensional rose diagrams of pebble orientation and contour diagrams of combined azimuth and plunge data for the three flutings:
(a) Fluting #1
(b) Fluting #3

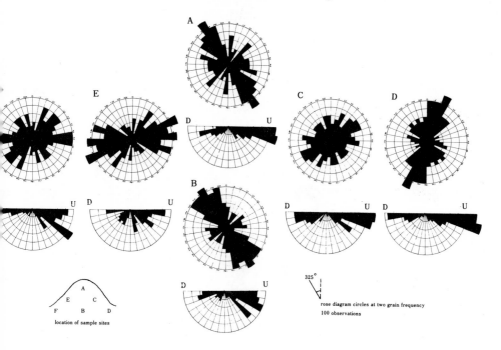

Figure 6. Two-dimensional rose diagrams of pebble orienta-
           tion and contour diagrams of combined azimuth and
           plunge data for the three flutings:
      (c) Fluting #5

compared to a chi-square table using a 95% confidence level
and two degrees of freedom. Any result <1.645 was deemed
insignificant. All microfabric statistical data are shown
in Table 2.

    A sample of approximately 150 g of till was collected
at each fabric site for textural analyses. Additional samples
were collected from numerous roadcuts situated throughout the
study area, and from auger holes drilled in the crests and
troughs of three flutings. All samples were analyzed using
hydrometer and sieving procedures. Further information was
obtained from auger holes and surface samples of the Alberta
Research Council Quaternary Geology Group.

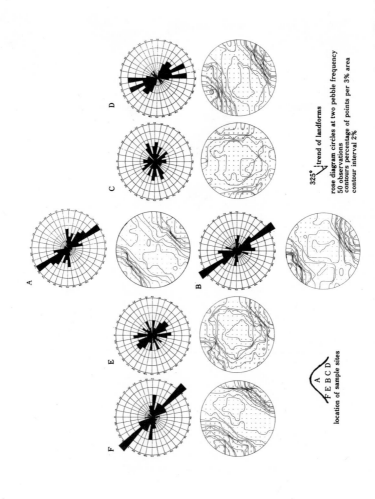

Figure 7. Two dimensional diagrams of microfabric data for the three flutings showing long axis orientation and plunge:
(a) fluting #1

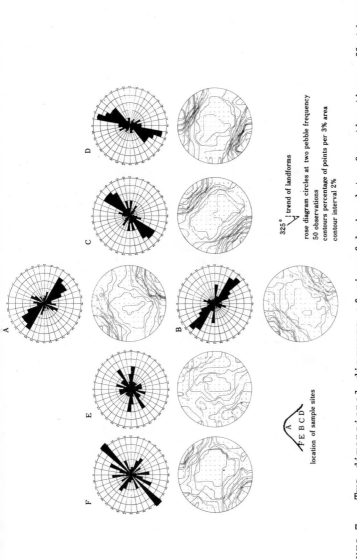

Figure 7. Two dimensional diagrams of microfabric data for the three flutings showing long axis orientation and plunge: (b) fluting #3

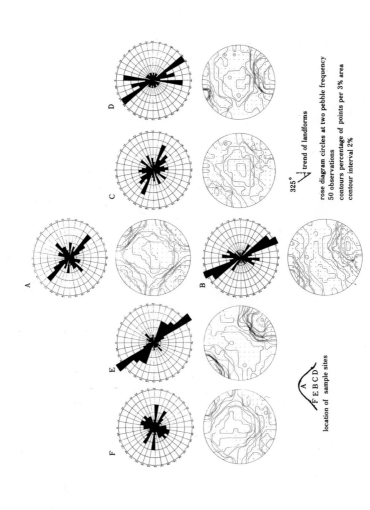

Figure 7. Two dimensional diagrams of microfabric data for the three flutings showing long axis orientation and plunge:
(c) fluting #5

Table 1. Macrofabric Statistical Data

Sample #	N	V(Deg.)	VM	R	K	A(Deg.)	E	I(Deg.)	D
1A	50	137	0.84	41.8	5.95	130.4	31.7	5.9 (D)	Bipolar
1B	50	321	0.77	38.5	4.28	329.9	32.0	0.5 (U)	Bipolar
1C	50	95	0.67	33.3	2.94	74.9	23.4	1.7 (N)	Girdle
1D	50	335	0.86	43.2	7.22	332.8	34.0	6.3 (U)	Asymmetric bipolar
1E	50	322	0.73	36.3	3.57	324.4	27.4	2.9 (U)	Girdle
1F	50	302	0.82	41.0	5.46	299.4	33.6	13.2 (U)	Asymmetric bipolar
3A	50	144	0.80	40.0	4.79	145.5	31.4	1.9 (D)	Asymmetric bipolar
3B	50	322	0.81	40.5	5.13	316.2	30.7	2.0 (U)	Asymmetric bipolar
3C	50	232	0.79	39.4	4.61	229.3	33.7	0.4 (D)	Asymmetric bipolar
3D	50	197	0.84	41.8	5.95	200.5	35.1	1.5 (D)	Asymmetric bipolar
3E	50	259	0.66	33.2	2.82	235.1	23.6	10.2 (N)	Girdle
3F	50	232	0.70	35.1	3.29	216.1	26.4	9.0 (N)	Girdle
5A	50	325	0.61	30.5	2.51	283.5	22.9	5.5 (U)	Girdle
5B	50	155	0.80	40.0	4.89	159.8	31.3	18.0 (D)	Bipolar
5C	50	356	0.65	32.7	2.83	319.6	24.8	1.2 (U)	Girdle
5D	50	161	0.77	38.4	4.24	163.9	29.2	8.4 (D)	Bipolar
5E	50	130	0.80	40.0	4.90	133.4	32.5	15.2 (D)	Bipolar
5F	50	204	0.61	30.9	2.57	213.9	25.4	15.8 (N)	Girdle

N = number of observations   A = azimuth of principal eigenvector   I = inclination of major plane
V = vector mean   E = eigenvalue of principal   (U) designates an up-ice inclination
VM = vector strength   eigenvector   (D) designates a down-ice inclination
R = vector strength   D = distribution pattern   (N) designates no preferred up- or down-ice
K = estimate of precision   inclination

Table 2. Microfabric Statistical Data

Sample #	N	$\bar{V}m$ (deg.)	$\bar{V}L$	X^2 value	10° Modal Class Midpoint	% Plunge up-ice	% Plunge down-ice	Plunge Significance value	Proportion value
1A	100	131.6	0.18	12.74	145	59	41		1.77
1B	100	144.7	0.31	9.45	145	63	37		2.51
1C	100	74.7	0.35	14.21	55	62	38		2.34
1D	100	9.7	0.31	14.37	15	65	35		2.87
1E	100	56.3	0.09	8.03	85	60	40		1.96
1F	100	40.2	0.19	15.31	55	66	34		3.05
3A	100	149.3	0.38	16.02	145	64	36		2.70
3B	100	12.7	0.09	14.66	5	54	46		0.81
3C	100	23.4	0.31	13.41	25	65	35		2.87
3D	100	14.2	0.29	10.07	15	55	45		1.00
3E	100	3.7	0.41	25.58	85	60	40		1.96
3F	100	87.2	0.18	27.19	85	61	39		2.15
5A	100	142.9	0.20	12.72	145	62	38		2.34
5B	100	145.8	0.43	17.76	145	62	38		2.34
5C	100	222.0	0.39	6.55	25	61	39		2.15
5D	100	17.1	0.51	18.34	25	63	37		2.52
5E	100	79.6	0.32	16.73	85	67	33		3.22
5F	100	77.2	0.32	19.52	95	66	34		3.05

N = number of observations $\bar{V}m$ = vector mean $\bar{V}l$ = mean vector length

DATA ANALYSIS

Fabric Data

Former ice movement may be discussed on the basis of till
fabric analyses (Harrison, 1957), and the flow conditions
present during formation of the streamlined landforms may
be estimated. For instance, if the arrangement of a till
fabric bears a close relationship to a landform, then a
common origin may be considered for both. The landform is,
therefore, depositional. Evidence of complex depositional
processes, those involved in the secondary flow mechanism,
may be present in the fabric of ice-moulded, streamlined
landforms. Shaw and Freschauf (1973) have shown this in
their study of flutings near Athabasca, Alberta, where a
'herring-bone' fabric pattern was found.

In the study area, the mean direction of ice advance,
based on the long axis orientations of the flutings present,
is from approximately 325°. The three flutings analyzed
possess an overall complex microfabric pattern. Microfabric
site 1 (Figure 7a) shows a trimodal fabric pattern, with
sites 1A and 1B having vector means which parallel the
fluting crest and primary ice flow direction, sites 1C and
1D having vector means which are rotated clockwise from the
fluting crest, implying secondary ice flow, and with the
vector means of sites 1E and 1F rotated anticlockwise from
the fluting crest. Sites 1E and 1F show a large anticlockwise rotation of their vector means and display a transverse
to primary ice flow orientation. All site 1 samples fit the
von Mises distribution satisfactorily.
This non-preferred state is reflected in its low mean vector
length value. All site 1 samples fit the von Mises distribution satisfactorily.

The site 3 microfabric azimuthal data (Figure 7b) display
a less consistent fabric pattern than the site 1 samples.
Data of site 3A show a preferred parallel to primary ice
flow orientation, but that of site 3B shows flow transverse
to this and also exhibit a very low mean vector length value.
This low mean vector length implies the sample does not have
a strong primary orientation, and resembles a uniform distribution. Distributions from sites 3C and 3D, conversely, have
relatively high mean vector length values, and show a strong
indication of secondary ice flow. Distributions from sites
3A, 3C and 3D all satisfactorily fit a von Mises distribution;
however those from sites 3E and 3F do not. This indicates
that fabrics at sites 3E and 3F do not show a significant
distribution of data points around their respective vector
means.

The microfabric site 5 orientation samples (Figure 7c)
show an excellent example of the 'herring-bone' pattern found
by Shaw and Freschauf (1973). The distributions located at
the fluting centre, 5A and 5B, display a parallel to primary
ice flow trend. Fabrics at sites 5C and 5D show an orientation rotated clockwise from the fluting crest, while those

at sites 5E and 5F show an orientation rotated anticlockwise from the fluting crest. Thus, a dominant secondary ice flow is indicated at sites 5C, 5D, 5E and 5F. All site 5 samples fit a von Mises distribution.

Although the significance of proportion test (Bruning and Kintz, 1968) showed that all samples, except 3B and 3D, have a significant up-ice plunge, it must be remembered that the vertical thin section used to determine grain plunge angles was cut parallel to the mean fluting orientation (325°), and thus, only diagrams with a vector mean which parallels this direction can be said to have a true up-ice plunge. Therefore, the grains at all A and B sites, except 3B, display an up-ice plunge. All other sites, except 3D, have a majority of grains which plunge towards 325°, but not necessarily in an up-ice direction for that sample.

The patterns shown by the macrofabric diagrams are less clear. All distributions were deemed to be significantly different from uniform, using the Fisher-Watson test of uniformity (Fara and Scheidegger, 1963). The diagrams of macrofabric site 1 (Figure 6a) show a tendency towards unimodal distributions with modes parallel to the fluting long axis, especially if site 1C is eliminated.

The Fisher-Watson analyses indicate samples 1A and 1B have bipolar distributions, 1D and 1F have asymmetric bipolar distributions, and 1C and 1E are girdle distributions. The well-defined bipolar distributions at 1A, 1B, 1D and 1F may indicate that more pronounced ice flow occurred at these locations, while the girdle distributions, which represent a wider scattering of pebble azimuths may indicate weaker ice flow, or, alternatively, more disturbance during deposition.

The diagrams for sites 3C and 3D (Figure 6b) reflect a clearer representation of secondary ice movement. The diagrams of 3A and 3B show a strong parallel to crest orientation is present in the till fabric at the fluting centre. Alternatively, diagrams of sites 3E and 3F show a preferred orientation transverse to primary ice flow. These transverse fabrics, which do not conform to a 'herring-bone' pattern, cannot be explained at present. However, if there is secondary flow, but without superimposed down-glacier flow, a flow at 90° to the fluting would be predicted. Sites 3A, 3B, 3C and 3D are asymmetric bipolar distributions possibly indicating pronounced ice flow, while 3E and 3F are girdle distributions indicating either weaker ice flow conditions, or disturbance during or after deposition.

The macrofabric diagrams for site 5 (Figure 6c) show a complex array of ice movements. Diagrams 5A, 5C and 5F show girdle distributions, although 5A could almost be said to represent a quadripolar distribution. Diagram 5A shows modes both parallel and transverse to primary ice flow. This situation is reflected in the statistical data (Table 1). The transverse mode may represent pebble rotation during transport about their 'A', or long axes, but insufficient data are available for this to be verified.

64

Diagrams, 5B, 5D and 5E have bipolar distribution patterns. Diagram 5B shows a preferred orientation parallel to fluting crest and primary ice flow. Diagrams 5D and 5E are somewhat similar but show some rotation of the vector means away from the fluting crest.

The Fisher-Watson analysis gives an indication of the plunge of the principal axis depicted by the principal eigenvector and eigenvalue of each three-dimensional microfabric diagram. Distributions 1B, 1D, 1E, 1F, 3B, 5A, and 5C have a preferred up-ice inclination of major axis (Table 1). Samples 1A, 3A, 3D, 5B, 5D, and 5E show preferred down-ice inclinations. Samples 1C, 3E, 3F and 5F show no preferred up- or down-ice inclination. Generally, in the macrofabrics, no preferred overall up- or down-ice inclination occurs. This lack of a preferred plunge in the macrofabrics, compared to the dominant up-ice plunge in the microfabrics, may indicate that post- and syndepositional rotation about a horizontal axis was more prevalent in the till pebbles than in the sand and silt matrix.

The complex micro- and macrofabric patterns clearly indicate the flutings of the study area resulted from a similarly complex process of transport. Part of this complexity may be attributed to secondary ice flow. Other processes, such as erosion and transport of frozen, nondeforming rafts of till, or post-depositional processes, such as freeze-thaw disturbance may also have been important.

The transport of the till as a frozen block of subglacially derived material may have been common. At fabric site 1C, a large block of fine to medium sand with its original bedding still intact was found in the till directly above the fabric location. The bedding could only have been preserved if the sand was transported and deposited as a rafted unit. If blocks of sand were transported in this way it seems reasonable to assume blocks of till underwent the same process.

Till Textural Data

Most grain-size analyses performed on till samples show a remarkably similar texture. The average textural percentages, and their respective standard deviations for till samples analyzed are: sand, 35.5, 8.6; silt, 27.1, 5.7; clay, 37.4, 7.5. The samples from auger holes drilled in fluting ridges and adjacent troughs also show a uniformity of till texture. As the same till was present within all of the flutings drilled, it is suggested that the material in them was derived from the same source area, and formation occurred during only one ice advance.

DISCUSSION

The preceding data and field analyses support the concept that secondary flow, and glaciotectonics are associated with the formation of large-scale flutings. This suggests a combination of two mechanisms introduced earlier, the secondary flow

Glacial erosion and deposition

of Shaw and Freschauf (1973), and the glaciotectonics of
Moran *et al.* (in press) which expands upon the work of
Weertman (1961).

The outstanding problem facing Shaw and Freschauf's
(1973) hypothesis is to provide a mechanism to initiate formation of the secondary flow cells. One hypothesis which may
provide a suitable mechanism is given by Hughes (1976) in
which he shows how a polygonal array of dikes created by
convection in an ice sheet becomes elongated into helicoidal
flow under ice flow. Hughes (1976) indicates the onset of
convection is controlled by ice thickness. However, once
again we are presented with a theoretical solution almost
impossible to verify practically.

Minell (1979) conducted a series of experiments with
media of different viscosities in order to present a situation
practically analogous to glacier flow. He found longitudinal
ridge surface patterns develop where the overflowing, less
viscous medium is accelerated (extending flow) and transverse
patterns exist where the overflowing medium is retarded
(compressive flow). Additionally, Minell (1979) found
transverse folds occur at the peripheries of the material,
while '.....longitudinal folds appeared in the lee of large
obstacles or on very flat areas...' (p.31).

In another experiment Minell (1979) exerted pressure on
a sand bed with a greased roller, and found longitudinal
ridges were best formed when high velocity movements, producing high shear, were introduced. This compares favourably
with Doornkamp and King's (1971) work, in which they postulate drumlin elongation is directly related to rapid, constant
ice flow.

Minells' (1979) work also has some significant application
to the St. Paul area, since his experiments show compressive
flow occurs where the medium is constricted and extending
flow where the medium is unrestricted, and especially where
acceleration occurs. In east-central Alberta, as has been
previously mentioned, the convergence of two separate ice
advances, the Lac la Biche lobe and the Cold Lake lobe,
occurred just northwest of St. Paul (Figure 4). The combined
flow of these two advances was then channelled to the southeast by the presence of two large, stagnant ice blocks. It
is postulated that at the point of convergence longitudinally
compressive flow occurred, and immediately down-ice, where
the ice was forced between the stagnant ice blocks, this
changed to extending flow.

The area in which longitudinally compressive flow is
thought to have occurred now contains a swarm of relatively
short, high drumlins and flutings (Figure 3), many of which
are directly down-ice of existing lakes which may be source
depressions for the landforms. Down-ice of this region, in
the area which probably experienced extending flow, long, low
flutings are now present (Figure 3). If, as Minell (1979)
has suggested, longitudinal folds occur on the surface of a
medium during extending flow, these folds would create a

differential transverse pressure system in the ice setting
up Shaw and Freschauf's (1973) helicoidal flow cells, and
producing fluting formation (Shaw, in press).

Moran *et al.* (in press) show that compressive flow
followed by continued ice advance, as in the zone of convergence in this case, can cause initial thrusting of blocks
of basal debris, and a subsequent moulding of these blocks
into streamlined landforms. The plucked blocks would
initiate a differential pressure system, with low pressure
on the downglacier side, including the secondary flow. Also,
Minell's (1979) tests showed that longitudinal folds occur
in the lee of large obstacles. These folds could also
initiate the secondary flow.

Wet-based conditions which are required in the depositional stage of Shaw and Freschauf's (1973) theory are assumed
to have occurred after thrusting, and during the moulding
stage of drumlin and fluting development. Deposition would
necessarily require extremely slow basal melt-out in order
for the streamlined features to be preserved. Menzies (1979)
emphasizes the rapid dissipation of porewater through stress
applied at the ice/glacier bed interface. The rate of dissipation will depend on the till texture and the consolidation
characteristics of the materials. Ice basal stresses would
be most important during this process, but stresses developed
at a freezing front within the material may also be a factor
(Menzies, 1979).

Shaw (1977) notes that removal of ice from till by sublimation is an important process in arid, polar environments.
A high degree of aridity in the study area is indicated from
the widespread occurrence of aeolian sands, and sand wedges
(Figure 3). Therefore, a sublimation process may have been
important during the deposition of the till in the flutings,
allowing passive, rather than highly active, deposition, and,
thus, a high degree of preservation of the till fabric
developed during the transportational phase. Any supraglacial
meltwaters are expected to have flowed into lateral channels
such as the Moosehills meltwater channel.

Moran *et al.* (in press) postulated that glacial thrust
blocks originate under frozen-bed conditions where high porewater pressures decrease the shear strength of the basal
material to a point less than the shear stress exerted by the
ice. This is thought to occur at the margin of the glacier
where the ice is thinnest, and cold conditions are present
at the bed. Other factors which accentuate the thrusting
process are the presence of pre-existing planes of weakness,
such as bedding or jointing in the sediment, and buried
aquifers which elevate the porewater pressure and reduce the
effective normal stress.

Streamlined terrain can be initiated through erosion of
the substrate or smoothing of thrust blocks and lee deposition.
Two elements exist here, convergence of volumes of debris in
lee zones, which may occur under frozen-bed conditions, and
deposition which usually requires thawing. The low pressure

on the downstream side of thrust blocks may cause flow convergence and accumulation of debris-rich ice. The till may retain evidence of this flow structure in a 'herring-bone' fabric pattern.

The size, especially the length of the resultant drumlin or fluting will be directly dependent upon the amount of material available for lee deposition, and the duration and consistency of direction of ice flow over the site. A direct correlation is expected between the type of resultant stream-lined landform and these factors, especially the consistency of ice advance. For example, drumlins may occur where the ice flows in short, discontinuous movements and debris availability is irregular, while glacial flutings may develop under periods of constant, continuous ice flow.

SUMMARY

Combination of the two hypotheses discussed (Shaw and Freschauf, 1973; Moran *et al.* in press) represents a major step towards explanation of the genesis of glacial flutings. Gravenor and Meneley's (1958) concept of high and low pressure zones provides a basis for Shaw and Freschauf's (1973) theory of secondary flow. The hypothesis of glacial thrusting and streamlining proposed by Moran *et al.* (in press) has an important function in fluting development as it provides a mechanism for initiating the secondary flows in the placement of resistant blocks of basal debris.

A combination of the two papers discussed, Shaw and Freschauf (1973) and Moran *et al.* (in press), seems most powerful in explaining the formation of streamlined landforms in the study area. The thrusting of blocks of basal debris during frozen-bed conditions and the subsequent creation of secondary flows and streamlining as ice advance continued adequately explains the formation of flutings in this region.

REFERENCES CITED

Aario, R. 1977, Classification and terminology of morainic landforms in Finland. *Boreas,* 6, 87-100

Allen, J.R.L. 1964, Primary current lineation in the Lower Old Red Sandstone (Devonian), Anglo-Welsh Basin, *Sedimentology,* 3, 89-108

Allen, J.R.L. 1968, On the geometry of current ripples in relation to stability of fluid flow. *Geografiska Annaler,* 51-A, 61-96

Baranowski, S. 1970, The origin of fluted moraine at the fronts of contemporary glaciers. *Geografiska Annaler,* 52, 68-75

Bretz, J.H. 1943, Keewatin and moraines in Alberta, Canada. *Geological Society of America Bulletin,* 54, 31-54

Bruning, J.L. and B.L. Kintz, 1968, *Computational Handbook of Statistics*. (Scott, Foresman and Co., Glenview, Illinois), 269 pp.

Corbató, C.E. 1966, *Fabric diagrams by computer*, (Department of Geology, U.C.L.A.), Spring

Doornkamp, J.C. and C.A.M. King, 1971, *Numerical Analysis in Geomorphology*, (Edward Arnold, London), 372 pp.

Dyson, J.L. 1952, Ice-ridged moraines and their relation to glaciers. *American Journal of Science*, 250, 204-211

Ellwood, R.D. 1960, *Surficial Geology of the Vermilion Area, Alberta, Canada*, (Unpublished Ph.D. thesis, University of Illinois), 131 pp.

Fara, H.D. and A.E. Scheidegger, 1963, An eigenvalue method for the statistical evaluation of fault plane solutions of earthquakes. *Bulletin Seismological Society of America*, 53, 811-816

Flint, R.F. 1971, *Glacial and Quaternary Geology*, (John Wiley and Sons Inc., New York), 892 pp.

Gravenor, C.P. 1953, The origin of drumlins. *American Journal of Science*, 251, 674-681

Gravenor, C.P. and W.A. Meneley, 1958, Glacial flutings in central and northern Alberta. *American Journal of Science*, 256, 715-728

Harrison, W. 1957, A clay-till fabric, its character and origin. *Journal of Geology*, 65, 275-308

Harvey, P.K. and C.C. Ferguson, 1976, On testing orientation data for Goodness-of-fit for a von Mises distribution. *Computers and Geosciences*, 2, 261-268

Hoppe, G. and V. Schytt, 1953, Some observations on fluted moraine surfaces. *Geografiska Annaler*, 35, 105-115

Hughes, T.J. 1976, The theory of thermal convection in polar ice sheets. *Journal of Glaciology*, 16, 41-73

Menzies, J. 1979, A review of the literature on the formation and location of drumlins. *Earth Science Reviews*, 14, 315-359

Minell, H. 1979, The genesis of tills in different moraine types and the deglaciation in a part of central Lappland. *Sveriges Geologiska Undersokning, serie C*, 754

Moran, S.R., Clayton, L., Hooke, R. Le B., Fenton, M.M. and L.D. Andriashek, (in press), Glacier-bed landforms of the prairie region of North America. *Journal of Glaciology*

Morris, E.M. and L.W. Morland, 1976, A theoretical analysis of the formation of glacial flutes. *Journal of Glaciology*, 17, 311-323

Shaw, J. 1977, Tills deposited in arid polar environments. *Canadian Journal of Earth Sciences*, 14, 1239-1245

Glacial erosion and deposition

Shaw, J. 1980, Drumlins and large-scale flutings related to glacier folds. *Arctic and Alpine Research*, 12(3), 287-298

Shaw, J. and R.C. Freschauf, 1973, A kinematic discussion of the formation of glacial flutings. *The Canadian Geographer*, 17, 19-35

Steinmetz, R. 1962, Analysis of vectorial data. *Journal of Sedimentary Petrology*, 32, 801-812

Weertman, J. 1961, Mechanism for the formation of inner moraines found near the edge of cold ice caps and ice sheets. *Journal of Glaciology*, 3, 965-978

4 Contemporary push moraine formation in the Yoho Valley, BC

R.J. Rogerson & M.J. Batterson

ABSTRACT

The characteristics and formation of minor push-moraine ridges are normally described for areas of terminal recession. Sometimes, ridge formation is described as an annual event. In the Yoho Valley a multi-year contemporary push-moraine ridge is forming at the margin of Emerald Glacier. The glacier appears to be in a state of still-stand or minor readvance. Two models of push moraine formation are apparent: one where ice annually decouples from the moraine during the summer, then readvances with the cessation of ice melt in the early winter; and a second where the ice remains in contact with the moraine throughout the summer due to a thick supraglacial cover reducing ice melt. In the latter case, subglacially transported fines are intruded into or emplaced upon the loose-textured moraine ridge resulting in a complex sedimentary arrangement. The models are supported by two years of observation of the ice terminus, and by an intensive sediment sampling program.

INTRODUCTION AND OBJECTIVES

The characteristics and formation of push-moraine ridges have been extensively documented (Dyson 1952; Rutten 1960; Bayrock 1967; Kalin 1971; Verbraeck 1975; Birnie 1977; Haeberli 1979; Rabassa *et al* 1979; etc.). Although Flint (1971) and Price (1973) suggest that push moraines are generally minor features of little significance, some contrasts of scale are apparent, possibly the result of frozen or unfrozen interstitial water within proglacial sediments. Large push features of reactivated ice-cored moraine or proglacial sediments have been described by Rutten (1960), Kalin (1971) and Johnson (1972), whereas small 'minor' push moraines containing recently discharged glacial sediments have been described by Worsley (1974), Boulton and Eyles (1979) and Rabassa *et al* (1979). This paper is concerned with the contemporary formation of the latter type of feature.

The term push moraine is attributed to Chamberlin (1894) and reflects the ice dynamics during or after deposition of proglacial material. In simple terms, till may be deposited

* R. J. Rogerson and M. J. Batterson
Memorial University of Newfoundland, St. John's, Newfoundland, Canada

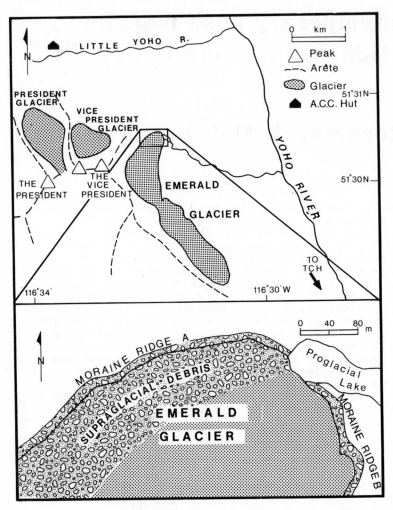

Figure 1.   Emerald Glacier: Location in the Yoho Valley, B.C.,
and detail of the northern terminus

at an ice terminus and then pushed by a minor readvance of
the ice. Such minor readvances are annual events at
the termini of temperate glaciers where recession induced by
ice melt ceases with the first effective cover of snow, but
basal sliding continues all winter (Hewitt 1967), or until the
ice is seasonally frozen to its bed.

Recent examination of moraine ridges and other till units
at the termini of cirque and valley glaciers has produced a
general description of the 'glaciated valley sediment/landform
association' (Boulton 1976; Boulton and Paul 1976; Boulton
and Eyles 1979) or the 'glaciated valley land system and
sediment association' (Eyles 1979).   Within these descriptions,
push moraines formed by winter readvance during a period of

general recession (Facies A_1; Boulton and Eyles 1979), are contrasted with dump moraines produced during standstill, with low glacial activity and no accompanying push moraine (Facies B).

Until recently, most temperate alpine glaciers were retreating, and push moraines were either not well developed, or were abandoned after a single year's activity and left as part of an 'annual' recessional moraine sequence (Worsley 1974). In the last decade recession has decreased in amount or ceased in many alpine glaciers in Western Canada (Gardner 1972). This has occurred either in response to climatic deterioration or because the glaciers reduced mass and higher elevation of termini are more in equilibrium with present climate. Thus, the opportunity now exists to examine multi-year push-moraine ridges where more than a single pushing event affects the constructional form. Such is the case at the northeastern teminus of Emerald Glacier (Figure 1), a small (less than 1 km^2) alpine glacier in the Yoho Valley, Rocky Mountains, British Columbia. The glacier erodes Cambrian sedimentary terrane, primarily limestone, dolomite and shale, and is perched on a distinct topographic shelf approximately 2300 m asl, which is an expression of the Wapta Mountain Thrust (Cook 1975).

The primary objective of this work is to analyse two parts of an active push-moraine ridge that are subject to two different modes of formation at a single glacier terminus. Included in this is a description of the morphology of the moraine ridge, its stratigraphy, sedimentology and certain geotechnical properties, as well as a preliminary examination of ice dynamics in the terminal region of Emerald glacier.

LOGISTICS AND METHODS

Field work at Emerald glacier was conducted in the summers of 1978 and 1979. Methods used were directed to particular aspects of the study.

(a)   morphological description:
      Uncontrolled ground photographs were supplemented by field sketches, and in August 1979, by a plane-table map of the terminal zone. Profiles of the moraine and ice surface were surveyed with a tape and Brunton compass at several locations.

(b)   stratigraphy:
      Sections were cut in the moraine ridge at nine points. Visible units were described by Munsell soil colour, pH, and by general textural appearance.

(c)   sediments:
      Samples were taken from all the stratigraphic units within the moraine, and from supraglacial, englacial and subglacial sources elsewhere on the glacier. Laboratory procedures included grain size analysis of the -2.5 to 13ϕ fraction, using the pipette method for the <4ϕ segment;

Figure 2. The northern terminus of Emerald glacier showing the debris-free and heavily debris-covered areas.

Figure 3. The push-moraine ridge in early July 1979

and the determination of Atterberg limits following standard
procedures outlined by Bowles (1975). Grain size distributions were plotted on a Hewlett-Packard desk-top computer
using a program devised by Slatt and Press (1976), and
analysed according to Friedman's (1961) method of moments.

(d) fabrics:
     The three-dimensional orientation of 50 clasts greater
than 1.5 cm long and with an a:b ratio of >3:2 was measured
with a Brunton compass in sites characterizing the major
stratigraphic units. Results were plotted and contoured on
a wolf net.

(e) ice and sediment dynamics:
     A preliminary determination of ice movement was under-
taken for a 25-day period in August 1979 using stakes drilled
into the ice at five locations. Measurements were taken on
a daily basis whenever possible from the stakes to fixed
reference points in the proglacial area. The direction of
movement was in all cases parallel to the ice slope.
     Ice-melt rates were measured at fixed points on both
debris-covered and debris-free sites on a daily basis.
     The downglacier movement of supraglacial debris was
measured along two transects parallel to the ice slope. For
each transect clasts of varying size and shape were marked
and their downglacier progression measured relative to a
fixed marker beyond the ice terminus. All measurements were
made with a steel tape.

PUSH MORAINE MORPHOLOGY

The northern terminus of Emerald glacier (Figure 2) is fringed
by a contemporary moraine ridge which,for most of its length
is between 1.5 and 3 m high (Figure 3). The ridge is continuous for 1500 m but for a 100 m section where the glacier
terminates in a small proglacial lake (Figure 1).

     To the west of the proglacial lake, the moraine ridge
(ridge A) lies at the margin of a moderate ice slope (16 to
32°) which is heavily covered with supraglacial debris
(Figure 4). The single crest of the ridge is well-defined and
composed of coarse shaley material. During the summers of
1978 and 1979 the ice remained in close contact with the
proximal side of moraine ridge A for most of its length.

     To the south of the proglacial lake the moraine ridge
(ridge B) lies at the margin of a steep ice slope (20 to 60°)
which is relatively free of supraglacial debris (Figure 5).
The ridge in this location is generally loose textured and
in parts has up to three superimposed 'push' units along the
crest (Figure 6). This type of unit has been described for
lateral moraines and Neoglacial end moraines (Humlum 1978;
Osborn 1978; Ahmed 1979; Luckman and Osborn 1979). During
the summers of 1978 and 1979 the ice along this section melted
back and lost contact with the proximal side of the moraine
by as much as four metres. This permitted easy observation
of the melt out of glacier sole debris from either minor
subglacial regelation layers (Figure 7) or from zones of more
massively impacted till (Figure 8).

75

Figure 4. Ridge A and the heavily debris-covered glacier
    behind it

Figure 5. Ridge B in late July 1978 with steep ice cliffs
    visible behind it

Figure 6. Three distinct push units on the crest of moraine ridge B, July 1979

Figure 9 summarizes the different profiles of the ice terminus and moraine ridge late in the melt season 1979. The contrasts between profiles in the vicinity of ridge A and ridge B are sufficiently well-defined to question whether both sections of the moraine can be formed by an identical process.

STRATIGRAPHY

Sections cut in the moraine reveal some further contrasts between ridge A and ridge B (Figure 10). At sample sites 2, 4, 6, 7, 8, and 9, all on ridge A, there exists a cohesive, hydroplastic, silt/clay sediment unit between 25 and 80 cm thick and inclined in a proximal direction within the moraine (Figure 11). At each site the unit contrasts markedly with the coarse, clastic textured material which both underlies and overlies the finer unit. Other fines were seen washed out of the distal base of the moraine. They were located in the area where a large block protrudes, as though thrust through or from the moraine (Figure 12).

In ridge B, to the south of the lake, composition appeared to be relatively homogeneous with no fine sediment unit being found. Thus the contrast is one of stratigraphic complexity in ridge A against homogeneity in ridge B. Nevertheless, some 'seasonal' complexity was noted in ridge B early in July 1979. At that time ice lay immediately proximal to the ridge for most of its length. Where decoupling was just beginning, a zone of buried snow could be seen underneath the ice and overlain by a part of the moraine. The snow had melted by the time stratigraphic sections and sediment samples were taken, and is not included in Figure 10.

Figure 7. Subglacial regelation ice and debris revealed
behind ridge B, late July 1978

Figure 8. The ice margin decoupled from behind moraine B
in the vicinity of sample site 1, late July 1978.
Sediments falling from underneath the ice include large
boulders and fine subglacial debris

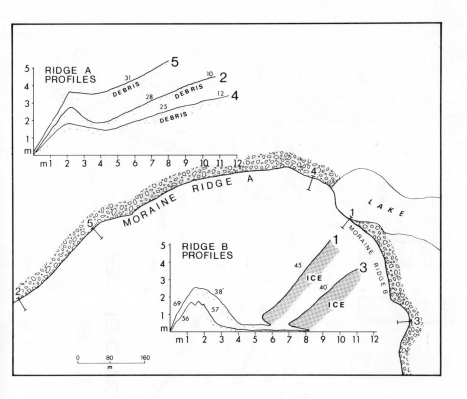

Figure 9. Profiles of the ice margin and moraines in late
August 1979

Till fabrics in the moraine (Figure 10) indicate moderate
to strong upglacier imbrication in three samples and weak
downglacier imbrication in two. The strongest fabric occurs
in the fine sediment layer at sample site 2 (ridge A) and
suggests active pushing or overriding of the ridge by proximal
ice. An origin related to the through-washing and catching
of supraglacial fines (Eyles 1979) can be discounted in this
case.

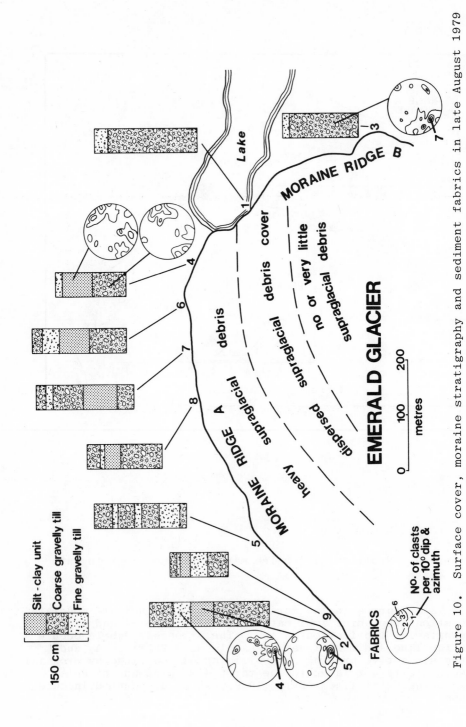

Figure 10. Surface cover, moraine stratigraphy and sediment fabrics in late August 1979

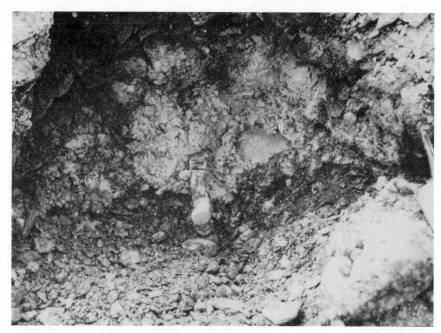

Figure 11.   A fine hydroplastic silt-clay layer in the
   vicinity of site 6, moraine ridge A.

Figure 12.   A large block thrust from moraine A, July 1978

SEDIMENT - TEXTURES AND GEOTECHNICAL PROPERTIES

An important question in the formation of push-moraine ridges concerns the source of sediments comprising the moraine. Is material derived from supraglacial, englacial or subglacial sources, or from a combination of all three? Sediments transported within these specific environments are known to differ texturally in the case of crystalline bedrocks and long valley glaciers (Slatt 1971; Boulton 1976; Eyles and Rogerson 1978). With small glaciers however, the short distance of transportation of the bed load reduces the intensity of comminution of subglacial debris; the primary cause of differentiation between it and other debris transported by the glacier (Eyles and Rogerson 1978; Boulton and Eyles 1979). Nevertheless, soft sedimentary bedrock may comminute rapidly beneath sliding ice. Certainly, textural differentiation between subglacial and other debris appears to exist at Emerald glacier. Grain size analysis reveals quite separate distributions for supraglacial and subglacial sediments in Figure 13 where mean size is plotted against standard deviation (first and second moments; Friedman 1961).

Sediments taken from the moraine ridge at Emerald glacier are also plotted on Figure 13. Samples from ridge A show a very broad spread of values in contrast to the narrow spread for those from ridge B. In ridge A this may be explained by the existence of separate units of coarse supraglacial and fine subglacial tills within the moraine. In ridge B, sediments are primarily derived from subglacial sources, but are not emplaced as an unmodified lodgement till. The till melts out (Figure 8), falls and is washed during the summer, prior to winter readvance when it is formed into a ridge. Thus the sediment is partly depleted of fines, and moves towards the coarser supraglacial distribution on Figure 13.

Atterberg limits indicate a very marked contrast between tills in ridge A and those in ridge B (Figure 14). All values lie below the 22-24 liquid limit where Boulton and Paul (1976) noted a considerable scatter of points away from the 'T-line', in tills from Spitsbergen and Iceland. Low liquid limits and plasticity indices are generally related to the 'dilution' effect of increases in the coarse fraction; while values far below the 'T-line' are characteristic of tills where depositional and post-depositional processes produce a grade different from the parent glacial debris (Boulton and Paul 1976).

At Emerald glacier, certain characteristics of the fine fraction of the till can be noted.

(1) Ridge A and Ridge B samples are clearly separate, with ridge A exhibiting generally higher plasticity indices and liquid limits.

(2) Samples from the fine silt-clay sediment units lie on the T-line, suggesting unmodified subglacial till.

(3) Other samples on the T-line are *in-situ* subglacial tills taken from underneath the ice behind moraine B, prior to natural melt-out.

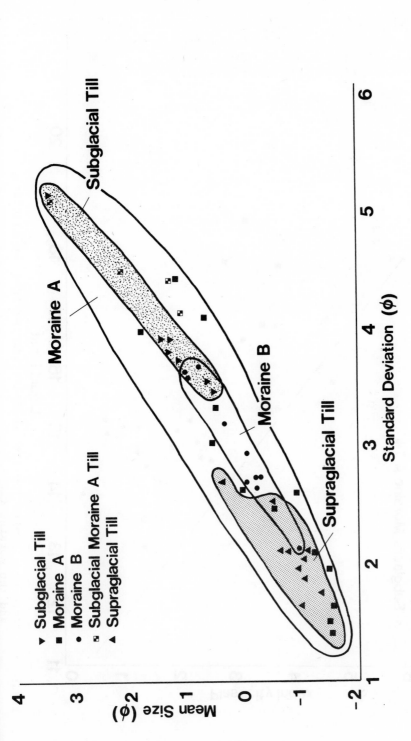

Figure 13. Mean grain size vs. standard deviation from the mean, for *in-situ* glacial sediments and for sediments taken from moraine ridges A and B

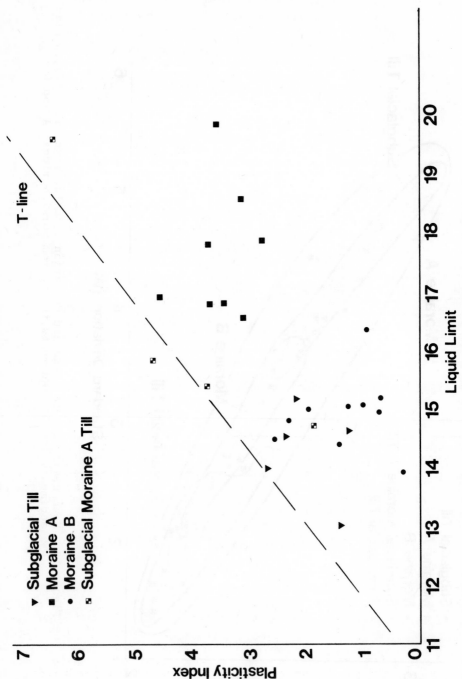

Figure 14. Atterberg limits for fine sediment samples from the glacier and the moraine ridge

(4) Samples from ridge B all lie below the T-line, indicating that post-depositional modification is characteristic of all the sediments in that ridge.

ICE DYNAMICS

Changes in the ice margin, surface slope and elevation during the summer occur in response to ice melt and glacier movement. Both factors were measured for a short period of time in the summer of 1979.

Surface ice melt, measured at (i) and (ii) on Figure 15, showed a marked contrast between heavily debris-covered ice proximal to ridge A and clean ice proximal to ridge B. Average melt for the former area, site (i), was 4.3 cm day^{-1} while for the latter area, site (ii), it was 14.6 cm day^{-1}. The major consequence of reduced melt in the area of supraglacial debris cover was that the ice remained in contact with ridge A throughout the summer for most of its length. In contrast, the ice decoupled from ridge B during the summer by as much as 4 m.

Downglacier ice movement was measured at six stakes in the terminal zone although a reasonable indication of movement can also be obtained from surface debris movements (Figure 15). A downglacier decrease in amount of debris movement indicates also a decrease in ice movement, and compressive longitudinal strain. Downglacier movement was greater in the area with no supraglacial debris where at sites B, D, E and F it averaged 5.6, 6.5, 6.7, and 6.9 cm day^{-1} respectively. Traverses behind sample sites 2 and 8 indicate maximum movements of 3.4 and 3.9 cm day^{-1} respectively. Longitudinal compressive strains were probably greater behind ridge A where the ice is partly supported by contact with the ridge. Markers on the ridge at sites 2 and 8 indicated that the ridge was pushed forward during August 1979 an average of 0.94 and 0.82 cm day^{-1} respectively. It is difficult to compare the magnitude of this push with that which affects ridge B. Higher rates may prevail at ridge B, but for a shorter period of time, once surface ice melt is prevented by winter snow cover, and the intervening gap between the glacier and the ridge has been closed. Early in July 1979 the ice behind moraine ridge B was observed to be actively pushing the ridge, although no measurements of the rate of pushing were made.

CONCLUSIONS

Examination of the morphology, stratigraphy, textures, fabrics, and geotechnical properties of sediments, as well as the ice dynamics at the margin of Emerald glacier support the conclusion that two types of push moraine may be formed at the margin of an active alpine glacier.

The first type (Figure 16) is represented by moraine ridge A, where a heavy supraglacial debris cover reduces the rate of ice melt such that contact is maintained between the moraine ridge and the glacier all summer. Much of this moraine is

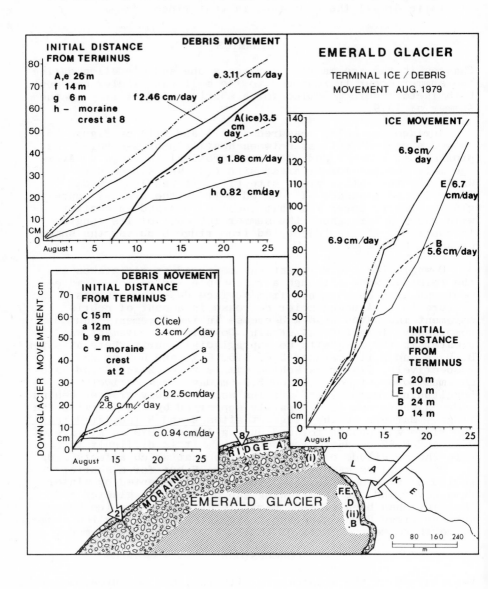

Figure 15. Terminal ice and supraglacial sediment dynamics
for August 1979

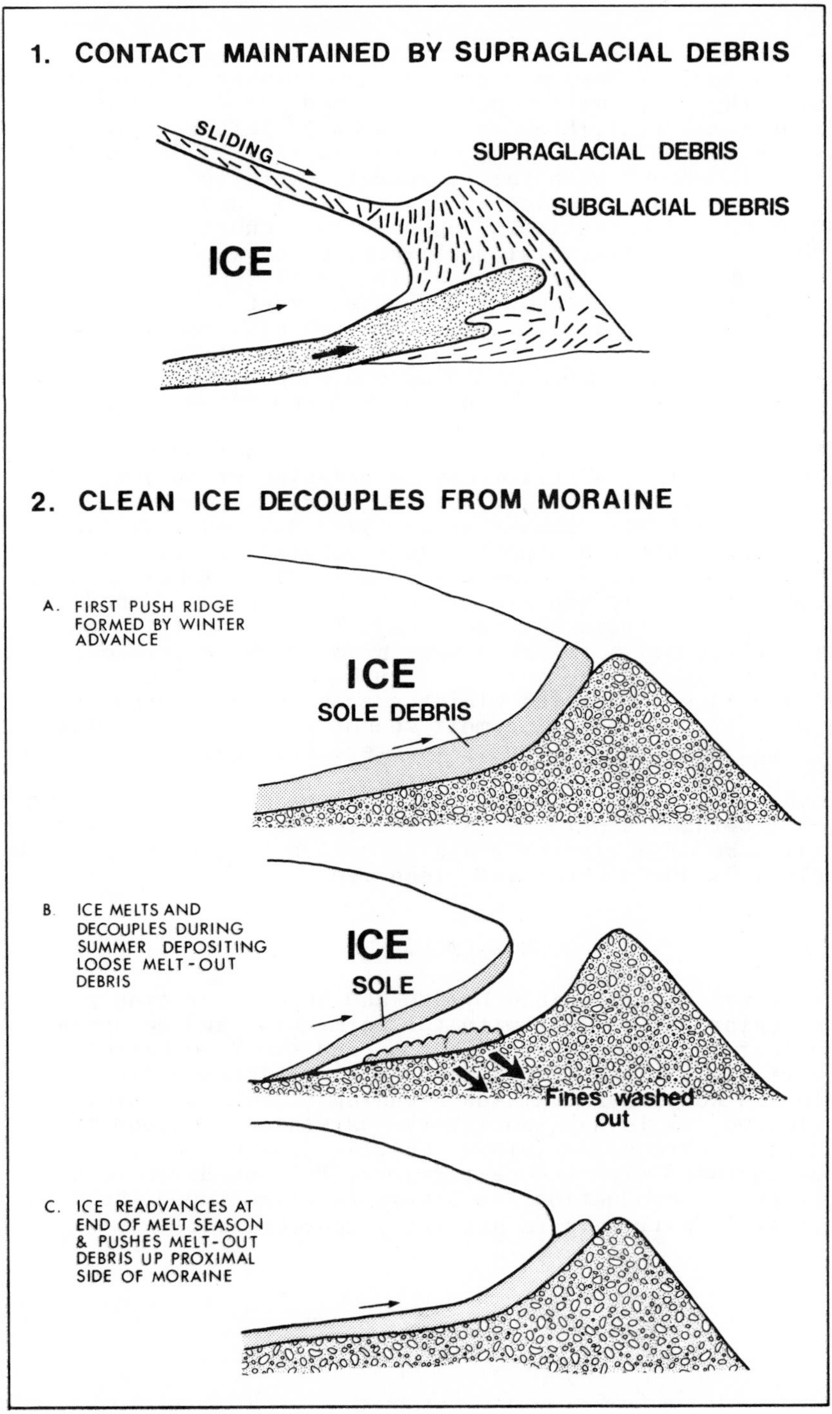

1. **CONTACT MAINTAINED BY SUPRAGLACIAL DEBRIS**

SLIDING

SUPRAGLACIAL DEBRIS

SUBGLACIAL DEBRIS

ICE

2. **CLEAN ICE DECOUPLES FROM MORAINE**

A. FIRST PUSH RIDGE
FORMED BY WINTER
ADVANCE

ICE
SOLE DEBRIS

B. ICE MELTS AND
DECOUPLES DURING
SUMMER DEPOSITING
LOOSE MELT-OUT
DEBRIS

ICE
SOLE

Fines washed out

C. ICE READVANCES AT
END OF MELT SEASON
& PUSHES MELT-OUT
DEBRIS UP PROXIMAL
SIDE OF MORAINE

Figure 16.   Models of push moraine formation

Glacial erosion and deposition

dumped from supraglacial sources as sediment is transported to the terminus on or by sliding over, the ice and accumulates as a talus apron. However, significant pushing by proximal ice forms the ridge morphology and causes the deposition of fine subglacial till which is subsequently left in a rela- tively unmodified state. The subglacial till is deposited either as lodgement when the ice margin over-rides the talus along a thrust, as observed by Hewitt (1967) and Whalley (1974) or by hydroplastic intrusion of wet subglacial till into the loose supraglacial sediments, or by a combination of both processes. The fact that a glacier is debris covered, has a reduced flow, and has a dumped sediment unit around its terminus, does not preclude the formation of a complex moraine with a pushed characteristic. This type of moraine thus combines elements of both the dump and push varieties which are given separate treatment by Boulton and Eyles (1979).

The second type of push moraine is represented by moraine ridge B adjacent to a relatively clean glacier surface. This type is recognizably similar to push moraines described else- where (Worsley 1974; Rabassa *et al* 1979; Boulton and Eyles (1979). Sediments are supplied from subglacial sources, but are not deposited as lodgement. Rather, glacier sole materials melt out (Figure 14) and are dropped into the gap formed between the ice margin and the ridge. They are partly depleted of fines which may be carried away by minor melt streams flowing through the base of the moraine. Pushing of the loose melt- out till occurs during the winter season and continues in the early part of the following melt season as long as the glacier remains unfrozen to its bed in the terminal zone.

Both types of push moraine may form at a single ice term- inus, and perhaps should be expected to coexist, wherever the terminal zone of a glacier contains contrasting zones of high supraglacial debris cover and clean ice.

ACKNOWLEDGEMENTS

This work was made possible by NRC and NSERC operating grants to the senior author; and with the permission and co-operation of the Western Region, Parks Canada, and the Yoho National Park personnel. Field assistance by Roger Jackson (1978) and Richard Kodybka and Alison Stenning (1979) is gratefully acknowledged, as is the laboratory assistance provided by Jeff Barnes. Michael McIntyre, Charles Conway and Gary McManus assisted with the cartography, Wilfred Marsh with photographic reproduction and Glenys Woodland typed the final manuscript. Their help is sincerely appreciated.

REFERENCES

Ahmed, N.   1979,   Morainic deposits in Kashmir Himalayas. in *Moraines and varves,* ed H. Schlüchter, (Balkema, Rotterdam), 59-64

Bayrock, L. A.   1967,   Catastrophic advance of the Steel Glacier, Yukon, Canada. *Boreal Institute, University of Alberta, Edmonton, Occasional Publication,* 3, 35pp.

Birnie, R.V.   1977,   A snow-bank push mechanism for the formation of some 'annual' moraine ridges. *Journal of Glaciology,* 18, 77-85

Boulton, G. S.   1976,   A genetic classification of tills and criteria for distinguishing tills of different origin. *Geografia,* 12, 65-80

Boulton, G. S. and N. Eyles, 1979,   Sedimentation by valley glaciers; a model and genetic classification.   in *Moraines and varves,* ed H. Schlüchter, (Balkema, Rotterdam),   11-23

Boulton, G.S. and M. A. Paul, 1976,   The influence of genetic processes on some geotechnical properties of glacial till.   *Quarterly Journal of Engineering Geology,* 9, 159-194

Bowles, J. E.   1975,   *Engineering properties of soil and their measurement,* (McGraw-Hill, New York)

Chamberlin, T. C.   1894,   Proposed genetic classification of Pleistocene glacial formations. *Journal of Glaciology,* 2, 517-538

Cook, D.G.   1975,   Structural style influenced by lithofacies, Rocky Mountain Main Ranges, Alberta-British Columbia, *Geological Survey of Canada Bulletin,* 233

Dyson, J. L.   1952,   Ice ridged moraines and their relationship to glaciers. *American Journal of Science,* 250, 204-211

Eyles, N.   1979,   Facies of supraglacial sedimentation on Icelandic and Alpine temperate glaciers. *Canadian Journal of Earth Sciences,* 16, 1341-1361

Eyles N. and R. J. Rogerson, 1978,   Sedimentology of medial moraines on Berendon Glacier, British Columbia, Canada: implications for debris transport in a glacierized basin. *Geological Society of America Bulletin,* 89, 1688-1693

Flint, R. F.   1971,   *Glacial and Quaternary Geology,* (Wiley, New York)

Friedman, G. M.   1961,   Distinction between dune, beach and river sands from their textural characteristics. *Journal of Sedimentary Petrology,* 31, 514-529

Gardner, J.   1972,   Recent glacial activity and some associated landforms in the Canadian Rocky Mountains. in *Mountain geomorphology,* ed O. Slaymaker and N. J. McPherson, (Tantalus Research Ltd., Vancouver), 55-62

Glacial erosion and deposition

Haeberli, W. 1979, Holocene push-moraines in alpine permafrost? *Geografiska Annaler A,* 61, 43-48

Hewitt, K. 1967, Ice front deposition and the seasonal
effect: a Himalayan example. *Transactions of the
Institute of British Geographers,* 42, 93-106

Humlum, O. 1978, Genesis of layered lateral moraines. Implications for paleoclimatology and lichenometry.
Geografisk Tiddsskrift, 77, 65-72

Johnson, P. G. 1972, The morphological effects of surges
of the Donjek Glacier, St. Elias Mountains, Yukon.
Journal of Glaciology, 11, 227-234

Kalin, M. 1971, Active push moraine of the Thompson Glacier,
Axel Heiberg Island, Canadian Arctic Archipelago.
*McGill University, Axel Heiberg Island, Research
Report, Glaciology,* 4

Luckman, B. H. and G. D. Osborn, 1979, Holocene glacier
fluctuations in the Middle Canadian Rocky Mountains.
Quaternary Research, 11, 52-77

Osborn, G. D. 1978, Fabric and origin of lateral moraines,
Bethartoli Glacier, Garhwal Himalaya, India. *Journal
of Glaciology,* 20, 547-553

Price, R. J. 1973, *Glacial and fluvioglacial landforms.*
(Oliver and Boyd, Edinburgh)

Rabassa, J., Rubulis, S. and J. Suarez, 1979, Rate of form-
ation and sedimentology of (1976-1978) push moraines,
Frias Glacier, Mount Tronador (41°10'S; 71°53'W),
Argentina. in *Moraines and varves,* ed H. Schlüchter,
(Balkema, Rotterdam), 65-79

Rutten, M. G. 1960, Ice-pushed ridges, permafrost and drainage. *American Journal of Science,* 258, 293-297

Slatt, R. M. 1971, Texture of ice-cored deposits from ten
Alaskan valley glaciers. *Journal of Sedimentary
Petrology,* 41, 828-834

Slatt, R. M. and D. E. Press, 1976, Computer program for
presentation of grain-size data by the graphic
method. *Sedimentology,* 23, 121-132

Verbraeck, A. 1975, Ice-pushed ridges in the eastern part
of the Netherlands River area. *Geologie en Mijnbouw,*
54, 82-84

Whalley, W. B. 1974, *Formation and characteristics of some
Alpine moraines.* (Unpublished Ph.D thesis, Downing
College, University of Cambridge)

Worsley, P. 1974, Recent 'annual' moraine ridges at Austre
Okstindbreen, Okstindan, North Norway. *Journal of
Glaciology,* 13, 265-277

PART 2

GLACIO–FLUVIAL
SEDIMENTATION
AND
PROCESSES

5 Subglacial fluvial erosion: a major source of stratified drift, Malaspina Glacier, Alaska

Thomas C. Gustavson & Jon C. Boothroyd

ABSTRACT

Studies of the sedimentary processes and hydrology of melt-water streams and proglacial lakes along the margin of the Malaspina Glacier suggest that most stratified drift is derived primarily from subglacial fluvial erosion and transport of basal till remote from the ice margin. Major outwash fans, kame deltas, and proglacial lakes originate at ice marginal fountains or meltwater tunnels. Meltwater from the Malaspina drainage area (2680 km^2) is discharged mostly via englacial and subglacial tunnels, and is derived from precipitation of 320 cm an^{-1} and ablation of over 393 cm an^{-1}. That meltwater in glacial tunnels far from the ice margin erodes and transports basal till is indicated by 1) direct observation, 2) high suspended sediment content (3.4 to 4.7 gl^{-1}), and 3) massive amounts of outwash supplied to ice-marginal fans. The longevity of fountains also suggests that networks of englacial and subglacial tunnels are relatively stable. Discharge into Malaspina Lake from meltwater tunnels is as much as 460 m^{3}s^{-1} and has occurred both at the base of the ice and part way up the ice contact face. Sediment is carried into the lake via continuous density flows issuing from the tunnel mouths.

Hydrology of the glacier system is reflected by water levels in sinkholes that mark a potentionmetric surface in the stagnant portions of the ice. Water within the higher or upglacier areas provides sufficient hydraulic head to maintain artesian conditions at the contact between ice and stratified drift at the glacier margin, and to move sediment entrained at the base of the glacier through glacial tunnels. Artesian springs or fountains are maintained as ice retreats, as outwash plains aggrade, or as lake levels change.

---

[1] Publication authorized by the Director, Bureau of Economic Geology, The University of Texas at Austin

[2] Bureau of Economic Geology, The University of Texas at Austin, Austin, Texas 78712

[3] Department of Geology, University of Rhode Island, Kingston, Rhode Island 02881

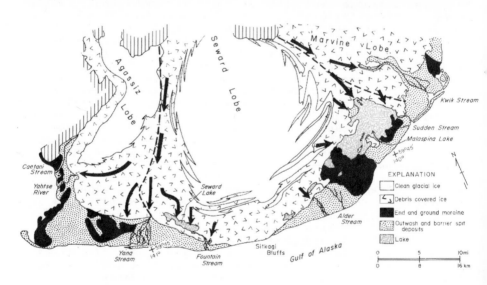

Figure 1. X-band SLAR image (1975) illustrates the Saint
Elias Range and the Agassiz, Seward, and Marvine Lobes
of the Malaspina Glacier. Glacial ice that is free or
nearly free of supraglacial debris is medium to dark grey.
Water and shadows are black. Bedrock and glacial drift
are light grey toned (image courtesy of P. Jan Cannon).
Map shows the generalized distribution of glacial drift.
Arrows show probable position and flow directions of major
englacial/subglacial drainage elements (after Plafker
and Miller, 1958b; Boothroyd and others, 1976)

94

PHYSICAL SETTING

The Malaspina Glacier lies at the foot of the Saint Elias Mountains along the southern coast of Alaska, U.S.A. (Figure 1). It is a piedmont glacier composed of lobes of ice contributed by the Agassiz Glacier on the west, the Seward Glacier on the north, and the Marvine Glacier on the east. The system of glaciers is one of the largest accumulations of glacier ice in North America, covering more than 4480 km^2 and containing an estimated 2050 km^3 of ice. The Malaspina Glacier, including only the piedmont bulb, covers approximately 2680 km^2 of the system.

The glacier is bounded on the east, south, and west by Recent glacial drift and shore deposits (Figure 1). Drift borders locally exceed 15 km in width although the southern-most extension of the Malaspina is exposed in ice cliffs along the shore at Sitkagi Bluffs. Ice rises from near sea level at the bluffs to approximately 610 m at the base of Mount Cook, 32 km to the north. The ice surface, except for very small areas near the terminus, does not maintain an integrated surface drainage. The peripheral portions of the glacier are partly to completely covered with ablation debris, which is rarely more than 1 m thick. In turn, the outer portion of the ablation zone is progressively covered by vegetation, including thick stands of alder and, locally, Sitka spruce and cottonwood.

The apparent terminus of the ice is marked by a series of ice-marginal lakes and a series of large meltwater streams that arise as fountains or from tunnels at the ice margin. Collapse of drift along the margin indicates that tongues of ice or isolated blocks of ice lie buried beneath the drift.

Little is known of the structure of the floor of the Malaspina Glacier apart from a single 19-km-long seismic reflection profile and a gravity map along a segment of the profile (Allen and Smith, 1953). The data indicate that the Malaspina occupies a broad shallow basin, which reaches at least 210 m below sea level. Along the middle of the profile the character of seismic reflectors suggests that the Mala-spina probably rests on bedrock. Additional seismic profiles near the snout of the glacier suggest that the margin of the glacier and the Malaspina Foreland are underlain by 150 to 250 m of glacial drift.

In Malaspina Lake, nearly 20 km east of the position of the seismic profile, the ice margin is approximately 80 m thick and extends to at least 60 m below sea level (Gustavson, 1975a). The western margin of the lake, however, is bordered by a series of drumlinoid hills approximately 50 m high, which illustrate that substantial relief exists along the margin of the glacier.

Substantial portions of the southern and eastern margins of the Malaspina Glacier are stagnant although the central portion of the glacier is probably still active (Sharp, 1963). On the east, most of the ice contributed by the Marvine Lobe

Figure 2. Aerial view of stagnant glacial ice covered with
ablation drift and contains several sinkholes. Large
sinkhole in the foreground is approximately 150 m in
diameter. Photograph is from the Seward-Marvine interlobate area east of Malaspina Lake

is stagnant, as is the interlobe area between it and the
Seward Lobe. To the southwest, much of the lower portion of
the Agassiz Lobe, including the interlobate area between it
and the Seward Lobe, is also stagnant. Areas of stagnation
are characterized by being partly to completely covered with
ablation debris and by the presence of collapse sinks (Figure
2). Glacial karst, including sinkholes, tunnels, sinking
streams, blind valleys, large springs, and ablation till, is
characteristic of stagnant glacial ice (Clayton, 1964), and
all these features are common to the debris-covered stagnant
periphery of the Malaspina.

CLIMATE AND GLACIAL REGIME

The Malaspina Glacier is bounded on three sides by waters of
Icy Bay, the Gulf of Alaska, and Yakutat Bay; consequently,
the peripheral portions of the glacier and the Malaspina
Foreland have a maritime climate. Both daily and seasonal
average temperatures vary only moderately (U.S. Department

of Commerce, 1969). Differences between mean maximum and minimum temperatures for Yakutat, Alaska, range from approximately $6^{0}C$ in October to approximately $9^{0}C$ in April and May. In a normal year Yakutat experiences only 10 days with temperatures below $-18^{0}C$. Temperature rarely exceeds $27^{0}C$.

Average annual precipitation is approximately 3.2 m along the glacier margin. In Yakutat for the period of record (January 1931 to the present) the average annual rainfall has never been less than 2.2 m, nor has it exceeded 4.75 m. June has the lowest monthly precipitation rate.

The most recent studies of accumulation and ablation on the Malaspina-Seward Glacier System were undertaken during 1948 and 1949 (Sharp, 1951). Sharp showed that the mean ablation rate during these periods was 394 cm an^{-1} for debris-free ice and approximately 39.4 cm an^{-1} for debris-covered ice. The volume of meltwater produced is 7.593 x $10^{15}cm^{3}an^{-1}$ without considering evaporation.

The volume of water available from precipitation is approximately 7.774 x $10^{15}cm^{3}an^{-1}$. Discharge from the Malaspina then may be estimated from the sum of precipitation plus meltwater, less evaporation, and is approximately 1.537 x $10^{10}m^{3}an^{-1}$ (Table 1). This is equivalent to a layer of water 6.1 m thick over the entire glacier or to a mean discharge of 487 $m^{3}sec^{-1}$.

Table 1. Estimated annual water discharge from the Malaspina Glacier

	Area[1] x	Mean ablation rate[1] =	Meltwater
Debris-covered ice	0.938 x $10^{13}cm^{2}$	39.37 cm	0.369 x $10^{15}cm^{3}$
Clean ice	1.742 x $10^{13}cm^{2}$	393.7 cm	6.863 x $10^{15}cm^{3}$
Total	2.68 x $10^{13}cm^{2}$		7.232 x $10^{15}cm^{3}$
Internal melting[1] = 5 per cent of surface melting			0.361 x $10^{15}cm^{3}$
Total melting			7.593 x $10^{15}cm^{3}$

	Area x	(Precipitation[2] - Evaporation[2]) =	Water available for infiltration
Total	2.68 x $10^{13}cm^{2}$	320 cm - 30 cm	7.774 x $10^{15}cm^{3}$

Discharge = Meltwater + Infiltration	1.537 x $10^{16}cm^{3}$

[1]Sharp, 1951
[2]U.S. Department of Commerce, 1969

Glacio-fluvial sedimentation and processes

PROGLACIAL DRAINAGE

Six major active drainage systems occur around the periphery
of the glacier; from west to east are the Yahtse, Yana,
Fountain, Alder, Sudden, and Kwik Streams (Figure 1). The
geographical limits of the basins drained by each of these
streams are not known, but on the basis of the positions of
the three ice lobes and the major streams, some speculations
can be offered. On the west, the Yahtse previously drained
the interlobate area between the Agassiz Lobe of the Malaspina
and ice that occupied the area of Icy Bay to the west. The
Yahtse, which has a maximum discharge of approximately
600 m^{3}sec^{-1}, drains the Agassiz Lobe. The Caetani River is an
ice-marginal stream that flows along the western edge of the
Agassiz Lobe. Yana Stream, with a known discharge of nearly
150 m^{3}sec^{-1}, arises as a fountain at the southern margin of
the interlobate area of the Agassiz and Seward Lobes (Boothroyd and Ashley, 1975). A large subglacial/englacial tunnel
has been partially unroofed at intervals extending 3 km
northward into the interlobate area. Fountain and Alder
Streams and Lake Malaspina provide the major active drainages
for the Seward Lobe although numerous smaller unnamed streams
also help drain this lobe. Along this portion of the terminus
several major channels, including Bader, Manby, Osar, Fotney,
and Kame Streams, are no longer active. Alder and Fountain
Streams arise as fountains at the glacier margin. Although
little is known about the history of development of these
streams, Fountain Stream, apparently named by Tarr and Martin
(1914), has been in existence since 1891.

Malaspina Lake receives drainage from a substantial portion of the southeastern margin of the glacier. The lake
drains via Sudden Stream southward to Yakutat Bay. During
July and August, 1971, Sudden Stream discharge ranged from
490 to 600 m^{3}sec^{-1} (Gustavson, 1973). Much of the discharge
into the lake is from a series of englacial and subglacial
streams (Gustavson, 1975a). Recent expansion of the northeast
quadrant of the lake has been enhanced by rapid wasting of
the stagnant zone developed between the Seward Lobe and the
Marvine Lobe. A major englacial stream drains into the northeast bay and has produced a large fan delta (Figure 1). A
pair of large ice-cored eskers occurs nearby and may be
related to an earlier stage of this system. An additional
portion of this drainage system is exposed nearly 1 km north
of the northeast limit of the lake where several segments of
a large englacial stream system have been unroofed. At the
western end of the lake, about 1 km north of the ice front,
a short segment of a subglacial stream has been unroofed.
The stream has cut a steep-walled tunnel valley 5 to 10 m deep.

Kwik Stream drains the eastern margin of the Marvine-
Hayden Lobe and arises from a tunnel at the point of contact
between the Marvine and Hayden Glaciers (Tarr and Martin,
1914). The position of the source of Kwik Stream has not
changed substantially when viewed in 1971 and 1979. Thus it
appears that englacial or subglacial tunnels containing streams
draining the Malaspina are in some cases stable or nearly
permanent features.

HYDROLOGY OF THE MALASPINA GLACIER

Some insight into the hydrology of the Malaspina Glacier can be obtained from observations of the processes and features that characterize the glacier, even though data from standard hydrologic instrumentation are not available. Previous sections have described the water budget and the external drainage system of the glacier. In essence, the glacier receives enormous amounts of water through rainfall and melting of snow and surface ice, most of which is drained from the glacier by a system of subglacial and englacial tunnels. The internal drainage system of the glacier is analogous to drainage systems developed in karstic limestone terrain. The generalized pattern of water movement through the glacier and sources of water is suggested in Figure 3.

Discharge from the Malaspina Glacier is approximately $1.537 \times 10^{10} m^3 an^{-1}$ and occurs primarily during July through September. Although full ranges of expected discharges of the major meltwater streams are not known, discharges from Sudden Stream and Yahtse Stream, typical large meltwater streams, range from 450 $m^3 s^{-1}$ to 600 $m^3 s^{-1}$ during the peak melting season. During this period, a hierarchy of fluctuations in discharge from the glacier occurs in response to long- and short-term climatic events such as annual climatic change, periods of rainfall (low-pressure weather systems), or warm cloud-free days (high-pressure weather systems). Short-term discharge fluctuations were recorded as lake-level changes in Lake Malaspina during July and August, 1970 and 1971. Lake level was recorded at a staff gauge at approximately the same time early each morning and compared with daily precipitation and temperature ranges for Yakutat, which lies 29 km to the southeast (Figure 4). Peaks in lake-level elevation lag from 1 to 2 days behind periods of rainfall. This relationship was true for 8 of 11 peaks in lake-level elevation that occurred during the period of record.

The relationship of cloud cover and air temperature to melting is not so clear. However, two periods of high temperatures, 22°C or above, are clearly associated with substantial rises in lake level. In this case, lake-level rises appear to lag one day behind high temperature conditions. During periods of relatively low daytime temperatures and clear skies, radiational cooling at night resulted in air temperatures of less than 4.5°C at the recording station. Minimum daily temperatures in this order also appear to decrease melting as reflected by lowering of the lake level following the cool periods.

Diurnal fluctuations in the rates of melting of ice and snow undoubtedly occur on the Malaspina as a result of changes in ambient air temperature. The direct relationship between daily air temperature ranges and water levels within glaciers or fluctuations in discharge of certain meltwater streams is well understood (Gudmundsson and Sigbjarnarson, 1972; Church, 1972). These relationships are especially clear where rainfall during the melting period is not common. For the Malaspina diurnal fluctuations in melting, glacier water level

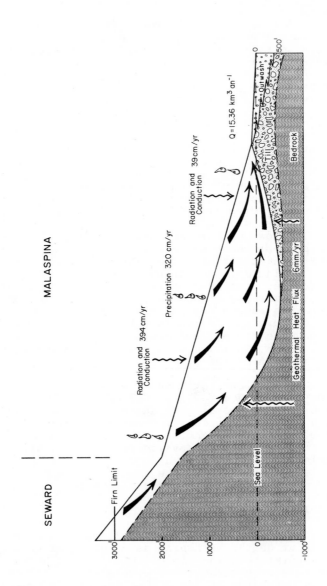

Figure 3. Arrows show the generalized paths of water movement within the Seward Lobe of the Malaspina Glacier. Sources of meltwater are precipitation and melting due to radiation and conduction. Melting at the margin is less because of the insulating effects of ablation drift.

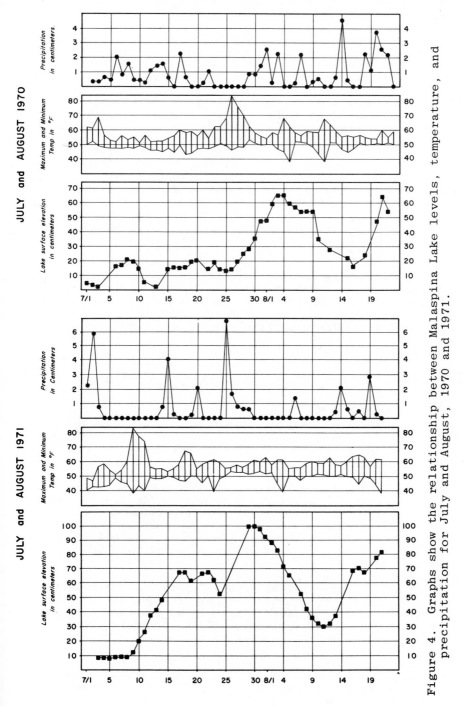

JULY and AUGUST 1970

JULY and AUGUST 1971

Figure 4. Graphs show the relationship between Malaspina Lake levels, temperature, and precipitation for July and August, 1970 and 1971.

and discharge are largely lost against a background of longer
term fluctuations in glacier water level and discharge as a
result of changing weather patterns. Similar relationships
between short-term weather changes and water levels within
the glacier have been observed in the South Cascade Glacier.
The South Cascade Glacier occurs in north-central Washington
and is subject to climatic conditions that are generally
similar to conditions in the vicinity of the Malaspina Glacier.
Hodge (1976) and Mathews (1964) have reported that the fluctuations in water levels in boreholes in the South Cascade
Glacier are related directly to water input at the glacier
surface, which varies with precipitation and melting. According
to Hodge (1976), peaks in water levels in boreholes often
occur roughly 2 days after a large increase in water input.
Data from Hodge (1976), from Krimmel and others (1973), and
from Figure 3 suggest that large fluctuations in glacier water
levels and thus discharge result from weather changes and
that the lag time may be a reflection of the length and
tortuosity of the paths water takes from the surface to the
water table as suggested by Shreve (1972).

Hodge (1976) is careful to point out that fluctuations
in borehole water levels may not be directly related to water-
pressure fluctuations at the glacier floor, although he
suggests that this is true. The relationships of weather
events and discharge data from Table 1 are readily explained
in the following manner: water levels within the Malaspina
fluctuate with the passage of weather systems that directly
cause changes in water levels and water pressures within the
glacier; these changes are manifested as fluctuations in
discharge observed as changes in lake level.

GLACIER DRAINAGE

Sedimentation in proglacial streams that drain the Malaspina
has been described by many workers (Boothroyd and Nummendal,
1978; Boothroyd et al, 1976; Boothroyd and Ashley, 1975;
Gustavson, 1974). Little is known of the extent of these
streams beneath the glacier. Tarr and Martin (1914) specu-
lated that the subglacial or englacial portion of Yana Stream
runs along the interlobate area between the Agassiz and
Seward lobes. A large englacial/subglacial tunnel is currently
being unroofed in the Agassiz/Seward interlobate area. As
suggested earlier, other major drainage systems may occur
along the interlobate zones, and at least the outlets of the
streams are relatively long lived (Figure 1). Mathematical
analysis of the development of water passages in glaciers
indicate that: 1) the flow in tunnels at the ice-till interface is stable; 2) a vertical network of passages leading
from the surface to the glacier is the normal end product in
the development of glacier drainage; and 3) the capacity of
the system adjusts to the supply of meltwater (Shreve, 1972).
Manifestations of active internal drainage include unroofed
portions of englacial and subglacial streams and sinkholes in
the portions of the glacier that are stagnant.

Glacier sinkholes, considered by Clayton (1964) to be
characteristic of stagnant ice, result from the combined
effects of melting and collapse over tunnels and from the
enlargement of moulins. Sinkholes are usually partly filled
with water during the summer months, and the water levels
mark the ground-water table or potentiometric surface of the
glacier. Small-scale topographic maps of the glacier terminus
are not available, and thus the elevations of sinkholes and
water levels are not precisely known. Nevertheless, the
locations of sinkholes are well known from aerial photographs
of several vintages, and from 1:250 000-scale topographic
maps. Collapse sinks in the interlobate areas extend northward from the ice margin nearly 35 km to the foot of the Saint
Elias Range. From this evidence it is apparent that the
elevation of both the sinks and water levels within the sinks
increases from near sea level to approximately 550 m as the
elevation of the glacier surface increases northward. If
waters in sinkhole lakes are an expression of the potentiometric surface of the glacier, then the gradient of the
surface parallels the surface slope of the glacier and is
approximately 0.0157 m km^{-1}.

Englacial Streams and Eskers

Five segments of large unroofed englacial streams were
observed in the lower portion of the Seward-Marvine interlobate area. These streams all occurred within 1 km of and
approximately 10 m above the northeast portion of Malaspina
Lake. Ice thickness measured at the northern margin of the
lake is a minimum of 73 m thick. Thus, the englacial streams
are flowing at least 83 m above the sole of the glacier.
Density current interflows and underflows into Malaspina Lake
may also be manifestations of deeper englacial streams
(Gustavson, 1975a and b) (Figures 5 and 6). Ice-cored eskers,
the remnants of former englacial streams, are common at the
periphery of the glacier and are preserved in front of the
glacier, at the glacier margin, and on the glacier surface.
An ice-cored esker is exposed on the glacier surface about
1.6 km north and 30 to 40 m above Lake Malaspina or about
100 m above the base of the glacier (Figure 6). Remnants of
the esker pass into and out of ice ridges, and locally, where
the former tunnel was breached, sediment has splayed out of
the main tunnel to form an outwash plain on the ice surface
(Figure 7). South of Malaspina Lake, two ice-cored eskers
lead out of an isolated block of stagnant ice approximately
20 m above the lake surface and about 50 m above the floor of
the glacier at this location. These eskers lead into a pitted
outwash plain that is graded to the coast, approximately 5 km
to the south. Several additional ice-cored eskers in the
vicinity of the lake were observed. Ice beneath these features
probably ranges from a few metres to over 100 m thick.

Observed englacial streams are extremely turbulent, and
their colour suggests high suspended-sediment load (Figure 8).
Suspended-sediment loads at streams issuing from fountains
along the glacier margin range from 1.7 g l^{-1} to 4.7 g l^{-1}.
That these streams also carry significant bed loads is clearly
illustrated by the sand and gravel that compose the ice-cored
eskers.

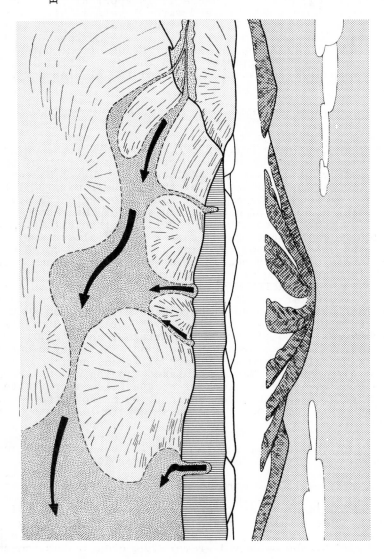

Figure 5. Density currents entering Malaspina Lake from the ice-face of the Malaspina Glacier (vertical lines) and from delta distributaries carry relatively dense sediment-charged meltwater across the lake floor to the deeper parts of the lake basin (derived from Gustavson, 1975a and b)

Figure 6. Aerial view of the southern margin of the Malaspina at Malaspina Lake (1971). Supraglacial esker
passes into and out of ablation-debris-covered ridges
of stagnant ice. Tonal differences in ridges reflect
differences in lithology of ablation drift.

Non-ice-cored eskers are common where recent back wasting
has exposed basal till. Basal till surfaces are replete with
fluted topography, drumlinoid hills, fracture fillings, and
eskers that show no evidence of having been underlain by ice.
Locally, kame deltas and kame plains occur at the end of
eskers.

The complex system of meltwater tunnels and eskers evinces
the dynamic processes that operate within and beneath the
Malaspina Glacier. During the melt season, high water levels

105

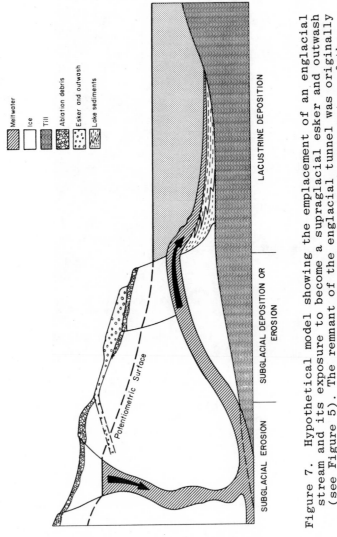

Figure 7. Hypothetical model showing the emplacement of an englacial stream and its exposure to become a supraglacial esker and outwash (see Figure 5). The remnant of the englacial tunnel was originally connected to a portion of the meltwater discharge system of the glacier. The model also shows discharge of relatively dense meltwater from an englacial stream into a proglacial lake. Deposits from the density flow are forming an ice-contact subaqueous fan. Rhythmites would be deposited in the deeper part of the basin.

Figure 8.   A large tunnel in the stagnant ice near the
    margin of the Malaspina Glacier (July, 1971).   Note
    man above tunnel for scale.   Debris mantling the ice
    is seldom more than 1 m thick.

are maintained within the glacier and provide the hydraulic
head necessary to move water through the glacier.   Sufficient
head is available to move water through englacial and subglacial
glacial streams and to form large fountains at the glacier
margin.

     More importantly, sufficient hydraulic energy is available
to erode the till floor beneath the glacier and to lift this
load as bed load including gravel-sized material at least
100 m above the floor of the glacier.   All of the suspended
sediment and bed load observed in meltwater tunnels and
streams, in proglacial lakes, and in eskers and outwash plains
on the Malaspina and Malaspina Foreland was derived primarily
by erosion of subglacial material. Essentially all stratified
drift is derived directly from till or from overridden
stratified drift beneath the glacier.   Insignificant amounts
of stratified drift are derived from other sources such as
drop stones, flow tills, or drift washed from the glacier
surface.

Subglacial Drainage

The subglacial drainage of the Malaspina was observed both
directly and indirectly. A single exposure of a subglacial

occurs approximately 1 km north of the northwest corner of
Lake Malaspina or approximately 1 km from the ice margin.
The stream is exposed along a short segment where collapse
of overlying ice has occurred to form a valley completely
surrounded by glacier ice (karst valley or uvala). The exposed portion of the subglacial stream is approximately 200 m
long, and it is incised into basal till to a maximum depth of
approximately 8 m. Although wet and unfrozen, the basal till
that forms the valley walls is extremely compact. Till is
yielded slowly to the stream as a thin saturated surface layer
moves down the steep valley walls to be picked up by the
stream. The floor of the stream is at least partly protected
by an armouring of boulders, many in excess of 50 cm in
diameter. Because of the armour, the stream was able to erode
its banks directly only during periods of high discharge.
Squeezing out of water-saturated till at the base of the ice
did not appear to be an important process in this area.
Perhaps the reason for this was that there was only about 5 m
of ice directly above the till along the stream valley sides.
Thus, most of the debris supplied to the stream along the
exposed reach was derived by local bank erosion during high
discharge and by small amounts of till flowing down the valley
walls.

Indirect evidence of subglacial drainage comes in three
forms: 1) well-preserved eskers lying on basal till, 2) a
single preserved tunnel valley, and 3) active streams carrying
high suspended and bed loads. On the recently deglaciated
surface west of Lake Malaspina, evidence of a subglacial
drainage system is preserved. The two drainage features that
occur here are eskers and a single tunnel valley segment. The
tunnel valley segment was identified from aerial photographs.
It is about 300 m long and 30 m wide with steep valley walls
and terminates abruptly at both ends against fluted ground
moraine. Furthermore, the valley notches the top of a small
drumlinoid hill, and there are no associated stratified drift
deposits preserved downslope from the tunnel valley. The tunnel
valley appears to have been formed by an englacial stream
that slowly incised through the ice. When the back of the
drumlin was encountered it was eroded by the meltwaters.
Tunnel incision and erosion continued until the present feature was formed. At that time the englacial stream was
abandoned. The tunnel valley was preserved because the
peripheral ice of the Malaspina is stagnant and melted in
place.

Numerous small eskers are preserved on fluted topography
west of Lake Malaspina. The eskers are sinuous, show little
evidence of collapse, and are mostly less than 1 km long.
Eskers were developed normal to the ice margin. Because these
eskers show little or no evidence of having been underlain by
ice, they probably represent the subglacial drainage of a
small portion of the Malaspina.

The major active and inactive meltwater streams that drain
the Malaspina issue from fountains or tunnels at the ice
margin (Figure 9). Although there is no practical way of
determining if these streams are at the base of the glacier

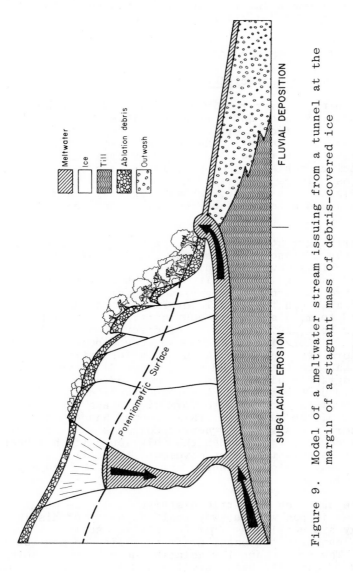

Figure 9. Model of a meltwater stream issuing from a tunnel at the margin of a stagnant mass of debris-covered ice

at the glacier margin, their heavy sediment load suggests
that they flow at the base of the ice. The sources of these
streams - Kwik, Sudden, Kame, Fotney, Osar, Manby, Alder,
Bader, Fountain, Yana, and Yahtse - mark the outlets of major
glacial drainage systems. The locations and flow directions
of the major englacial and subglacial drainage elements of
the Malaspina are summarized in Figure 1.

SOURCES OF STRATIFIED DRIFT

Supraglacial and Englacial Debris

The Malaspina Glacier receives ice and entrained sediment from
the Agassiz, Seward, and Marvine Glaciers, which in turn
receive ice and rock debris from numerous valley glaciers
that drain the Saint Elias Range. A variety of rock debris
is contributed to these glaciers as lateral moraines. Rock
types include schists, gneisses, intrusives, greywackes,
argillites, slates, tillites, and marine and continental sediments (Plafker and Miller, 1958a). In many cases the lateral
moraines are distinctive and consist of only one or two rock
types.

As tributary streams of ice coalesce to form the Agassiz,
Seward, and Marvine Glaciers, the lateral moraines become
medial moraines, but the medial moraines maintain both their
integrity and distinctive lithologic character. As the ice
lobes merge to form the Malaspina Glacier, severe folding
occurs; although the medial moraines are folded and attenuated
they tend to maintain their continuity and distinctive lithology (see Post, 1972, for a brief discussion of the folding
mechanism). Ablation of the ice surface exposes the folded
medial moraines. Ice beneath the ablation drift melts more
slowly than ice not mantled by ablation drift and tends to
form topographic highs. Mass movement of ablation drift down
the slopes of the ice ridges spreads the rock debris of the
medial moraines laterally to form wide bands. Near the stagnant edge of the Malaspina, this process has proceeded to the
point where the surface is nearly completely covered with
ablation debris. Even though the ablation drift has been
subject to substantial mass movement, it still retains its
distinctive lithologic banding parallel to the ice margin
(Figure 6).

There has been so little disturbance of the margin of the
glacier as it has wasted away that the bands of distinctive
lithology are contiguous from the glacier surface across the
terminus and onto the basal drift that lies beyond the ice
margin. The coarse angular ablation debris simply forms a
thin veneer over the basal drift and does not obscure basal
drift landforms.

Observations from the ice surface, from low-flying air-
craft and from aerial photographs of several vintages indicate
that little debris is supplied to the surface of the Malaspina
by movement along shear planes. Fluctuations of the active
margin of the Agassiz Lobe, however, have overridden the

stagnant margin, thrusting up fluvial sediments and till.
It seems, therefore, that nearly all of the debris that
mantles the margins of the Malaspina is derived from a system
of medial moraines that originated in the valley glaciers of
the Saint Elias Mountains. Although the base of the Malaspina was observed only in a few areas, it is significant that the
ice was very clean. Since the Malaspina is a temperate glacier,
the process of regelation does not occur and sediment is not
frozen onto the base of the glacier. Bands of englacial
sediment (of undetermined origin) are relatively thin and
widely distributed.

Subglacial Debris

Nearly all of the sediment supplied to meltwater streams from
the Malaspina Glacier appears to be derived from subglacial
drift. Streams draining the Malaspina carry large suspended
loads and bed loads. Suspended sediment content of seven major
streams draining the Malaspina Glacier ranged from 1.7 to
4.7 g l^{-1} (Gustavson, 1975b; Boothroyd and Ashley, 1975;
Boothroyd, unpublished data). If, to simplify calculations,
an average suspended sediment load of 3.0 g l^{-1} is assumed
and a sediment specific gravity of 3.0 is also assumed, then
each litre of meltwater discharged from the glacier contains
1 cm of sediment. The 1.537 x 10^{16} cm^{3}an^{-1} discharge from
the glacier yields 1.537 x 10^{13}cm^{3}an^{-1} or about 1.537 x 10^3
ha m suspended sediment. All suspended sediment samples were
collected in relatively slow moving water at the edges of
meltwater streams. Certainly the suspended sediment values
observed in these samples are lower than the suspended sediment loads carried by the much more rapid but inaccessible
portions of the streams. Under these circumstances it may be
that the value of 4.7 g l^{-1} more nearly approaches the actual
suspended load for Malaspina meltwater streams. If this is
correct, then the annual suspended load for streams draining
the Malaspina may reach 2.4 x 10^3 ha m.

Bed-load transport data for the streams draining the
Malaspina Glacier are not available. The paucity of bed-load
sediment transport data is such that any comments on the sediment yield of these streams must be considered speculative.
A minor exception is that Gustavson and others (1975) reported
that a small kame delta with a surface area of 0.5 km^2 and
an approximate volume of 8 x 10^6m^3 was deposited in Malaspina
Lake in less than 10 years. Qualitatively, however, it is
obvious that transport and deposition of bed load are major
processes. Since the last recession of the Malaspina began
(1700-1791 A.D.), several large outwash plains, large elongated barrier spits, kame deltas, and fan deltas have been
built and maintained along the Malaspina Foreland (Plafker
and Miller, 1958b). Numerous forested chenier-like ridges
landward of the present coast attest to the progradation of
the shoreline and indicate that large volumes of bed-load
sediment are supplied to the beach area to nourish the beaches
and allow spit growth.

Church and Gilbert (1975) discussed the general problem
of determining bed-load and total sediment yields for

111

proglacial streams. They compare contributions of suspended
and bed-load sediment transport for two proglacial rivers.
It is interesting that the suspended load of these streams
accounts for 78% to 90% of the total sediment load. Although
no direct comparison should be made between these streams
and meltwater streams on the Malaspina Foreland, the percentage of total sediment yield attributed to suspended load
may also be true for streams draining the Malaspina Glacier.
If so, then the total annual sediment yield from the Malaspina Glacier may exceed 2.7×10^3 ha m (2.2×10^4 ac ft),
equivalent to a layer of sediment 0.9 cm (0.35 in) thick
covering the entire floor of the glacier.

The observed processes of acquisition and transport of
this material are almost exclusively fluvial. However, there
are probably mass movement processes at the base of the
glacier that also contribute to erosion of the bed. Although
not directly observed, water-saturated till may be squeezed
laterally into tunnels at the base of the ice. This process
has been used to explain the origin of numerous till landforms by suggesting that they were formed from water-saturated
till, statically pressed up into cavities in the glacier base
by the weight of the overlying ice (Hoppe, 1952; Stalker,
1960; Schutt, 1959). Crevasse fillings and fluted topography
similar to features described by Stalker (1960) and Dyson
(1952) are common in areas of exposed basal drift along the
margin of the Malaspina and indicate that till at the base
of the Malaspina is mobile. If true, this process would be
an important mechanism for providing continued sediment load
to subglacial streams.

SUBGLACIAL EROSION ZONE

Models have been developed recently to describe the processes
of erosion and landform development beneath glaciers or along
glacier margins (Boulton, 1974; Clayton and Moran, 1974; and
Koteff, 1974). To these models we wish to add the concept
that during stagnation and downwasting of large temperate ice
masses, the dominant process is subglacial erosion by fluvial
processes.

Although no practical means exist for defining the limits
of a zone of predominantly fluvial erosion at the base of the
glacier, it is probably better developed beneath areas of
stagnant ice at the glacier margin and along interlobate areas.
The presence of stagnant ice is a form of stability that
allows major subglacial drainage elements to become established.
It is an area where the volume of eroded sediment is not even
partly replaced by sediment brought in by active ice.

SUMMARY

The directly and indirectly observed englacial and subglacial
drainage features of the Malaspina provide a fragmentary
picture of the three-dimensional drainage system of a large
temperate glacier. It is an arborescent system of passages

that is in part similar to the drainage network described by
Shreve (1972) in his theoretical discussion of the movement
of water in glaciers.

Surface drainage is accomplished partly by flow into
moulins and sinkholes. Water movement also occurs along the
boundaries of ice crystals. (For a discussion of this
phenomenon see Nye and Frank, 1970.) The absence of an integrated surface drainage system coupled with heavy precipitation and rapid ablation suggests that surface drainage of
the Malaspina by intergranular flow may be an important process. Englacial drainage consists of systems of passages
that penetrate the glacier from its surface to its bed.
Water generally moves downward from the surface until it
reaches the glacier water table. From here water moves toward discharge points along paths that are controlled by the
hydraulic gradient and available passages through the ice.
Many of the drainage conduits reach to the bed of the glacier.
Water that moves to the bed of the glacier scours the drift
and bedrock floor. Contribution of water and sediment to
these subglacial streams by basal melting is minor, however,
for basal melting of the Malaspina accounts for less than
1 percent of the meltwater discharge. Major drainage elements
of the Malaspina flow along the bed of the glacier to discharge at the glacier margin. The presence of supraglacial
eskers and englacial tunnels and streams choked with sediment
indicates that subglacial streams and conduits locally lose
contact with glacier bed and may carry sediment over 100 m
up into the glacier. Preserved eskers showing little evidence
of collapse indicate the extensive previously existing subglacial drainage system. Modern fountains at the margin of
the glacier mark the present outlets of the glacier's drainage system.

Annual meltwater discharge probably exceeds 15 km^3 and
probably carries more than $1.5 \times 10^7 m^3$ and maybe as much as
$2.4 \times 10^7 m^3$ of suspended sediment with it. Qualitative evidence in the form of a prograding shoreline and aggrading
outwash fans also indicates that a large load of coarse
sediment is derived from the glacier. Sediment appears to be
derived primarily by erosion of subglacial channels, with
additional till probably being squeezed into the channels by
the weight of overlying ice. The resulting impression is that
the Malaspina, a stagnating temperate glacier, is undergoing
active fluvial erosion at its bed and by this mechanism
provides essentially all of the stratified drift deposited
along its margin.

ACKNOWLEDGEMENTS

We would like to thank Marc B. Edwards, Charles W. Kreitler,
and William Simpkins for their critical review of this manuscript. Gail Ashley, Mark Cable, Kerry Campbell, Lorie Dunn,
Ray Levey, and James Morrisson provided invaluable assistance
in the field. Funds for this research were provided by the
Office of Naval Research, Geography Branch (Contract Number
N00014-67-A-0230-0001; Miles O. Hayes, Principal Investigator),

Glacio-fluvial sedimentation and processes

National Oceanographic and Atmospheric Administration/OCSEP
(Grant Number 03-5-022-82, Miles O. Hayes and Jon C. Boothroyd, co-Principal Investigators); NASA Planetary Geology
Program (Grant Number NSG 7414, Jon C. Boothroyd, Principal
Investigator). Additional support was provided by the Bureau
of Economic Geology, The University of Texas at Austin, and
by the Departments of Geology at the Universities of Massachusetts, Rhode Island, and South Carolina.

REFERENCES CITED

Allen, C.R. and G. I. Smith, 1953, Seismic and gravity investigations on the Malaspina Glacier, Alaska.
American Geophysical Union, 34, 755-760

Boothroyd, J.C. and G. M. Ashley, 1975, Processes, bar
morphology, and sedimentary structures on braided
outwash fans, northeastern Gulf of Alaska. in
Glaciofluvial and glaciolacustrine sedimentation,
ed A.V.Jopling and B.C.McDonald, (Society of Economic Paleontologists and Mineralogists Special
Publication, 23), 193-222

Boothroyd, J.C., Cable, M.S. and R.A.Levey, 1976, *Coastal
morphology and sedimentation, Gulf Coast of Alaska
(glacial sedimentology),* (Annual Report for NOAA
Contract No.03-5-022-82), 84 pp, 4 maps

Boothroyd, J.C. and D. Nummendal, 1978, Proglacial braided
outwash: a model for humid alluvial fan deposits.
in *Fluvial sedimentology,* ed A. D. Miall, (Canadian
Society of Petroleum Geologists, Memoir 5), 631-668

Boulton, G.S. 1974, Processes and patterns of glacial
erosion. in *Glacial geomorphology,* ed D. R. Coates,
(State University of New York, Binghamton, N.Y.),
398

Church, M. 1972, Baffin Island sandurs: a study of arctic
fluvial processes. *Geological Survey of Canada
Bulletin,* 216, 208

Church, M. and R. Gilbert, 1975, Proglacial fluvial and
lacustrine environments. in *Glaciofluvial and glaciolacustrine sedimentation,* ed A.V.Jopling and B.C.
McDonald, (Society of Economic Paleontologists and
Mineralogists Special Publication, 23), 22-100

Clayton, L., 1964, Karst topography on stagnant glaciers.
Journal of Glaciology, 3, 107-112

Clayton, L. and S.R.Moran, 1974, A glacial process-form
model. in *Glacial geomorphology,* ed D.R.Coates,
(State University of New York, Binghamton, N.Y.),
398 pp.

Dyson, J.L. 1952, Ice-ridged moraines and their relation
to glaciers. *American Journal of Science,* 250,
204-211

Gudmundsson, G. and G. Sigbjarnarson, 1972, Analysis of
glacier run-off and meteorological observations.
Journal of Glaciology, 11, 303-318

Gustavson, T.C. 1973, *Fluvial and lacustrine sedimentation in the proglacial environment, Malaspina Glacier Foreland, Alaska.* (Ph.D. dissertation, University Microfilms, Ann Arbor, Michigan), 177 pp.

Gustavson, T.C. 1974, Sedimentation on gravel outwash fans: Malaspina Glacier Foreland, Alaska. *Journal of Sedimentary Petrology,* 44, 374-389

Gustavson, T.C. 1975a, Bathymetry and sediment distribution in proglacial Malaspina Lake, Alaska. *Journal of Sedimentary Petrology,* 45, 450-461

Gustavson, T.C. 1975b, Sedimentation and physical limnology in proglacial Malaspina Lake, southeastern Alaska, in *Glaciofluvial and glaciolacustrine sedimentation,* ed A.V.Jopling and B.C.McDonald, (Society Economic Paleontologists and Mineralogists, Special Publication, 23), 249-263

Gustavson, T.C., Ashley, G.M. and J.C.Boothroyd, 1975, Depositional sequences in glaciolacustrine deltas, in *Glaciofluvial and glaciolacustrine sedimentation,* Paleontologists and Mineralogists, Special Publication, 23), 264-280

Hodge, S. M. 1976, Direct measurement of basal water pressures: a pilot study. *Journal of Glaciology,* 16, 205-218

Hoppe, G. 1952, Hummocky moraine regions, with special reference to the interior of Morrboten. *Geografiska Annaler, A,* 34, 1-72

Koteff, C. 1974, The morphologic sequence concept and deglaciation of southern New England, in *Glacial geomorphology,* ed D.R.Coates, (State University of New York, Binghamton, N.Y.), 398 pp.

Krimmel, R.M., Tangborn, W.V. and M.F.Meier, 1973, Water flow through a temperate glacier, in *International Hydrological Decade; The role of snow and ice in hydrology, Proceedings of the Banff symposia, September, 1972,* (Paris, UNESCO; Geneva, WMO; Budapest, IAHS), 1, 401-416

Mathews, W.H. 1964, Water pressure under a glacier. *Journal of Glaciology,* 5, 235-240

Nye, J.F. and F.C.Frank, 1970, *The hydrology of the intergranular veins in a temperate glacier. Union Geodesique et Geophysique Internationale. Association Internationale d'Hydrologie Scientifique. Commission de Neiges et Glaces. Symposium on the hydrology of glaciers, Cambridge, 7-13 September 1969, organized by the Glaciological Society.*

Plafker, G. and D.J.Miller, 1958a, Reconnaissance geology of the Malaspina District, Alaska. *U.S. Geological Survey, Oil and Gas Investigations Map,* OM 189

Glacio-fluvial sedimentation and processes

Plafker, G. and D.J.Miller, 1958b, Glacial features and surficial deposits of the Malaspina District, *U.S. Geological Survey, Miscellaneous Geological Inv. Map*, 1-271

Post, A. 1972, Periodic surge origin of folded medial moraines on Bering Piedmont Glacier, Alaska. *Journal of Glaciology*, 11, 219-226

Schutt, V. 1959, The glaciers of the Kebnekaise-Massif. *Geografiska Annaler, A*, 41, 213-227

Sharp, R.P. 1951, Accumulation and ablation on the Seward-Malaspina Glacier System, Canada, Alaska. *Geological Society of America Bulletin*, 62, 725-744

Sharp, R.P. 1963, Deformation of bore hole in Malaspina Glacier, Alaska. *Geological Society of America Bulletin*, 64, 97-100

Shreve, R.L. 1972, Movement of water in glaciers. *Journal of Glaciology*, 11, 205-214

Stalker, A.M. 1960, Ice-pressed drift forms and associated deposits in Alberta. *Geological Survey of Canada Bulletin*, 57, 38

Tarr, R.S. and L.Martin, 1914, *Alaskan glacier studies*, (National Geographic Society, Washington, D.C.), 498 pp.

U.S. Department of Commerce, 1969, *Local climatological data, Annual summary with comparative data*, (Yakutat, Alaska)

6 Depositional processes in the development of eskers in Manitoba

Susan Ringrose

ABSTRACT

In an attempt to arrive at a comprehensive theory for the
origin of eskers, different eskers occurring in northern,
central and southern Manitoba are compared in terms of morphology and sedimentology. Northern eskers, which occur as
continuous ridges in subparallel swarms are longer, higher,
and narrower than southern eskers which occur relatively
infrequently, in beads which are shorter, lower and wider.
Nineteen major facies types are identified and interpreted
relative to the current literature on closed conduit and open
channel bedform types. This, used in conjunction with vertical,
lateral and downstream facies relationships, provides evidence
to suggest that the northern eskers are produced primarily by
surges of sediment deposited in heterogeneous suspension in
a closed tunnel, whereas central and southern eskers (where
observed) are the products of braided stream, open channel
environments. The different types may be related to the
prevailing ice regime with southern, beaded eskers being
formed initially in the relatively narrow ablation zone at
the margin of a 'polar' ice sheet, which may have become
inactive during the later (observed) stage of esker deposition.
The northern Leaf Rapids esker is thought to have been probably
formed under active ice during more temperate conditions,
where rapid melt and ice movement cause sliding bed conditions
in vertical tunnels.

INTRODUCTION

The origin of eskers has previously been viewed from the
perspective of the location of the tunnel within the ice sheet,
or various sedimentation patterns into pro-glacial lakes;
and with speculation as to the increase in elevation downstream as this relates to hydrostatic head changes in the
subglacial environment (Price, 1973). Such speculation
naturally results from the characteristics of eskers in
differing morphologies and differing combinations of
sedimentary textures and structures. The early abundance of

---

*Department of Energy and Mines
Mineral Resources Division
989 Century Street,
Winnipeg, Manitoba
R3H 0W4

Present Address:
Geo-Analysis Ltd.
Box 173, Station A
Ottawa, Ontario
KIN 8Y2

relatively simplistic origins is being replaced by more comprehensive theories, for instance that developed by Banerjee and McDonald (1975). Their Figure 4(p.137) provides the most comprehensive model of esker sedimentation to date as it relates nature of the conduit and site of deposition.

This paper concentrates on the mode of esker deposition and attempts to identify diagnostic criteria in order to recognize depositional sequences formed in a closed conduit environment or conversely under 'normal fluvial' conditions. These considerations are related to the broad geographic frequency of eskers and differing ice melt regimes in Manitoba.

FIELD EXAMPLES

One example from each of three series of eskers were analysed in detail. Northern eskers are exemplified by the Leaf Rapids esker which is oriented north-south across the Churchill River at about 56°30'N. This feature, a semi-continuous ridge, occurs in an area of relatively high esker frequency, comprising subparallel esker swarms. Individual eskers range from 10 to 30 m high (Ringrose and Large, 1977) and hundreds of km in length (Figure 1). The Axis Lake esker is oriented east-northeast to west-southwest at about 54°30'N, between Setting Lake and Clark Lake. The area is one of intermediate esker frequency with some parallel esker development, displaying bead - like morphology in features 7 to 10 m high and tens of km in length (Ringrose, 1977). The Birds Hill deposit is a unique esker which is fused at its eastern margin and has a beaded morphology (Figure 2). The two esker sections are referred to as Birds Hill south, which runs south to north, and Birds Hill west, which runs west to east. The feature fans out into an outwash complex in the north. This deposit occurs in the Red River basin to the northeast of Winnipeg at 50°00'N. Each of these eskers was deposited during the last or Classical period of Wisconsin recession and all either flowed into or were surrounded by pro-glacial lakes.

MORPHOLOGY

The morphology of the eskers was ascertained using 1:16 000 aerial photography and contours on National Topographic Series maps, augmented by benchmark elevations emplaced by the Geodetic Survey in 1974/75. Contours for the more northern eskers (Leaf Rapids and Axis Lake) were available from 1:50 000 maps using a 25 foot (~8.0 m) interval. Heights for the Birds Hill esker were taken from 1:25 000 maps using a 10 foot (~3.1 m) interval. The morphological distinction between the three esker types is shown on Figure 2 and Table 1. Generally the absolute length varies from about 31 km for the Leaf Rapids esker, to 12 km for the Axis Lake esker to 10 km and 13 km for the Birds Hill eskers. Width to height ratios show a similar transition from north to south. In the case of the Leaf Rapids esker, the average width ($\bar{w}$) is 41h (h=height);

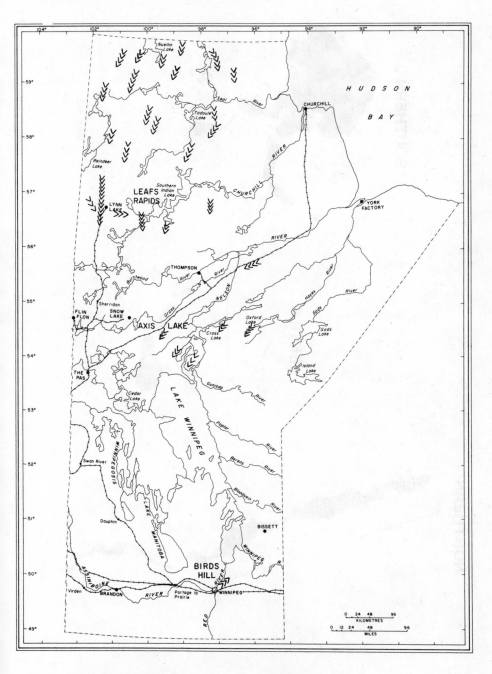

Figure 1.   Distribution of eskers in Manitoba.

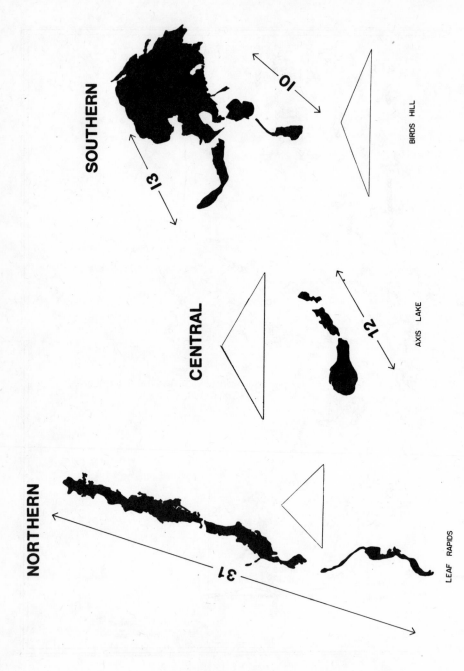

SOUTHERN

13

10

BIRDS HILL

CENTRAL

12

AXIS LAKE

NORTHERN

31

LEAF RAPIDS

Figure 2.   General morphology of the northern, central and southern esker systems.

Table 1. Comparison of esker morphology

(1) Esker Segment		(2) Segment Length(m)	(3) Maximum Height(m)	(4) Total Length with gaps(m)	(5) Total Length to Maximum Height Ratio
Leaf Rapids	1	5400	15.25	31 500	1032.79
	2	6000	30.50		
	3	9400	15.25		
	4	10 000	15.25		
Axis Lake	1	2000	15.25	12 000	786.89
	2	3000	15.25		
	3	4800	15.25		
Birds Hill West	1	2500	6.12	13 000	852.46
	2	3400	15.25		
	3	5900	15.25		
Birds Hill South	1	2000	12.23	10 500	490.43
	2	1400	15.25		
	3	3800	21.41		

$\bar{x}$=5267 $\bar{y}$=17.04
S_x=3018 S_y=6.48

Correlation of 2 and 3 r = 0.224
Correlation of 3 and 4 r = 0.907

121

for Axis Lake, $\bar{w}$ = 71h and for Birds Hill south $\bar{w}$ = 110h.
The correlation between maximum height and total length is
high and the total length (l) to maximum height ratio differs
for the three groups of eskers such that l = 1033h for Leaf
Rapids, l = 787h for Axis Lake, l = 853h for Birds Hill west
and l = 491h for Birds Hill south. The northern eskers,
therefore, tend to be longer, higher and narrower than the
southern eskers. Supposing a differing shape of the conduit,
and incidently the frequency of eskers in each category,
differing hydrodynamic activity in terms of sediment accumulation may be anticipated.

FACIES TYPES

A quantitative assessment of the depositional environment of
each esker was undertaken through the identification of lithofacies based on similarity of texture and sedimentary structure. The procedure used involved the development of textural envelopes cross-referenced with structures as outlined
by Ringrose (1979). Comparable facies can be identified in
each of the three eskers; and these are similar to others
in the literature (e.g. Saunderson, 1975, 1977a, 1977b).
Nineteen of the major facies types are considered here.
Bedform definitions and origins are those used by Harms *et al.*
(1975).

The main facies types and characteristic structures are
listed in Figure 3. Sand is defined as comprising 90% material
finer than 1.0ϕ, gravel comprises 70% granules, pebbles and
cobbles (>-1.0ϕ) and 30% sand; sand and gravel is defined
as comprising 50% gravel and 50% sand (terminology of Folk,
1968). Examples of the kinds of sedimentary structures
identified are shown as Figure 4. Interpretation of the
facies was considered in comparison to the literature on
closed conduit (tunnel) bedform development and open channel
bedform development under increasing bed shear strength. The
hydrodynamic interpretation of sand size bedforms follows the
work of Simons *et al.*(1965) and Harms *et al.*(1975). Sediment
accumulation of coarse clasts is less readily quantified
under laboratory conditions. Gravel deposition in coarse
outwash systems has been described in detail by Gustavson *et
al.*(1975), Hein and Walker (1977), Church and Gilbert (1975),
Rust and Romanelli (1975) and Eynon and Walker (1974).
Reviews of coarse clastic depositional environments are found
in Miall's work (1977) and that of Rust (1978). The major
depositional forms include longitudinal and transverse bars
in which gravel, .transported during flood stage activity, is
deposited during the subsequent period of waning flow as a
diffuse gravel sheet. Massive or crudely horizontally bedded
gravel forms longitudinal bars during conditions of shallow
flow, and high sediment and fluid discharge. Slip faces may
be developed on transverse bars when the flow deepens and
the sediment and fluvial discharge are low (Hein, 1974, in
Harms *et al.*,1975). Reviews of the kinds of bedforms anticipated in closed conduit or tunnel conditions have been
undertaken by Saunderson (1977b) and Ringrose (1979). The
work of McDonald and Vincent (1972) indicates that a series

FACIES		CHARACTERISTIC STRUCTURE		ORIGIN	
				CLOSED CONDUIT	OPEN CONDUIT
Sand	A_1	Parallel bedded or laminated	FLUVIAL	Plane bedded	Traction carpet
Sand	A_2	Massive, faint horizontal bedding	FLUVIAL	Heterogeneous suspension	Rapid subaqueous dumping
Sand	A_3	Cross-laminated	FLUVIAL	Ripple	Ripple - low flow
Sand	A_4	Trough cross-stratified	FLUVIAL	Dune	Dune - high flow
Sand	A_5	Tabular cross-stratified	FLUVIAL	Dune	Sand wave - high flow
Sand	A_6	Cut and fill	FLUVIAL	-	Open channelling
Gravel	B_1	Massive matrix supported gravel	FLUVIAL	Heterogeneous suspension	Longitudinal transverse bar, later infiltration
Gravel	B_2	Open-work gravel	FLUVIAL	-	Longitudinal bar
Gravel	B_3	Cross-bedded	FLUVIAL	-	Transverse bar - rapid flow
Gravel	B_4	Horizontally bedded	FLUVIAL	-	Gravel bar - rapid flow
Gravel	B_5	Backset bedded	FLUVIAL	-	Antidune regime - rapid flow
Sand & Gravel	C_1	Horizontally bedded	FLUVIAL	-	Gravel bar - rapid flow
Sand & Gravel	C_2	Massive, unsorted	FLUVIAL	Heterogeneous suspension	Gravel bar - rapid flow
Silt & Clay	D_6	Cross-laminated sandy silt	FLUVIAL	Dune	Ripple - low flow
Silt & Clay	D	Silt and clay rhythmites	NOT FLUVIAL	Lacustrine deposits	
S & G	E	Unsorted sand and gravel with silt clasts	NOT FLUVIAL	Mixed deposition (?)	
S&G	F	Reworked shoreline sediments	NOT FLUVIAL	Littoral reworking	
Sand	G	Horizontally bedded sand	NOT FLUVIAL	Eolian	
Till	H	Unsorted and flow tills	NOT FLUVIAL	Glacial melting	

Figure 3. Main facies types and characteristics structures of Manitoba eskers

Figure 4

4a Facies Type A (parallel bedded sand) in the
Leaf Rapids esker, lateral to the coarse central
core, showing minor tectonic structures.
Height of section is 7m.

4b Facies Type A_3 in the Leaf Rapids esker showing
showing ripple drift cross lamination.

4c Facies Type A_6 in the Axis Lake esker showing
cut and fill development.

4d Facies Type B_1 in the Axis Lake esker showing
coarse, matrix supported gravel and silt beds
above with soft sediment deformation

4e Facies Type B_2 in the Axis Lake esker showing
openwork gravel.

Figure 4b

Figure 4c

Fig 4d

Fig 4e

of bedforms may be produced with increasing shear flow
velocity. This generally changes under conditions of low flow
velocity from a stationary bed, through dune and plane bed
development. With further increases in velocity the sediment
is transported as heterogeneous suspension (typified by a
gradation from coarse to fine grain sizes in the sediment
column) to homogeneous suspension (their Figure 2a). Hence
it becomes clear that the presence of any facies can rarely
be regarded as diagnostic of open or closed conduit flow.
As these criteria are significant in terms of the depositional
history of an esker and proglacial lake, further consideration is given to the identification of such criteria in the
literature.

Criteria for subaqueous deposition is found in ball and
pillow and dish structures identified by Rust and Romanelli
(1975) in subaqueous outwash deposits south of Ottawa. Sliding
bed facies have been ascribed to heterogeneous suspension in
a pipe flowing full by Saunderson (1977b). The facies however comprise coarse matrix supported gravel, which may
equally be deposited during gravel bar development and later
sand infiltration under open channel, normal fluvial conditions (Eynon and Walker, 1974). Lack of complete flow
separation in dune bedform development is quoted by McDonald
and Vincent (1972) as causing oversteepening of material at
the brink point and the reverse grading of sediment down foreset beds. If a number of diagnostic features can be identified with certainty, then some evidence of closed conduit
flow may be assumed. Finally the presence of backset bedding,
resulting from antidune migration upstream, is regarded as
being relatively diagnostic as a 'free surface' bedform.
Problems arise in the identification of such structures.
Many of the antidune bedform features resemble cut and fill
structures (Middleton, 1965). Others appear as massive or
gently dipping gravel beds (Shaw and Kellerhals, 1977).

RESULTS

The present work takes the position that the subjective causal
interpretation of individual facies may be overcome by looking
at facies in terms of downstream, vertical and lateral associations and the relationship of sediment accumulation to
morphological characteristics.

The relative frequency of facies in each esker grouping
was considered (Figure 5). The northern Leaf Rapids esker
contains a relatively high frequency of coarse gravel facies
(Types B_1 and B_2) and a low frequency of sand facies. The
Axis Lake esker has a relatively even coarse gravel (Type B)
to sand (Type A) ratio with an abundance of mixed facies
(Type C). The composite frequency of the Birds Hill eskers
show proportionately more sand than gravel, indicating a
higher incidence of finer sediment. A further point of
interest is the relative abundance of till in the three esker
groupings. No till was found associated with the northern
esker. Till represents under 10% of the Axis Lake esker and
forms about 20% of the Birds Hill esker occurring peripheral
to and overlying, coarse clastic deposits.

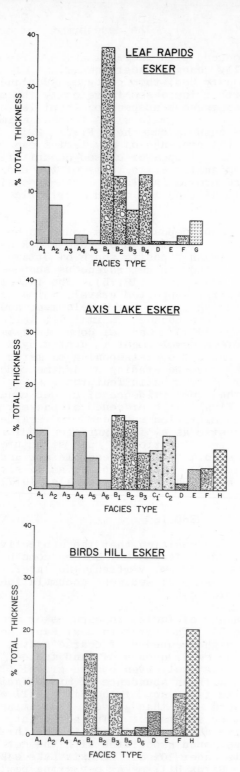

Figure 5. The relative frequency of facies types in each esker grouping

Vertical facies changes were analyzed using transitional matrices, following a method advocated by Selley (1971) and exemplified by Shaw (1975). In the case of the Leaf Rapids esker, 52 transitions occurred between the 14 identified facies and a lag pebble sediment. Positive values on the residual transition probability matrix indicate that a particular transition occurs more frequently, and a negative value less frequently, than it would if the sequence was the result of random selection.

The vertical facies transition diagram (Figure 6a) for the Leaf Rapids esker, derived from the residual transition probability matrix, shows that the facies sequence $B_1 \rightarrow A_1 \rightarrow B_1 \rightarrow B_2 \rightarrow B_1$ predominates, with a close genetic affiliation between Types A_1 and B_2, and that a secondary transition from facies $B_1 \rightarrow A_2 \rightarrow B_3 \rightarrow B_1$ is evident. Facies Type B_1, massive matrix supported gravel, predominates and is associated with openwork gravel, cross-bedded gravel, parallel bedded and massive sand.

Facies associations in the Axis Lake esker were obtained by using a transitional matrix to establish vertical trends. A total of 60 vertical transitions were noted between 18 facies types. Residual transition probabilities show a wide range of variation, which resolve into two distinct trends on the vertical facies transition diagram (Figure 6b). A close association appears between facies Types B_2, C_2 and E and facies A_1 (horizontally bedded sand), in two sequences. The sequence $A_5 \rightarrow F$ suggests that late stage outwash conditions prevailed, with facies A_5 representing sand waves in the outwash sequence, which were later reworked by shoreline activity.

In the Birds Hill esker, western section, 88 transitions occurred between 15 facies types and a minor pebble lag. The vertical facies transitions derived from residual transition probabilities are shown as Figure 6c. The transition tree shows two distinct, although interrelated vertical sequences. The most direct goes from backset bedded gravel (B_3) and trough cross-stratified sand (A_4) through parallel bedded sand (A_1) and reworked shoreline sediment (F).

A total of 70 transitions were noted for the southern segment of the Birds Hill esker which relate 15 facies and a pebble lag. The southern section differs from the western section in that it contains a preponderance of gravel and a till cap in the vertical axis but the southern segment is more cyclic (BABAB) in vertical section (Figure 6d).

INTERPRETATION

In the Leaf Rapids esker, the vertical extent and downstream continuity of Type B gravel is greater than that normally accorded to gravel bar development under braided stream conditions (Rust, 1978). Facies Type B is interpreted as resulting from closed conduit, sliding bed conditions based on the vertical extent and downstream continuity of the gravel beds. An explanation is forthcoming regarding the relationship

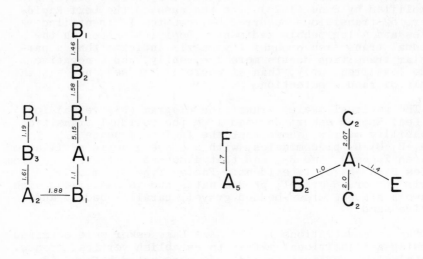

a. *LEAF RAPIDS* b. *AXIS LAKE*

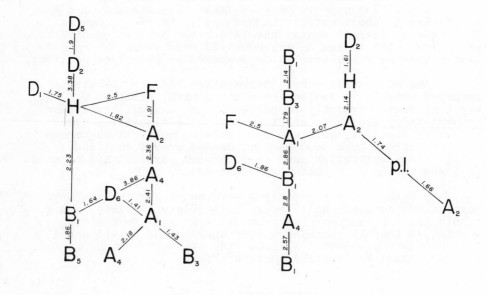

c. *BIRDS HILL WEST* d. *BIRDS HILL SOUTH*

Figure 6. Vertical facies transition diagrams

of 'sliding bed' faces to parallel bedded sand in what appears
to be the main vertical sequence and cross-bedded gravel and
homogeneous sand in the lateral sequence. Using all the evidence available, it appears that the central core of the Leaf
Rapids esker accumulated as a result of repeated surges of
sediment transported in a relatively confined tunnel as
heterogeneous suspension. The flow appears to have been
intermittent and interrupted by periods of more normal fluvial
flow which took place in an open tunnel.

Lack of total sediment incorporation during the subsequent
heterogeneous surge could have been due to frozen conditions
at the base of the conduit, but if this were the case, rip
up structures (which were not evident) would be formed.
Alternatively, heterogeneous suspension may have occurred
only in the early summer, when thin sheets of ice protected
the sediments below producing a zero resistant surface, which
may have assisted in the downstream perpetuation of turbulent
suspension. After a period of coarse sediment deposition,
melting and expansion of the tunnel periphery took place
concurrently with a decrease in meltwater flow. More 'normal'
sediment deposition prevailed through late summer to early
autumn, with in-channel lateral bar development and sand
accumulation. During the subsequent winter, active ice movement led to further tunnel confinement, with low meltwater
or no flow taking place through the system. The tunnel radius
may thus have become relatively small prior to spring thaw
and enlarged consequent upon surges of meltwater draining the
system and removing coarse debris from the sole and flanks of
the esker tunnel. With melting and tunnel expansion, more
normal fluvial conditions prevail and the cycle is repeated.
Hence, a rapid melt, northern esker depositional model may
be devised which consists of a narrow vertical column of
coarse sediment, accumulated under temperate ice conditions,
with free flow to the ice front in an active ice regime.
Deposition occurs as a result of periods of heterogeneous
suspension. Coarse matrix supported gravel is deposited
while the conduit flows full in the early summer. This probably alternates with periods during which normal fluvial
conditions prevail (Figure 7).

The vertical sequence of the Axis Lake esker comprises
horizontally bedded sand forming an integral part of three
plausibly separate sequence groupings. Although the overall
vertical sequence may be explained in terms of heterogeneous
suspension, the strong lateral facies relationship with Type
B_2 open work gravel suggests the accumulation of gravel bars
in a braided channel. In this case channel widening is more
prevalent than vertical deposition. Gravel bar deposits were
later succeeded by in-channel sand deposition, followed by
late stage bar evolution. The overall beaded form of the
esker contrasts with the longitudinal continuity of the Leaf
Rapids esker. It appears that individual tunnels or channels
were used relatively infrequently and that each bead appears
to comprise a single surge event (in contrast to the superimposed surges in Leaf Rapids). Figure 7 shows the central
esker depositional model depicting mainly coarse gravel bar
accumulation, alternating with, and grading laterally into,
in-channel sand deposition.

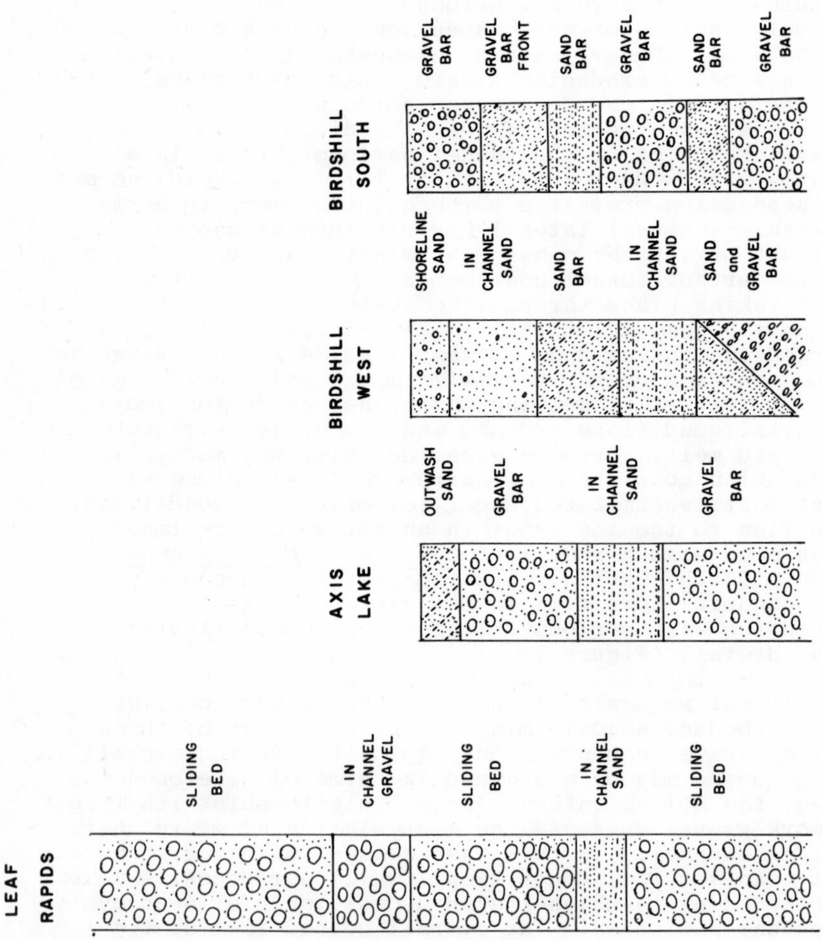

Figure 7. Vertical facies transition diagrams

The western and southern sections of the Birds Hill esker also comprise rapidly alternating facies with strong lateral continuity, suggestive of deposition in a braided stream environment. In this case facies Type B_1 is not vertically extensive and was probably not deposited under sliding bed conditions. The genetic relationship of this facies type with backset bedded gravel tends to support this view. The vertical association of gravel with till indicates that gravel bar development continued towards the close of fluvial deposition. The southern section differs from the western section in that it contains a preponderance of gravel and a capping of till in the vertical axis and is more cyclic (BABAB) in vertical section (Figure 7). The presence of trough cross-stratified sand and cross-bedded gravel suggest sand in-filling between gravel braid bars. Deposition may have taken place over a relatively short time span. Individual beads and the braided outwash sequence were probably finally deposited in a broad enclave between vertically upstanding ice walls. The width of the beads denotes lateral erosion, not compensated for by active ice movement back into the channel, which in turn suggests that the channel walls were composed of stationary ice which may have become separated from the main ice margin.

DISCUSSION

The question of ice regime can be addressed in terms of predominant fluvial mode of deposition and till content. The more rapid vertical, relative to lateral, melting in northern eskers may relate to a steep ice gradient and higher ambient temperatures which result in chute-like rapid meltwater escape down extensive conduits extending for up to 30 km back from the ice front. The more rapid lateral, relative to vertical melting in southern eskers, and bead type depositional form appear to relate to lower overall temperatures, slower recession, relatively low flow and deep (though wide) sediment accumulation. The high till content appears to substantiate this, as till appears to be carried higher into the marginal ice in shear planes resulting from basal freezing under relatively 'polar' conditions, whereas relatively little till is carried high into the marginal zone of temperate (wet based) ice (Boulton, 1972).

Two different hydrological regimes appear to have prevailed (Figure 8). Hooke (1977) suggests that the marginal zone of a large ice sheet which consists mainly of cold, dry based ice may contain a narrow ablation area of subglacial melting at pressure melting point. The limited extent of the ablation area may restrict upstream linear esker development such that individual bead deposition occurs. Dislocation of the frozen toe may cause large blocks of ice to become detached from the ice margin, providing, at least during the later stages of bead development, relatively stagnant walls which allow lateral erosion of an entrapped braided stream system. The level of Lake Agassiz is inferred as being too low to cause subaqueous deposition. The structures are interpreted as being formed by bedforms under normal fluvial conditions.

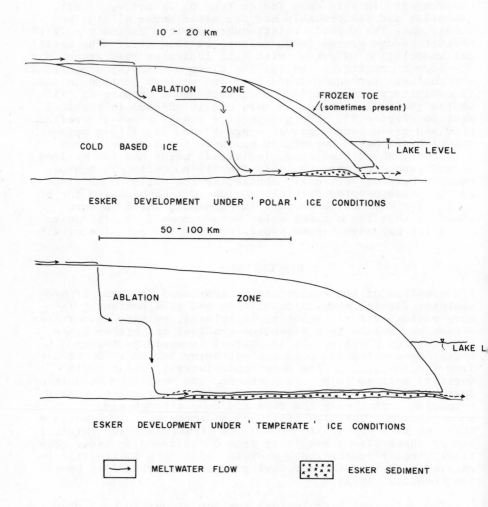

10 - 20 Km

ABLATION ZONE

FROZEN TOE
(sometimes present)

COLD BASED ICE

LAKE LEVEL

ESKER DEVELOPMENT UNDER ' POLAR ' ICE CONDITIONS

50 - 100 Km

ABLATION ZONE

LAKE L

ESKER DEVELOPMENT UNDER ' TEMPERATE ' ICE CONDITIONS

MELTWATER FLOW   ESKER SEDIMENT

Figure 8.   Different hydrological regimes under polar and
temperate ice conditions

Conversely the northern eskers appear to have formed as a result of meltwater catchment throughout an extensive ablation area, with meltwater concentration at low pressure points towards the base of the glacier (Figure 8). Additions to the esker take place by headward accretion possibly on an annual basis. The length of a temperate esker, may potentially extend throughout the length of the ablation zone. This kind of closed conduit rapid melt flow appears to take place generally independently of the presence of an adjacent pro-glacial lake.

The above theory appears to accord broadly with the climatic history of deglaciation throughout the Prairies. After a period of maximum ice advance in Iowa 12 000 years B.P., recession to approximately the position of Birds Hill, may have taken place at about 11 000 years B.P. During this period, the high pressure system centred on the Laurentide ice mass perpetuated relatively cold, polar air along the ice front (Bryson and Wendland, 1976). After considerable recession to about 7000 or 8000 years B.P. more temperate conditions are believed to have prevailed, concurrent with extensive melting and water impoundment in the Tyrrell Sea - Hudson Bay basin. During the 'hypsithermal' interval, therefore, rapid melting was instrumental in producing extensive esker swarms in northern Manitoba.

Hence, basically two types of eskers are found in the active ice basinal portions of Manitoba. Beaded eskers which owe their origin to limited meltwater developed in the ablation zone of an otherwise cold-based glacier; and long continuous ridge eskers developed in the extensive subglacial tunnels of temperate ice.

REFERENCES CITED

Banerjee, I and B.C.McDonald, 1975, Nature of esker sedimentation, in *Glaciofluvial and glaciolacustrine sedimentation,* ed A.V.Jopling and B.C.McDonald, (Society of Economic Paleontologists and Mineralogists, Special Publication 23), 132-154

Boulton, G.S. 1972, Modern arctic glaciers as depositional models for former ice sheets. *Journal Geological Society London,* 128, 361-393

Bryson, R.A. and W.M.Wendland, 1967, Tentative climatic patterns for some Late Glacial and Post Glacial episodes in central North America, in *Life, land and water,* ed W.J.Mayer-Oakes, 271-298

Church, M. and R. Gilbert, 1975, Proglacial and lacustrine environments, in *Glaciofluvial and glaciolacustrine sedimentation,* ed A.V.Jopling and B.C.McDonald, (Society of Economic Paleontologists and Mineralogists, Special Publication 23), 22-100

Glacio-fluvial sedimentation and processes

Glacio-fluvial sedimentation and processes

Gustavson, T.C., Ashley, G.M. and J.C.Boothroyd, 1975, Depositional sequences in glaciolacustrine deltas in *Glaciofluvial and glaciolacustrine sedimentation,* ed A.V.Jopling and B.C.McDonald, (Society of Economic Paleontologists and Mineralogists, Special publication 23), 264-280

Harms, J.C., Southard, J.B., Spearing, D.R. and R.G.Walker, 1975, *Depositional environments as interpreted from primary sedimentary structures and stratified sequences,* (Society of Economic Paleontologists and Mineralogists. Short Course No.2), 161 pp.

Hein, F.J. and R.G.Walker, 1977, Bar evolution and development of stratification in the gravelly, braided Kicking Horse River, B.C. *Canadian Journal of Earth Sciences,* 14, 562-571

Hooke, R. Le B., 1977, Basal temperatures in polar ice sheets, a qualitative review. *Quaternary Research,* 7, 1-13

Miall, A.D. 1977, A review of the braided river depositional environment. *Earth Science Reviews,* 13(1), 1-62

McDonald, B.C. and J.S.Vincent, 1972, Fluvial sedimentary structures formed experimentally in a pipe and their implications for interpretation of subglacial sedimentary environments. *Geological Survey of Canada, Paper,* 72-27, 30 pp.

Middleton, G.V. 1965, Antidune cross-bedding in a large flume. *Journal of Sedimentary Petrology,* 35, 922-927

Price, R.J. 1973, *Glacial and fluvioglacial landforms.* (Oliver and Boyd, Edinburgh), 242 pp.

Ringrose, S. 1977, Quaternary geology of the Kiski-Hill Lakes area. *Preliminary Map Series. Manitoba Mineral Resources Division.*

Ringrose, S. 1979, *The sedimentology of esker deposits in Manitoba, with particular reference to coarse sediment deposition and implications for the Late Glacial history of Manitoba.* (Unpublished Ph.D. thesis, University of London), 395 pp.

Ringrose, S. and P. Large, 1977, Quaternary geology and gravel resources of the Leaf Rapids local government district. *Manitoba Mineral Resources Division Geological Report,* 77-2, 93 pp.

Rust, R.B. 1978, Depositional models for braided alluvium, in *Fluvial sedimentology,* ed A.D.Miall, (Canadian Society of Petroleum Geologists, Memoir 5), 605-626

Rust, B.R. and R. Romanelli, 1975, Late Quaternary subaqueous outwash deposits near Ottawa, Canada, in *Glaciofluvial and glaciolacustrine sedimentation,* ed A.V.Jopling and B.C.McDonald, (Society of Economic Paleontologists and Mineralogists, Special Publication 23), 177-192

Saunderson, H.C. 1975, Sedimentology of the Brampton esker and its associated deposits: an empirical test of theory, in *Glaciofluvial and glaciolacustrine sedimentation,* ed A.V.Jopling and B.C.McDonald, (Society of Economic Paleontologists and Mineralogists, Special Publication 23), 155-176

Saunderson, H.C. 1977a, Grain size characteristics of sands from the Brampton esker. *Zeitschrift Geomorphologie,* 21(1), 46-56

Saunderson, H.C. 1977b, The sliding bed facies in esker sands and gravels: a criterion for pipe fill (tunnel) flow? *Sedimentology,* 24, 623-638

Shaw, J. and R. Kellerhals, 1977, Paleohydraulic interpretation to antidune bedforms with applications in antidunes in gravel. *Journal of Sedimentary Petrology,* 97, 257-266

Simons, D.B., Richardson, E.V. and C.F.Nordin Jr., 1965 Sedimentary structures generated by flow in alluvial channels, in *Primary sedimentary structures and their hydrodynamic interpretation,* ed G.V.Middleton, (Society of Economic Paleontologists and Mineralogists, Special Publication 12), 34-53.

Wright, H.E. Jr., 1973, Tunnel valleys, glacial surges and subglacial hydrology of the Superior lobe, Minnesota. *Geological Society of America Memoir,* 13b, 251-276

Acknowledgement

Publication of the foregoing paper was made possible by the generosity of the Province of Manitoba, Mineral Resources Division who funded the fieldwork and afforded overall support for the project. Individuals who provided constructive assistance and comment include Ms. Peggy Large, Dr. Erik Neilsen and Mr. B. Bannatyne. Academic support and encouragement was provided by Prof. E.H. Brown, University College London and Prof. B. Price, University of Glasgow, Scotland.

7 Bed form diagrams and the interpretation of eskers

Houston C. Saunderson

ABSTRACT

Bedform stability diagrams offer considerable potential as an aid in the interpretation of glaciofluvial structures preserved in eskers. Structures of open channel and sub-glacial, free-surface flows are easier to interpret because of the abundance of experimental data available. Competency diagrams and stability diagrams may be used to obtain estimates of palaeovelocity and palaeodepth, from which other hydraulic parameters may be extrapolated. Although structures of sub-glacial, full-pipe flows are less well documented, some assistance to interpretation is forthcoming from pipe flow stability diagrams. Of particular note is the absence of antidunes from full pipe flows: recent experiments indicate that antidunes are replaced by a plane bed in sands where a bed is already in existence. Experiments by others show the presence of a sliding bed mode of transport between a plane bed and total suspension of sediment.

INTRODUCTION

Although hydraulic interpretations of the structural anatomy of eskers are not particularly new, recent experimental work on bed form mechanics has expanded greatly our knowledge of sediment transport and deposition in fluvial channels. Parallel research using pipes has likewise provided new evidence useful to geomorphologists struggling with the interpretation of glaciofluvial landforms. Both open and enclosed channel flows have been reviewed extensively elsewhere (Graf, 1971; Vanoni, 1975) and need not be repeated here. The purpose of this paper is to select for emphasis a trend established by Gilbert and Murphy (1914), Simons and Richardson (1960, 1961), Simons et. al. (1965), Southard (1971), Fredsøe and Engelund (1975) among others: this trend concentrates on ways of summarising bed form stability fields on plots of flow and particle parameters. Such plots are useful in the hydraulic interpretation of primary sedimentary structures preserved in eskers.

---

* Department of Geography, Wilfrid Laurier University, Waterloo, Ontario, Canada.

Estimates of palaeohydraulic parameters of shallow palaeo-flow regimes may be enhanced by these diagrams which can be used quickly from knowledge of only field structures and particle size. Further refinement of the estimates may be obtained using more detailed reconstruction methods such as the inverse path line method of Jopling (1965, 1966).

BED FORM STABILITY DIAGRAMS

With the literature on sand transport in open channels quite voluminous, any attempt to summarize the wealth of information is encouraging. Particularly so is the effort to produce three-dimensional plots (cf. Southard, 1971; Southard and Boguchwal, 1973) of hydraulic parameters and bed states on which a given bed state falls in an unique location. Plots of flow depth, flow velocity, and particle size have provided clear separation of bed forms into distinct fields, albeit often with diffuse boundaries where data are deficient. Nevertheless, the potential is quite clear for these diagrams as aids in the palaeohydraulic interpretation of eskers deposited during both free-surface and full-pipe flows.

Free-surface stability diagrams

Free-surface flows include open-channel flows and pipe flows where the pipe is not completely filled throughout its cross-sectional area. As there is little reason to believe that there are major dynamic differences between the two, it is convenient to treat them both together in general terms.

The very detailed flume research of Simons and Richardson (1960, 1961, 1966), Simons et. al. (1965) and Guy et. al. (1966) showed that bed forms in medium sands fell into discrete parts of velocity-depth and stream power-fall diameter (Fig. 1) diagrams. More specifically, for a constant depth the bed form sequence is ripples -- ripples-on-dunes -- dunes -- transition -- plane bed -- standing waves and antidunes -- chutes-and-pools as the flow velocity increases above the threshold for general grain movement. Likewise, Figure 1 shows a similar sequence in medium sands for stream power ($\tau_0\bar{u}$) versus median fall diameter, where τ_0 is the bed shear stress and $\bar{u}$ the mean flow velocity. Southard (1971) expanded the applicability of velocity-depth diagrams by adding information on bed forms developed in fine sands and coarse sands (Fig. 2).

Palaeohydraulic application

The great potential for these bed form stability diagrams lies in their ease of use and in the valuable parameters of palaeoflow regimes yielded from their application. Field exposures of eskers often contain primary sedimentary structures in sand that are of the same dimensions as those produced experimentally in flumes. These structures may

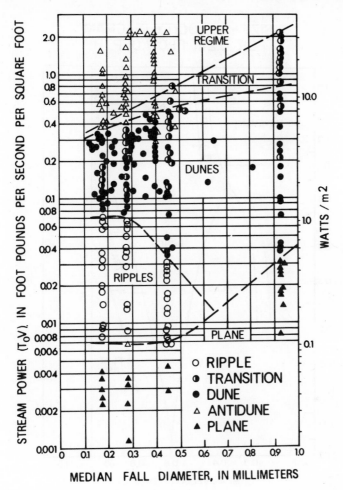

Figure 1.   Redrafted stream power diagram of Simons and
            Richardson (1966). Stream power (τυ) has the
            dimensions of power per unit of area. Stream
            power limits for different bed forms may be
            deduced from this diagram for sands. Metric
            scale added by present author. Courtesy of
            United States Geological Survey.
            $\tau_0 \bar{u}(\text{text}) = \tau_0 V(\text{diagram})$

then be deduced to be the relict features of particular
ancient bed forms for which the stability diagrams provide
estimates of the hydraulic conditions under which such forms
would have been stable. Knowledge of both bed form and
particle size then make it possible to estimate a range of
flow velocities (using Figure 2) at the time of transport
and deposition. An alternative would be to use Figure 2 to
cross-check one's interpretation of bed form from structure:

SIZE - VELOCITY DIAGRAM
FOR 0.2m FLOW DEPTH

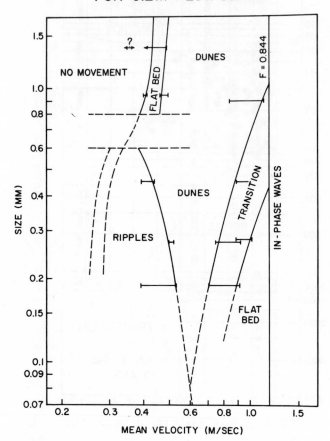

Figure 2.   Redrafted Figure 4 of Southard (1971).   Size-
velocity diagram for 0.2 m flow depth.   A mean
flow velocity of 0.65 m/sec and particle size
of 0.2 mm intersect in the dune field, thus
confirming the interpretation of the tabular,
cross-bedded sand as relict dune structures.
Redrafted with permission of Society of Economic
Paleontologists and Mineralogists.

for a given particle size, the competency diagrams of
Sundborg (1956) or Ljunggren and Sundborg (1968) provide an
estimate for palaeovelocity which, when combined with particle diameter, can be used to locate the appropriate bed
form on Figure 2.

This alternative approach aided the interpretation of
tabular units of sand (Fig. 3) overlying a thicker tabular
unit of cross-bedded sand in the Brampton esker, Ontario

Figure 3.   Cross-bedded sand from the Brampton esker.   The
            upper tabular sets have an average thickness of
            0.15 m and were probably deposited as topsets on
            top of a thicker (0.51 m) set of cross-beds
            interpreted as the micro-deltaic infilling of a
            depression.   The 0.51 m thick unit is partly
            shown in the lower part of the photograph.

(Saunderson and Jopling, 1980).   The small, tabular units
had an average thickness of 0.15 m and were interpreted as
dunes migrating over the topset part of a micro-delta (the
unit 0.51 m thick, Fig. 3).   Median particle diameter of a
bulk sample of the micro-delta was 0.2 mm, which gave a
threshold velocity estimate of about 0.35 m/sec.   This estimate was then multiplied by 2.25 because bottomsets in the
micro-delta provided abundant evidence for transport of sand
in suspension, and suspension of sand is well developed at
velocities of about 2.25 times the threshold velocity
(Jopling, 1966).   Thus, a velocity of about 0.8 m/sec is
probably closer to the true palaeo-velocity of the flow.
This estimate is one for the surface velocity rather than
the mean velocity because the competency diagrams of Sundborg
(1956) and Ljunggren and Sundborg (1968) were constructed
for flows of at least 1.0 m depth.   The mean velocity is
commonly calculated as 0.8 times the surface velocity, thus
giving in this example, an estimate of about 0.65 m/sec for
mean palaeo-velocity.

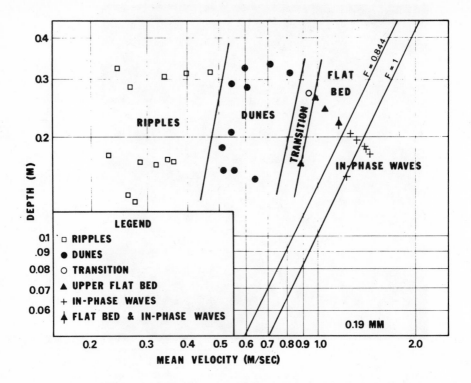

Figure 4.   Depth-velocity-bed form diagram for a particle
size of O.19 mm (Fig. 2a of Southard, 1971).
Dunes are stable over a range of depths from
about O.15 m to O.35 m.   Redrafted with permission of Society of Economic Paleontologists and
Mineralogists.

This estimate can be checked using the size-velocity
diagram of Southard (1971) for O.2 m flow depth (Fig. 2).
For a particle diameter of O.2 mm, given an interpretation
of the top set deposit as dunes, this diagram shows that
dunes can exist in a range of velocities from about O.5 to
O.7 m/sec. Dunes are also stable over a range of flow depths,
namely from about O.15 m to O.35 m (Fig. 4) at a velocity
of O.65 m/sec. Set thickness of the dune cross-beds was used
to check these estimates of depth (Saunderson and Jopling,
1980) using dune height to stream depth ratios recorded from
flume experiments (Guy et. al., 1966). Good preservation
of topset, foreset and bottomsets in the deposit made it
possible to use the inverse path line technique (Jopling,
1966) to reconstruct flow depth, and a value of approximately
O.3 m was obtained.

With the estimates of mean flow velocity, water depth
($\sim$ hydraulic radius) and median fall diameter it was then
feasible to use the stream power diagram (Fig. 1) of Simons

and Richardson (1966). The only value in the ordinate which is unknown is S, the energy gradient, because stream power $\tau_0\bar{u} = \rho gRS\bar{u}$ where ρ is fluid density (constant), g is gravitational acceleration (constant), R is hydraulic radius ($\sim$ flow depth, $\sim$ 0.3 m), S is energy gradient, and $\bar{u}$ is mean flow velocity ($\sim$ 0.65 m/sec.). Dune structures were preserved in the topset and should be stable over a stream power range of 0.07 to 0.35 foot pounds per second per square foot for a fall diameter of 0.2 mm. Thus, the only unknown quantity, S, should range from about 0.005 to 0.002. From these fundamental parameters -- palaeo-velocity, palaeodepth and palaeoslope -- other parameters can be calculated: these include Froude number (0.38), Reynolds number (1.24 X 10^5), Chezy coefficient (30.4), dimensionless Chezy coefficient (9.7), Darcy-Weisbach friction factor (0.085) and bed-material sediment discharge (19 tonnes/day/m). Details of these calculations may be found in Saunderson and Jopling (1980).

Full-pipe stability diagrams

Pipe-flow data are more fragmentary than free-surface information on transport and bed form mechanics. One reason is that hydraulic engineers have been more concerned with predicting head losses and particularly the velocity at which a bed starts to form for decelerating flow than with the structural characteristics of bed forms. Nevertheless, some stimulating relationships do exist and, once there is more concern for sedimentological and geomorphological aspects of transport and deposition, such diagrams can be modified if necessary and extended to include larger pipe diameters and coarser particles.

Information on the collective transport of sands, and more particularly of gravels, is not very abundant; but a few of the recent contributions to pipe transport may be emphasized because of their sedimentological content. Newitt et. al. (1955) distinguished four transport regimes: (a) at low velocities a stationary bed with bedload and saltation, and ripples as the primary bed form; (b) at higher velocities a moving or sliding bed, particularly for coarser particle sizes; (c) heterogeneous suspension, in which all of the sediment available is in suspension, the finer sizes distributed uniformly throughout the pipe cross-section and the coarser confined to the lower half of the cross-section; and (d) homogeneous suspension in which the sediment available is all in suspension but all sizes distributed uniformly throughout the cross-section. Of particular note is the separation by these authors of a sliding bed as a distinct mode of transport.

Wilson (1965) provided a fuller description of sliding in solid-liquid pipe flows, showing that when a flow decelerates from a velocity at which heterogeneous suspension occurs to one at which a bed starts to form on the invert of the pipe, namely at or just below the limit deposit velocity, the incipient bed starts to move as a whole unit along the bottom of the pipe. A sliding bed occurs if this motion

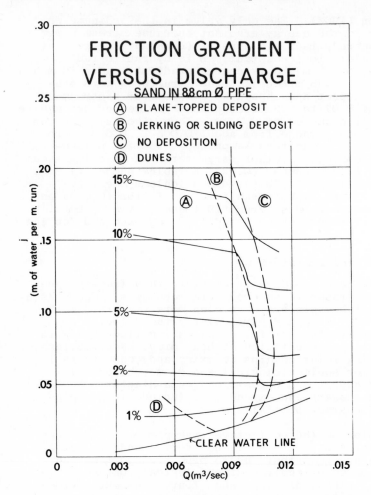

Figure 5. Friction gradient-flow discharge-bed form
diagram of Wilson (1965, his Fig. B-1).
Friction gradient is the hydraulic gradient
of the solid-liquid mixture. Note that this
gradient increases sharply for all mixtures
when a bed starts to form on the bottom of the
pipe. This sharp increase results in re-
entrainment of the bed with consequent sliding
or jerky motion.

is continuous whereas the bed jerks along the bottom if the
motion is intermittent. Figure 5 has been redrafted from
Wilson (1965, his Fig. B-1) to show the bed form sequence
found when sand was in transport. At the highest flow discharges all sediment is in suspension, i.e. a bed is absent
from the pipe; at slightly lower discharges a bed starts to
form, but slides or jerks along the pipe invert, and at this

stage the friction gradient increases markedly causing re-
entrainment of the bed and the maintenance of a sliding or
jerky motion; at still lower flow discharges a plane bed
forms; and at the lowest discharges a plane bed or dunes
(probably ripples according to the nomenclature of sedimen-
tologists and geomorphologists).

Acaroglu and Graf (1968) concluded that the sliding
bed was probably the pipe flow counterpart of antidunes
found in open-channel flows, a conclusion which was challenged by Wilson (1969). To test this hypothesis, a series
of experiments were run by the present author to observe the
transformation of antidunes when they become damped by the
presence of a tunnel roof: when antidunes and breaking antidunes formed in the open-channel sections of the two flumes
used, a plane bed formed inside the tunnel section. Thus
a plane bed, and not a sliding bed, is the tunnel counterpart
to antidunes of open channels. It should be emphasized that
the experiments just mentioned were conducted with a bed
already in existence in the flumes. Had it been possible
to begin the experiments with sediment already in uniform
suspension, then upon deceleration a plane bed might not
have formed in the tunnel. Thus the conclusion that antidunes are transformed to a plane bed is confirmed only for
accelerating flows with a bed already in existence, and may
not be appropriate for high-magnitude, decelerating flows
with no pre-existing bed. A sliding bed could form possibly
in these decelerating flows; but further experimental tests
need to be performed on this speculation.

Matrix-supported gravels in the Guelph esker have been
interpreted as sliding bed deposits (Saunderson, 1977) and
have been found subsequently to be common structures in the
Hopeville esker (Fig. 6) in Ontario. The suggestion (Saunderson, 1977) that sliding bed deposits might be an exclusive
trait of tunnel conditions, and therefore of subglacial
eskers, has been challenged by Boulton and Eyles (1979)
largely because matrix-supported gravels were found in proximal outwash deposits and thus may be formed by open-channel
flows.

CONCLUSIONS

To date, most of the information used to compile stability diagrams has come from shallow flows usually less than
1.0 m deep. Moreover, the variation of bed states with respect to changes in particle size have not yet been fully
established. This is especially true for gravel sizes, but
is due in part to the inability of most experimental facilities to recirculate gravel. If technological innovation
fails to produce flumes capable of recirculating gravel, the
theory of scale modelling still holds promise for investigations of gravel transport.

Figure 6.   Matrix-supported sandy gravel from the Hopeville
esker, Ontario.   Interpreted as a sliding bed
deposit transported by a high-magnitude flow
discharge, probably of flood proportions.

Despite these current limitations, the stability diagrams already available for medium to coarse sands offer
considerable potential for palaeohydraulic interpretations
of glaciofluvial landforms.   By providing estimates of the
lower and upper limits of hydraulic parameters between which
bed forms are stable, these diagrams offer a way to obtain
first approximations of the parameters defining palaeoflow
regimes.   Reconstruction of these parameters such as flow
depth and flow velocity, leads on to the extrapolation of
other characteristics of regime such as Froude number,
Reynolds number, energy gradient, bed shear stress, friction
factor and bed material discharge.

Solid-liquid flow in pipes needs to be studied further
in larger diameter pipes and for gravel sizes.   Investigations
focussed on high-magnitude discharges and their attendant
transport modes would be particularly useful in the interpretation of gravel facies in eskers.

REFERENCES

Acaroglu, E.R., and Graf, W.H. 1968, Sediment transport
    in conveyance systems - Part 2: *Bull. Internat.*
    Assoc. Sci. Hydrol., 13, 123-135.

Boulton, G.S., and Eyles, N. 1979, Sedimentation by valley
    glaciers; a model and genetic classification. in:
    Ch. Schluchter (ed.) *Moraines and Varves*, Balkema,
    Rotterdam, 11-24.

Fredsøe, J., and Engelund, F. 1975, Bed configurations in
    open and closed alluvial channels. *Inst. Hydrodyn.*
    Hydraul. Eng., Techn. Univ. Denmark Ser. Paper 8,
    39 pp.

Gilbert, G.K. and Murphy, E.C. 1914, The transportation
    of debris by running water. *U.S. Geol. Surv. Prof.*
    Paper 86, 263 pp.

Graf, W.H. 1971, *Hydraulics of Sediment Transport*.
    McGraw-Hill, New York, 513 pp.

Guy, H.P., Simons, D.B., and Richardson, E.V. 1966,
    Summary of alluvial channel data from flume exper-
    iments, 1956-1961. *U.S. Geol. Surv. Prof. Paper*
    462-I, I1-I96.

Jopling, A.V. 1965, Laboratory study of the distribution
    of grain sizes in cross-bedded deposits. in: G.V.
    Middleton (ed.) *Primary Sedimentary Structures and*
    their Hydrodynamic Interpretation. Soc. Econ.
    Paleont. and Mineral., Spec. Pub., 12, 53-65.

——— 1966, Some principles and techniques used in re-
    constructing the hydraulic parameters of a paleo-
    flow regime. *Jour. Sed. Petrology*, 36, 5-49.

Ljunggren, P., and Sundborg, A. 1968, Some aspects on
    fluvial sediments and fluvial morphology II. A
    study of some heavy mineral deposits in the valley
    of the Lule Alv. *Geog. Annaler*, 50A, 121-135.

Newitt, D.M., Richardson, J.F., Abbott, M., and Turtle, R.B.
    1955, Hydraulic conveying of solids in horizontal
    pipes. *Trans. Inst. Chem. Engrs.*, 33, 93-190.

Saunderson, H.C. 1977, The sliding bed facies in esker
    sands and gravels: a criterion for full-pipe
    (tunnel) flow? *Sedimentology*, 24, 623-638.

——— and Jopling, A.V. 1980, Palaeohydraulics of a
    tabular, cross-stratified sand in the Brampton esker,
    Ontario. *Sed. Geology*, 25, 169-188.

Simons, D.B., and Richardson, E.V. 1960, Resistance to
    flow in alluvial channels. *Amer. Soc. Civ. Engrs.*
    Proc., 86, 73-99.

——— 1961, Forms of bed roughness in alluvial channels.
    Amer. Soc. Civ. Engrs. Proc., 87, 87-105.

——— 1966, Resistance to flow in alluvial channels.
    U.S. Geol. Surv. Prof. Paper, 422-J, J1-J61.

Simons, D.B., Richardson, E.V., and Nordin, C.F. 1965, Sedimentary structures generated by flow in alluvial channels: in Middleton, G.V. (ed.), *Primary Sedimentary Structures and their Hydrodynamic Interpretation,* Soc. Econ. Paleont. and Mineral., Spec. Pub. 12, 34-52.

Southard, J.B. 1971, Representation of bed configurations in depth-velocity size diagrams. *Jour. Sed. Petrology,* 41, 903-915.

—— and Boguchwal, L.A. 1973, Flume experiments on the transition from ripples to lower flat bed with increasing grain size. *Jour. Sed. Petrology,* 43, 1114-1121.

Sundborg, A. 1956, The river Klaralven: a study of fluvial processes. *Geog. Annaler,* 38, 127-316.

Vanoni, V.A. (Editor), 1975, *Sedimentation Engineering.* Amer. Soc. Civ. Engrs., Manuals and Reports on Engineering Practice, 54, New York, 745 pp.

Wilson, K.C. 1965, Derivation of the regime equations from relationships for pressurized flow by use of the principle of minimum energy-degradation rate. *Civ. Eng. Report* 51, Queen's Univ., Kingston, Ontario.

—— 1969, Comments on 'Sediment transport in conveyance systems'. *Bull. Int. Assoc. Sci. Hydrol.,* 14, 131-134.

8 The hydraulic geometry of the lower portion of the Sunwapta River valley train, Jasper National Park, Alberta

Randy J. Rice

ABSTRACT

Morphologic and hydraulic data were gathered from 60 gravel channels (20/reach) on the Beauty Creek Flats section of the proglacial Sunwapta River during August 4-15, 1977. Four power functions (log-linear: width, average depth, average surface velocity and water surface slope) are determined for each reach and for Beauty Creek Flats as a whole with discharge as the independent parameter in all cases. A downstream hydraulic geometry interpretation indicates that the downstream reduction in the median grain size is mainly responsible for the variation in channel behaviour. In all three reaches of Beauty Creek Flats the primary adjustment of the channels to an increased discharge is an increase in the width of the flow.

It appears that the width exponent (b) may be used as an index of braiding intensity.

On Beauty Creek Flats slope is an independent parameter and is not a significant influence in the nature of the anabranch adjustment.

The hydraulic geometry relations determined for Beauty Creek Flats as a whole are compared to corresponding relations from other gravelly, glaciofluvial environments (Fahnestock, 1963; Church, 1972; and Arnborg, 1955). The comparison suggests that Arctic and non-Arctic outwash may be distinguished by the magnitude of the width and velocity exponents. The former is lower in an Arctic environment while the latter is higher. This suggests that there may be a similarity in channel response among areas of braided gravel outwash provided associated climatic conditions are similar. If additional data on channel adjustment on areas of gravelly outwash supports a similarity there may be potential for the development of a set of hydraulic geometry equations for each environment which could be used as predictors of channel behaviour.

* Amoco Canada Petroleum Company Limited, Calgary, Alberta, Canada

INTRODUCTION

This paper describes the nature of braid channel adjustment on a portion of the gravelly valley train of the proglacial Sunwapta River. Although studies of braided rivers are numerous, very few have dealt exclusively with braid channel behaviour on areas of gravelly outwash, be it a valley train or outwash plain. The first serious attempt to study such channels was associated with the Swedish expeditions to Iceland in 1951-52 to study the Hoffelssandur, an outwash plain adjoining a lobe of the Vatnajokull. The fluvial studies associated with these expeditions were largely qualitative and no comprehensive data set on channel hydraulics or morphology resulted. A small amount of data on channel adjustment did come from Arnborg's (1955) study of the glacial river Austurfljot on the Hoffellssandur, however his data was taken from only one cross section. The next and first of such studies to produce a comprehensive data set was Fahnestock's (1963) investigation of the valley train of the White River flowing from the Emmons Glacier on Mt. Rainier, Washington. The most recent study was conducted by Church (1972) on the braided outwash of Ekalugad Fiord on east-central Baffin Island. Channel behaviour was investigated as a part of this comprehensive study of Arctic fluvial processes, however the data were gathered from only several stations on the outwash.

The approach used in this study was similar to that used by Fahnestock. Data were acquired from as many channels as possible within the period of investigation and advantage was taken of the stepwise increase in total discharge down the study area to investigate variation in braid channel behaviour. The channel behaviour is described by four power functions (log-linear) of the general form $y = ax^b$. Width, average depth, average surface velocity and water surface slope are regressed against discharge using morphologic and hydraulic data gathered from 60 active gravel channels during August 4-15, 1977. By developing a set of the four power functions for each of an upper, middle and lower reach of the study area a downstream variation in channel adjustment is determined and interpreted. Finally, the braid channel behaviour of the Sunwapta River is related to channel behaviour on other areas of gravelly braided outwash by comparison with the limited number of channel data sets available on this depositional environment.

LOCATION AND DESCRIPTION OF THE STUDY AREA

Location

The Sunwapta River is located at the southern end of Jasper National Park in western Alberta (Figure 1), and is approximately 50 km in length. The upper 20 km of the river is discontinuously braided and flows through gravelly outwash left behind as glacial ice retreated up the Sunwapta River valley. The lowermost 9 km of the upper 20 km is a continuous stretch of braided gravel flats which are locally known as Beauty Creek Flats. These gravel flats were chosen as the study area (Figure 2).

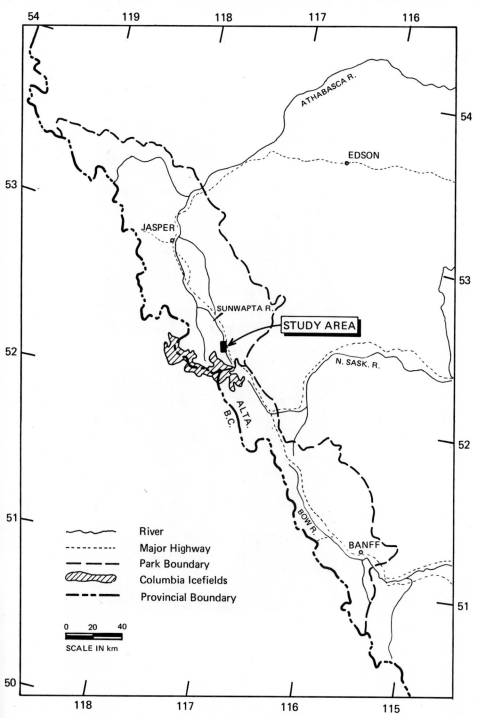

Figure 1. Location of the study area

Figure 2. The Beauty Creek Flats section of the Sunwapta River showing the three reaches of the study area. The old position of Highway 93 is shown on the photograph, the highway now runs along the eastern margin of the gravel flats. Use of the photo is through the courtesy of the Alberta Department of Energy and Natural Resources

Description

The Sunwapta River derives most of its meltwater from two
outlet glaciers of the Columbia Icefields, Athabasca and
Dome glaciers. Along Beauty Creek Flats the river receives
additional discharge contributions from two sources. An unnamed meltwater creek joins the flats from the west at
approximately one third of the distance down their length.
At approximately two thirds of their length, a snowmelt and
pluvial runoff creek known as Beauty Creek, joins the flats
from the east. As a result, the two creeks conveniently
divide the gravel flats into an upper, middle and lower
reach and causes a stepwise increase in total discharge down
the study area (Figure 2). A meandering regime exists on the
braided channel network of the gravel flats. As a result of
this the active channel area shifts from the west along the
upper half of the flats (upper reach) to the east along the
bottom half (middle and lower reaches). Adjacent inactive
areas have been stabilized to varying degrees by vegetation
which includes several isolated patches of infant and/or
stunted softwood. An abandoned alluvial fan constricts fluvial
activity to one channel at the bottom end of Beauty Creek
Flats (Figure 2). The fan creates a local base level for
the channels of the study area resulting in a drastic downstream decrease in the water surface slope of the dominant
active channel from 0.010 in the upper reach to 0.005 in the
middle reach and 0.001 in the lower reach. As a consequence
of this decrease in slope the calibre of the channel bed
sediment decreases markedly down the flats.

Views of the three reaches of the study area are presented
in Figure 3.

The weather in the study area during the summer of 1977
was mainly cold and rainy. In early August longer periods
of clear, hot weather began to occur and initiated the peak
discharge period for that summer. The daily mean discharge
entering Beauty Creek Flats, the average temperature and the
average estimated percent cloud cover for the period July 21 -
August 15, 1977 are shown in Figure 4. The data was acquired
at a gauging station established by the author at the top end
of Beauty Creek Flats where the flow is confined to a single
channel.

DATA ACQUISITION

Equipment

The fieldwork consisted mainly of levelling and the determination of flow velocities with current meters. The former was
used for obtaining accurate information on channel dimensions
as well as for establishing the long profile of the study area.
Flow velocities of the anabranches were obtained by the use
of current meters attached to wading rods. The velocities
were obtained both as primary data and for combination with
cross sectional area data for determination of the discharge
values of the theoretical discharge data set (see Methodology).

Figure 3a
Figure 3b

Figure 3. Photographs of Beauty Creek Flats
    (a)   The upper reach during a high flow period. Note
    the sheet flow over the bar in the centre foreground
    (b)   The middle reach of Beauty Creek Flats in July,
    1977. Highway 93 is in the foreground
    (c)   The lower reach of Beauty Creek Flats as seen from
    Highway 93 in mid summer 1977. Flow is from left to
    right in all three photographs

At depths in excess of 0.31 m a Price type AA current meter
was used. Velocities of shallower flows were determined with
a pygmy current meter. A Stevens type F stage recorder was
employed at the gauging station established at the top end
of Beauty Creek Flats.

Flow Conditions At The Time Of Data Acquisition

As stated above the data was gathered during the first two
weeks of August, 1977, coinciding with the beginning of the
peak discharge period for Beauty Creek Flats. Throughout
the study period a significant diurnal discharge variation
occurred in the anabranches with stage usually fluctuating
from half bankfull (pre 10 A.M.) to bankfull or slightly
above 6-9 P.M.). For this reason the adopted dominant
discharge of this study was bankfull discharge. A 1.5-2 day
lag usually occurred between weather change and discharge
response.

    Although bedload transport was not measured, significant
gravel transport did occur throughout the data gathering
interval. The bankfull discharges were capable of moving
only the smaller gravel sizes of the channels. Varying rates

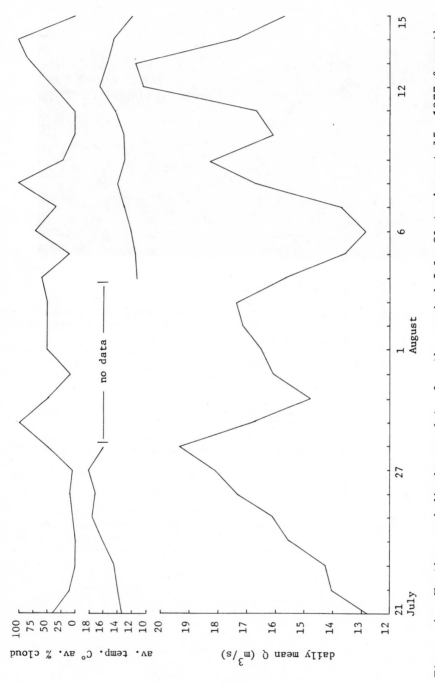

Figure 4. Weather and discharge data for the period July 21 to August 15, 1977 from the gauging station established at the top of the study area

of sand transport occurred throughout the summer, the amount being dependent on the weather controlled discharge conditions. During this period it could be observed that the most active braiding was occurring in the middle reach. It was also obvious that the maximum suspended sediment load yet carried by the anabranches was occurring. The average water temperature in the channels of the upper, middle and lower reach was 6.28, 8.05 and 9.20 C°, respectively.

The discharge entering the upper reach during August 4-15, varied between 13-21 m³/s as determined from a stage-discharge relation established for the gauging station at the top of the study area. Unfortunately the total discharge of the middle and lower reach is not known since neither the unnamed creek or Beauty Creek was gauged. However, visual comparison of their individual flow magnitudes to that of the gauging station during August 4-15, suggested that its discharge was being approximated. Under this assumption an estimate of the total discharge being transmitted by the braid channels of Beauty Creek Flats during the period of investigation would be 39-63 m³/s.

The variation in stage for the period August 5-10 is presented on Figure 5 so as to provide an indication of the magnitude of the discharge variations during the investigation.

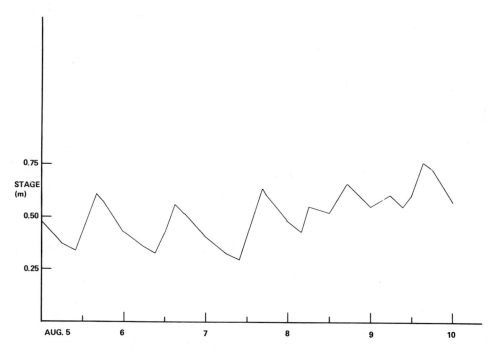

Figure 5. The variation in stage for August 5-10, 1977 from the gauging station at the top of the study area

Glacio-fluvial sedimentation and processes

Methodology

The three reaches of Beauty Creek Flats are basically very similar, the principal difference between them being the number of active channels which increases down the study area. Morphologic and hydraulic data was gathered from 20 channels per reach. Because of the prohibitive amount of time involved in making velocity-area measurements in the field, and since only the author and an assistant were involved in data gathering it was decided to obtain the information according to two formats. The principal difference between the two formats lies in the manner in which the discharge values were determined. The measured discharge data set included those channels for which the discharge was determined by velocity-area measurements in the field. A total of 30 channels, 10 per reach, were examined in this manner. The theoretical discharge data set included those active channels, 10 from each reach, 30 in total, whose discharge values were determined according to a relationship suggested by G. Parker and for which bed material grab samples were taken. This relation is based on Keulegan's 1938 logarithmic velocity distribution equation for turbulent open channel flow which assumed the channel to be rectangular in cross section. The relation suggested by Parker determines the dimensionless discharge of the channel in a manner which incorporates the reality of sloping channel margins. This was accomplished through the use of a corrected average depth. For use in the hydraulic geometry equations presented subsequently the discharge was converted to a dimensional form and a correction factor applied which allowed for a non-logarithmic velocity profile. The correction factor for a particular channel was the ratio of the measured thalweg surface velocity to a surface velocity determined from Keulegan's relation. Data on channel dimensions and slope were also obtained for this data set through the use of a level and levelling rod.

The channels of the measured discharge data set were chosen at random from amongst the active channels of the three reaches. The channels of the theoretical discharge data set were chosen by running transects across the valley train in each reach. The location of these transects, 1 and 2 in the upper reach, 3, 4 and 5 in the middle reach and 6 and 7 in the lower reach is indicated on Figure 2.

For a detailed explanation of the field procedures used in gathering the morphologic and hydraulic information and a more thorough explanation of the use of the theoretical discharge relation the reader is referred to Rice (1979).

Table 1 provides a statistical summary of the data. The reader is referred to Rice (1979) for tables containing the raw data.

Table 1 (part 1). Statistical summary of the morphologic and hydraulic data gathered from the channels of Beauty Creek Flats

parameter	reach	$\bar{X}$	std. dev.	N	Beauty Creek Flats max.	min.	$\bar{X}$	std. dev.	N
flow area (m^2)	upper	2.64	2.72	20	9.86	0.19	2.39	2.49	60
	middle	1.92	1.97	20					
	lower	2.60	2.78	20					
length (m)	upper	157.83	56.57	10	252.37	26.52	100.89	67.88	30
	middle	103.27	60.49	10					
	lower	41.58	21.68	10					
S_w	upper	0.011	0.001	10	0.016	0.002	0.008	0.004	29
	middle	0.010	0.003	10					
	lower	0.004	0.001	9					
S_b	upper	0.011	0.004	10	0.015	+ 0.010	0.008	0.005	30
	middle	0.010	0.003	10					
	lower	0.004	0.004	10					
av. width (m)	upper	8.10	5.29	20	24.38	1.68	8.05	5.00	60
	middle	7.63	5.02	20					
	lower	8.41	4.89	20					

Table 1 (part 2). Statistical summary of the morphologic and hydraulic data gathered from the channels of Beauty Creek Flats

parameter	reach	$\bar{X}$	std. dev.	N	max.	Beauty Creek Flats min.	$\bar{X}$	std. dev.	N
av. depth (m)	upper	0.26	0.10	20	0.49	0.10	0.23	0.10	60
	middle	0.21	0.07	20					
	lower	0.22	0.11	20					
av. w:d	upper	30.76	10.87	20	67.37	13.63	35.21	13.05	60
	middle	36.63	15.59	20					
	lower	38.24	11.61	20					
$\bar{V}_s$ (m/s)	upper	1.48	0.46	20	2.44	0.58	1.25	0.43	60
	middle	1.28	0.36	20					
	lower	0.99	0.31	20					
$\bar{\tau}_o$ (kg/m^2)	upper	31.69	11.40	10	48.06	5.44	20.62	12.47	30
	middle	18.67	4.67	10					
	lower	11.50	10.79	10					
Fr	upper	0.72	0.15	20	1.05	0.29	0.66	0.17	60
	middle	0.72	0.16	20					
	lower	0.54	0.12	20					

Table 1 (part 3). Statistical summary of the morphologic and hydraulic data gathered from the channels of Beauty Creek Flats

parameter	reach	$\bar{X}$	std. dev.	N	max.	min.	Beauty Creek Flats $\bar{X}$	std. dev.	N
Re_{ch}	upper	220810	142715	20	513333	36667	174005	120245	60
	middle	165577	105476	20					
	lower	135628	97338	20					
n	upper	0.055	0.009	10	0.084	0.033	0.051	0.013	30
	middle	0.050	0.014	10					
	lower	0.047	0.015	10					
D_{50} (mm)	upper	45.16	14.74	10	69.55	8.28	30.21	16.63	30
	middle	31.73	10.36	10					
	lower	13.74	3.75	10					
D_{90} (mm)	upper	99.60	10.76	10	116.15	18.64	68.34	32.28	30
	middle	71.08	26.43	10					
	lower	34.34	12.85	10					
gravel to sand ratio	upper	30.75	30.49	10	111.98	3.24	19.06	23.58	30
	middle	20.54	22.57	10					
	lower	5.90	2.51	10					
Q (m^3/s)	upper	3.27	4.17	20	14.59	0.08	2.47	3.20	60
	middle	2.14	2.72	20					
	lower	2.02	2.45	20					

CHANNEL CHARACTERISTICS AND ADJUSTMENT

Channel Characteristics

It is estimated that the data collected represent approximately 70% of the active channels present on Beauty Creek
Flats in the period August 4-15. Seven morphologic and
seven hydraulic parameters are described in Table 1. Review
of this table indicates that the mean value of the parameters
progressively decreases from the upper to the lower reach,
excepting Froude number, width to depth ratio, depth, width
and area. Of these width to depth ratio progressively
increases down the study area while the remainder show no
consistent down valley behaviour. The effect of the alluvial
fan at the bottom of Beauty Creek Flats is manifest in an
order of magnitude difference between the water surface slope
of the upper and middle reach and the water surface slope of
the lower reach which is reduced due to the proximity of the
fan. Corresponding to this drastic decrease in water surface
slope is a strong progressive decrease in bed material grain
size.

The shovel and bucket method of obtaining the channel
bottom grab samples for the channels of the theoretical
discharge data set resulted in the loss of the majority of
the silt and clay sized sediment causing a strong positive
skewness in the samples. However, since the weight lost
would only be a small percentage of the total weight the
percentiles given in Table 1 are in excess of the true value
by only a small amount.

Channel Adjustment

Figures 6, 7 and 8 present the hydraulic geometry relations
determined for the three reaches of the study area. These
were derived by collating the data of the measured and
theoretical discharge data sets and then breaking this
composite data set into the data obtained for the upper,
middle and lower reach of Beauty Creek Flats. In this manner
the variation in channel behaviour down the study area could
be determined and interpreted.

Since the interpretation constitutes an explanation of
the downstream hydraulic geometry the principle of constant
frequency of discharge becomes of paramount importance. For
this study the concern had to be for a similar average discharge for the three reaches period of investigation since
no records exist for Beauty Creek Flats. As determined in
Rice (1979) the average stage (representing discharge) of the
upper, middle and lower reach during their period of
investigation was 0.16, 0.11 and 0.15 m, respectively. This
indicates that the variation in channel behaviour between
the three reaches is real and not attributable to the time
at which the data for each reach was gathered.

A standard notation exists for the exponents of the power
functions for the four channel characteristics whose downstream variation is interpreted. The letters b, f, m and z

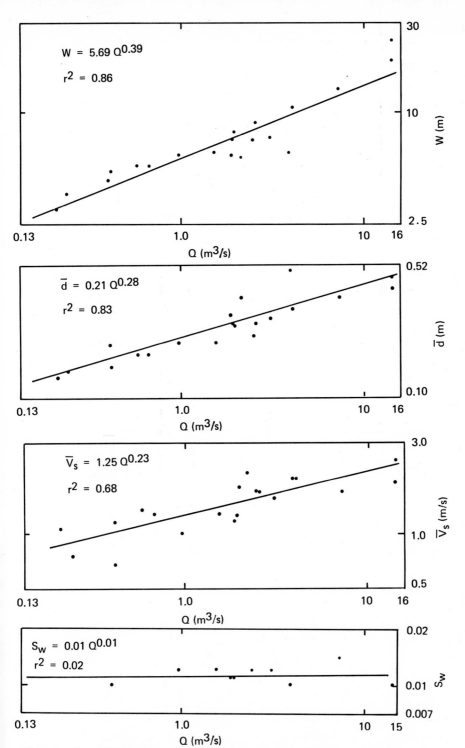

Figure 6. The hydraulic geometry relations determined for the upper reach of Beauty Creek Flats

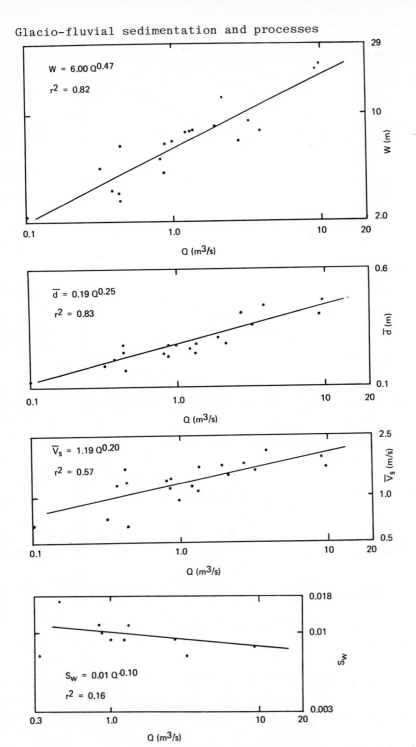

Figure 7. The hydraulic geometry relations determined for the middle reach of Beauty Creek Flats

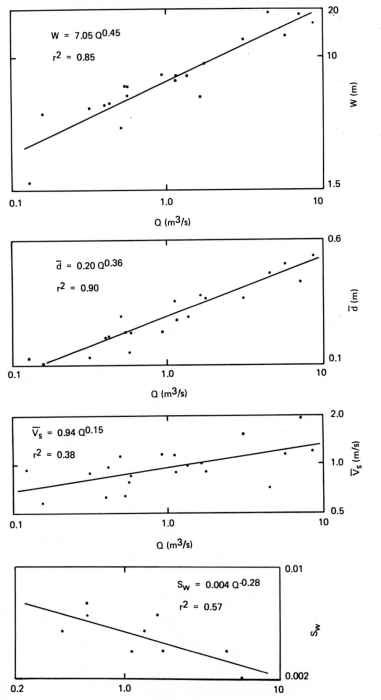

Figure 8. The hydraulic geometry relations determined for the lower reach of Beauty Creek Flats

167

represent respectively the rates of change of width, depth, velocity and slope with changing discharge.

In the following interpretation dominant or control parameters were chosen. These are felt to *most adequately* explain the downstream variation in the channel characteristic examined.

In recent literature the applicability of log-linear power functions as accurate representations of the response of the channel characteristics to varying discharge has been severely questioned (Richards, 1973, 1976). A discussion of this with respect to the channels of Beauty Creek Flats is contained in Rice (1979), in which it is concluded that the power functions developed for the study area do not constitute severe oversimplifications.

Width

reach	b value
upper	0.39
middle	0.47
lower	0.45

dominant parameters: average bottom shear stress, average median grain size

On Beauty Creek Flats the rate of increase of width with increasing discharge increases in the middle reach channels and decreases slightly in the channels of the lower reach. Despite the increase in total discharge in the middle reach due to the discharge contribution from the unnamed creek a concurrent increase in the number of active channels results in an average discharge per channel which is less than that in the upper reach ($2.14 \ m^3/s$ vs $3.27 \ m^3/s$). In light of the larger b value for the middle reach this would initially seem anomalous. This can be explained by reference to the average bottom shear stress and average median grain size values for the upper and middle reach channels. The middle reach channels are increasing their width at a greater rate, therefore the differential between the actual bank shear stress and the critical shear stress is larger than it is in the upper reach despite a lower average discharge per channel and a lower average bottom shear stress ($18.67 \ kg/m^2$ vs $31.69 \ kg/m^2$; average bottom shear stress is taken as representative of average bank shear stress). This is interpreted to be the result of a marked decrease in the average median grain size (decreased by approximately 30%) in the middle reach chanels causing the banks to be more easily eroded by creating a larger differential between the actual and critical bank shear stress (bed material grain size is assumed to be representative of bank material).

The coincidence of the most active braiding and the largest b value in the middle reach suggests that this exponent may be used as a braiding intensity index.

From the middle to the lower reach the decrease in average median grain size is much greater (57% vs 30%), the decrease in average bottom shear stress is less (38% vs 41%) and the decrease in the average discharge per channel is less (6% vs 35%). Rather than suggest a slight decrease in the value of b, this would cause one to anticipate an increase in its value. The source of this seemingly anomalous behaviour is interpreted to be the percentage of interstitial sand in the bank gravel. The increase in the percentage of sand from the upper to the middle reach is approximately 42% (5.41% vs 7.69%) while the increase from the middle to the lower reach is approximately 111%(7.69% vs 16.23%; percent sand of bed is assumed to be representative of bank sand content). The ultimate reason for this increase is the decreased areal slope due to increasing proximity to the alluvial fan at the bottom of Beauty Creek Flats. The increased interstitial sand serves a supportive function which becomes a significant factor affecting a slight decrease in the rate of increase of width in the lower reach.

Average Depth

reach	f value
upper	0.28
middle	0.25
lower	0.36

dominant parameters: average bottom shear stress, average median grain size

The average depth-discharge relations for Beauty Creek Flats indicates that the rate of increase of average depth decreases slightly in the middle reach channels and increases markedly in the channels of the lower reach. The dominant parameters are felt to be the same that determined the width response. From the upper to the middle reach the average median grain size drops by 30% while the average bottom shear stress of the middle reach channels decreases by 41%. The greater decrease in the latter is interpreted as overriding the drop in the average median grain size, resulting in an f value slightly lower than that of the upper reach. The lowest f value of the middle reach combined with the observation that the most active braiding occurred here, indicates that this is also the area of most rapid sediment deposition.

In the lower reach a smaller drop in average bottom shear stress (38%) and a much larger decrease in average median grain size (57%) occurs with the net result being more erodible channel beds and an accompanying increase in the rate of increase of channel depth.

The presence of channel armouring in all reaches rules out any control over the f value by interstitial sand.

Average Surface Velocity

reach	m value
upper	0.23
middle	0.20
lower	0.15

dominant parameter: water surface slope

Glacio-fluvial sedimentation and processes

The interpretation of the variation in m down Beauty Creek Flats is straightforward and is an excellent example of the influence of a more dominant factor in controlling the behaviour of a particular channel characteristic. Table 1 indicates that the average roughness value decreased down Beauty Creek Flats, an expected response in light of the decrease in the average median grain size. If one were to consider only roughness the expected behaviour of m would be to increase down the study area. However, rather than increase from the upper to the lower reach m decreases. This behaviour is the result of the decreasing value of the water surface slope as the alluvial fan at the bottom of the study area is approached.

Water Surface Slope

The slope-discharge relations for Beauty Creek Flats are very poor as indicated by the very low values of the coefficient of determination presented in Figures 6-8. This indicates that slope is only minimally, if at all, dependent on discharge and that it is effectively, an independent parameter.

In many streams slope is readily adjusted by scour and/or deposition on the channel bed. On Beauty Creek Flats the slope of the gravel anabranches is in a state of non-adjustment due to the inability of the majority of flows to move the coarse sediment, the degree of non-adjustment varying from one anabranch to another. The lack of slope adjustment by discharge is manifest in the large amount of scatter shown on the slope-discharge plots.

BEAUTY CREEK FLATS COMPARED TO OTHER OUTWASH AREAS

Power functions representing the behaviour of the same four channel characteristics were developed for Beauty Creek Flats as a whole by combining the data from the three reaches. These equations and their corresponding graphs are presented as Figure 9.

The only other significant channel studies on gravelly outwash are those of Arnborg (1955), Fahnestock (1963) and Church (1972) given in the introduction.

Figure 10 provides a comparison of the hydraulic geometry exponents of this study to the other three. The comparison indicates a distinction between gravel channel adjustment on non-Arctic (Sunwapta and White Rivers) and Arctic outwash (Hoffellssandur and Baffin Island sandar). The primary adjustment of the Arctic channels is a rapid increase in velocity while the primary response of the non-Arctic channels is an increase in channel width. The depth exponent is similar amongst the four studies. It had been previously suggested (Rice, 1979) that the distinction between these two groups in terms of the width and velocity exponents was due to increased bank stability of the Arctic outwash channels caused by freezing of bank sediment moisture during the night when the stage had dropped. Subsequent discussions with both Boothroyd

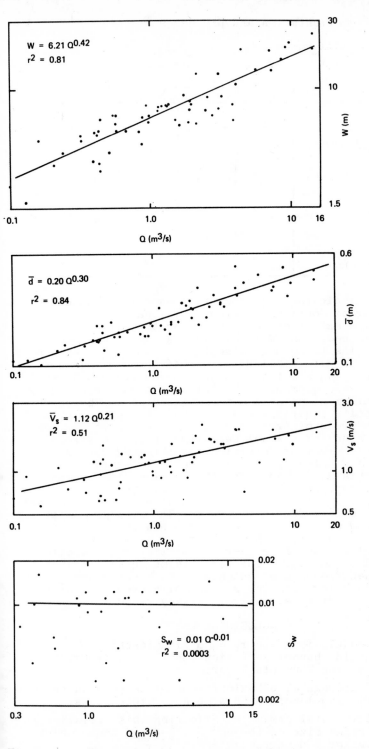

Figure 9. The hydraulic geometry relations determined for Beauty Creek Flats as a whole

Figure 10. Comparison of hydraulic geometry exponents
for areas of gravelly outwash

source	exponent			
	W	d	$\bar{v}$	S_w
Baffin Island sandar, Church (1972)	0.22	0.31	0.48	/
Hoffellssandur, Arnborg (1955)	0.17	0.39	0.44	/
White River, Fahnestock (1963)	0.38	0.33	0.27	0.13
Sunwapta River at Beauty Creek Flats	0.42	0.30	0.21	-0.01

and Church has indicated that nocturnal bank freezing does
not occur on Arctic outwash, thereby invalidating that
suggestion. The extent of and reason for the difference
between the two geographically distinct areas of outwash
occurrence remains to be determined. The similarity within
the two groups of Figure 10 indicates that a potential may
exist for developing a set of hydraulic geometry equations
that could be used to predict channel adjustment on gravelly
outwash of similar geographic setting. At present Church's
width and velocity equations would be best suited for predictive use on areas of Arctic outwash since his is the most
comprehensive study of channel behaviour in this environment.
The higher coefficient of determination obtained for Fahnestock's width and velocity relations relative to the same
relations of this study indicates that they would presently
be best suited for predictive use on non-Arctic outwash.
As mentioned previously the depth exponent was similar amongst
all four studies included in Figure 10. The highest coefficient
of determination was obtained from the depth relation of this
study suggesting that it might be used for predicting channel
depth on gravel outwash in either the Arctic or non-Arctic
environment. However, until further data on channel adjustment is obtained from gravel outwash in both environments
the validity of using these or any set of hydraulic geometry
equations in a predictive manner is highly suspect.

CONCLUSIONS

The following conclusions are reached with respect to the
nature of the braid channel adjustment on the Beauty Creek
Flats segment of the Sunwapta River:

1) A variation in channel behaviour does exist between an
   upper, middle and lower reach of Beauty Creek Flats.

2) The most influential parameter affecting this variation is
   the median grain size of the channel bed and banks which
   decreases markedly downstream.

3) In all three reaches of Beauty Creek Flats the primary,
   secondary and tertiary adjustment of the channels to an

increase in discharge is an increase in width, depth and velocity respectively.

4) Bankfull flow exceeds the critical condition required for significant gravel movement in all three reaches.

5) The highest rate of sediment deposition occurs in the channels of the middle reach.

6) The alluvial fan at the lower end of Beauty Creek Flats exerts a dominant control only over the velocity-discharge relation.

7) The width exponent may be used as a braiding intensity index.

8) Slope is effectively an independent parameter and is not a significant factor in channel adjustment on Beauty Creek Flats.

The comparison of the data from Beauty Creek Flats to other areas of gravelly outwash suggests the following:

1) Channel adjustment on gravelly outwash in an Arctic environment is distinguishable from that on non-Arctic outwash by the width and velocity exponents, the former being lower and the latter higher in an Arctic climate. The depth exponent is similar in both environments.

ACKNOWLEDGEMENTS

The material presented in this paper constitutes research done for a Master of Science thesis in the Department of Geology at the University of Alberta. Funding for the project was provided by the Boreal Institute for Northern Studies as well as by contributions from the supervisor's N.R.C. grant. The supervisor for the project was Dr. N.W. Rutter. Throughout the project invaluable advice was received from Dr. J. Shaw of the Geography Department and Dr. G. Parker of the Civil Engineering Department.

REFERENCES

Arnborg, L.   1955, Hydrology of the glacial river Austurfljot: ch. 7 of the Hoffellssandur - a glacial outwash plain. *Geografiska Annaler,* 37, 185-201

Church, M.   1972, Baffin Island sandurs: a study of Arctic fluvial processes. *Bulletin Geological Survey Canada,* 216

Fahnestock, R.K.   1963, Morphology and hydrology of a glacial stream - White River, Mt. Rainier, Washington. *U.S. Geological Survey, Professional Paper,* 422-A

Rice, R.J.   1979, *The hydraulic geometry of the lower portion of the Sunwapta River valley train, Jasper National Park, Alberta,* (Department of Geology, University of Alberta, unpublished Master of Science thesis).

Richards, K.S.   1973,   Hydraulic geometry and channel roughness - a non-linear system. *American Journal of Science,* 273, 877-896

Richards, K.S.   1976, Complex width-discharge relations in natural river sections. *Bulletin Geological Society of America,* 87, 199-206

9 Derivation of a summary facies sequence based on Markov chain analysis of the Caledon outwash: a Pleistocene braided glacial fluvial deposit

J.Z. Fraser

ABSTRACT

The Caledon Outwash is a Late Pleistocene, ice-marginal glaciofluvial sequence in southern Ontario. Identification of the facies assemblage, and Markov chain analysis of facies transitions indicate that the sequence is similar to that of generalized facies models proposed for the gravelly braided stream environment.

The assemblage comprises eight distinct facies, and three coarse-grained facies predominate. The Gm facies (terminology of Miall, 1977) consists of horizontally stratified clast-supported gravel with a well developed imbricate fabric. It is the deposit of mid-channel, longitudinal primary bedforms, aggraded at high flow stage. Coarse-grained Gp and Gt facies are characterized by planar and trough cross-stratification respectively, and are the deposits of high flow stage, transverse primary bedforms.

Fine-grained facies reflect the migration of dunes and sand waves at moderate flow stage and consist of trough (St), or less frequently, planar (Sp) cross-stratified sand and horizontally stratified sand (Sh). Ripple laminated sand (Sr) and silt (Fl) facies reflect deposition by low water accretion processes, and are uncommon in the depositional sequence.

Markov chain analysis was employed to detect and enhance non-random facies transitions in the deposit. The derived summary sequence is dominated by superposed, truncated, upward fining and thinning sequences which represent repeated channel-fill events. The base of the summary sequence is defined by the initiation of a channel-fill cycle, often marked by the scour of large-scale Gt facies sets into

*Ontario Geological Survey, Toronto, Ontario M5S 1B3

*underlying, finer grained facies of a previous cycle. The
channel-fill sediments are predominantly multistorey sequences
of Gm facies which represent aggradation by successive longitudinal bars. Occasional solitary Gp and Gt facies sets in
these sequences represent slight decreases in flow stage.
The upper portions of channel-fill cycles are marked by
aggradation of sand-dominant facies (St, Sp, Sh) and by
general upward fining to low water accretion deposits (Sr
and Fl facies). The fine-grained upper portions of the
sequences are often partially removed by scour at the
initiation of the next channel-fill cycle.*

INTRODUCTION

Earlier studies of the braided stream depositional environment concentrated on the morphology of modern examples, and
on the hydrodynamic conditions which influence the braiding
process (Leopold and Wolman, 1957; Krigstrom, 1962; Fahnestock, 1963; Church, 1972). More recent work has focused
on the patterns and sequence of deposition in both modern and
ancient braided streams (Smith, 1970; Costello and Walker,
1972; Miall, 1973; Eynon and Walker, 1974; Cant and Walker,
1976). In the last several years, a synthesis of previous
studies has developed generalized normative and predictive
depositional models similar to those developed for the
meandering stream depositional environment (Miall, 1977, 1978;
Cant, 1978; Rust, 1978,1979). Miall (1977) reviewed the
literature, and on the basis of predominantly descriptive
data, identified the main constituent facies of the braided
stream sequence and derived four general depositional models.
The number of models has since been increased to six (Miall,
1978; Rust, 1978), representing a continuum of sub-environments from proximal alluvial fans to distal ephemeral streams,
and a progression of textures from coarse gravel to silt and
clay.

Validation and further refinement of the general models
require that they be tested against the depositional sequences
observed in local examples (Walker, 1979). To achieve this
objective, and to facilitate cross-comparison, a quantitative
approach based on Markov chain analysis, has been employed
for the description of depositional sequences (Miall, 1973;
Cant and Walker, 1976; Cant, 1978). This statistical technique identifies non-random patterns and cyclic repetitions
in a given sequence of elements and has been used in the
study of meandering stream deposits (Allen, 1970), Coal-
measure cyclothems (Read, 1969) and a variety of other
depositional environments (Schwarzacher, 1969).

In the present study, Markov chain analysis is applied to
the Caledon Outwash, a Pleistocene braided fluvial deposit
in southern Ontario (Cowan, 1976). The study has two
objectives: the first is to identify and describe the facies
which make up the depositional sequence in the context of the
facies code proposed by Miall (1977) and modified by Rust
(1978). The second objective is to identify non-random

patterns in the deposition of these sediments and to relate
the patterns to the generalized depositional models proposed
for the braided fluvial environment.

GEOLOGICAL SETTING

The Caledon Outwash was deposited in a Pleistocene ice-
marginal meltwater channel located approximately 65 km northwest of Toronto (Figure 1). The fluvial origin of the deposit
was first recognised by Taylor (1912), Chapman and Putnam
(1966) later delineated the deposit and linked it to an
extensive meltwater channel system which trends south-
westerly through southern Ontario. Detailed local mapping
of the deposit was carried out by White (1975) and Cowan
(1976). Aggregate resources of parts of the deposit have
been discussed by Hewitt and Karrow (1963) and Fraser (1976).

The main depositional period occurred during the latter
part of the Port Bruce Stadial, Wisconsinan Substage, 14 000
to 13 000 years B.P. (Cowan, 1976). At this time, the margins
of the Ontario and Simcoe lobes of the Laurentide ice sheet
stood at or near the Paris and Gibraltar Moraines respectively
(Figure 1) (Cowan 1976; White, 1975). The channel was formed
by meltwaters which flowed to the southwest, being confined
on the north by the Niagara Escarpment and on the south by
the moraines and ice margins.

The portion of the outwash chosen for detailed study lies
in an area of extensive gravel operations just south of the
village of Caledon, where numerous pit faces expose more than
12 m of outwash gravel. Three stratigraphic units may be
recognized in the section. The lower 2 to 5 m consist
predominantly of coarse, horizontally stratified gravel with
well developed imbricate fabric. Isolated units of matrix-
rich coarse gravel with poorly developed imbricate fabric also
occur. Considerable lateral variation exists from the coarse
units to thick sequences of ripple laminated and trough cross-
stratified sand. Paleoflow directions measured from imbricate
clasts are normal to the orientation of the Paris Moraine.
The coarse texture, lateral variability and paleoflow direction
are evidence for a very proximal depositional environment at
the margin of the Paris moraine during early phases of
deposition.

The lower unit is overlain by a stony, sandy silt to silt
till identified as the Wentworth Till (Cowan pers.comm.).
The till grades laterally into massive to ripple laminated
silt and fine sand and may represent either a local advance
of the Ontario lobe over the flood plain, or an episode of
flow till deposition. The till unit serves as a convenient
marker horizon and divides the section into two depositional
periods.

The upper 4 to 8 m of the section consist of multistorey
sequences of horizontally stratified imbricate gravel, interlayered with trough and planar cross-stratified gravel,
grading upwards into finer grained facies. These sequences

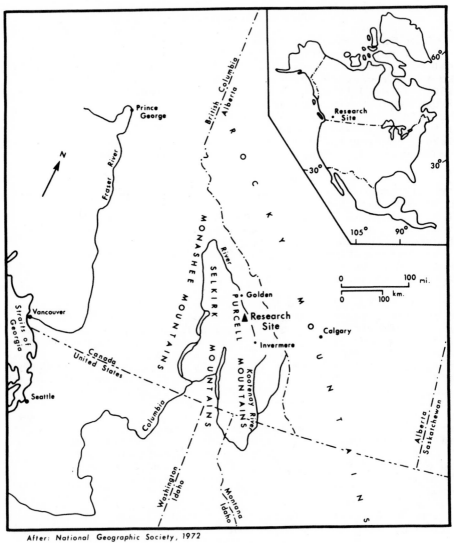

After: National Geographic Society, 1972

Figure 1.   Location of the research site.

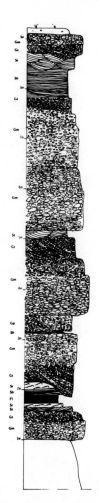

Figure 2. Measured vertical
profile through the Caledon
Outwash, showing several
truncated, superposed channel-
fill cycles. The facies code
is explained in the text.

are interpreted to be superposed channel-fill cycles. Paleoflow measurements on imbricate clasts indicate a flow direction
parallel to the orientation of the Paris moraine. Meltwaters
from the Ontario and Simcoe lobes are thought to have breached
the Singhampton moraine (Figure 1) during the second depositional phase and flowed along the ice margin, forming a narrow
braided flood plain. As the Ontario lobe ice-margin retreated
from the Paris moraine, the volume of meltwater decreased
and the upper most parts of the section are generally fine-
grained.

FACIES DESCRIPTIONS

Vertical profiles selected for detailed study in the central
portion of the outwash were measured and all upward facies
transitions were recorded. An example of one such vertical
profile is shown in Figure 2. Facies definitions were based
on primary structure and texture and follow the facies code
proposed by Miall (1977,1978) and modified by Rust (1978).
Examples of selected facies are given in Figures 3 to 6.

Figure 3. Trough cross-stratified gravel (facies Gt) scoured
       into horizontally statified sand (facies Sh) at the
       initiation of a channel-fill cycle. The Gt set is
       overlain transitionally by crudely horizontally strati-
       fied gravel (facies Gm) with well developed imbricate
       fabric. The scale is 9 cm long.

Figure 4. Planar cross-stratified gravel (facies Gp) de-
       posited within a multistorey sequence of Gm gravels.
       The upper and lower bounding surfaces of the Gp set are
       transitional. The scale divisions are 30 cm long.

Figure 5. Cosets of trough cross-stratified gravel (facies
Gt) in a coarsening upwards sequence grading into horizontally stratified gravel (facies Gm). . The Gm sediments are marked by an imbricate gravel lag which is
overalin by finer-grained Gm gravels. Horizontally
stratified sands (facies Sh) overlie the Gm sequence
at the top of the section. The scale is approximately
2 m long.

Figure 6. Ripple laminated sand and silt (facies Sr) grading
upwards into ripple and horizontally laminated silt
and fine sand (facies Fl).

Table 1.   Caledon Outwash facies assemblage –
statistical parameters

Facies code (Miall,1977)	Proportion (fixed probability vector)	Mean	Standard deviation	Skewness	Kurtosis	Modality
			TEXTURE (methods of moments)			
Gm (n=19)	.238	-2.5	2.8	.45	2.4	polymodal (4-5 modes)
Gp (n=10)	.064	-2.6	2.3	.79	3.5	polymodal (3-5 modes)
Gt (n=9)	.134	-1.7	2.1	.50	3.5	bimodal to trimodal
Sp (n=9)	.048	0.6	1.6	.34	4.6	bimodal to trimodal
Sn (n=22)	.174	1.7	1.1	.68	5.9	unimodal to trimodal
St (n=18)	.195	1.8	0.8	1.35	7.5	unimodal
Sr (n=9)	.078	2.5	0.7	.53	6.4	unimodal
Fl (n=12)	.061	4.0	1.5	2.40	11.5	polymodal

The grain size distributions of the eight facies identified
in the field were determined using the method of moments
(Swan *et al*.1978) and are summarized in Table 1.   The proportion of each facies in the assemblage is also shown in Table 1
and is based on the determination of the fixed probability
vector for the facies Transition Probability Matrix (Harbaugh
and Bonham-Carter, 1970).   The values relate to the proportion
of occurrence of each facies rather than to the volume of
sediment.   The following sections briefly describe the
characteristics of the facies. Their interpretation in terms
of depositional processes will be given after the depositional
sequence has been established.

HORIZONTALLY STRATIFIED GRAVEL FACIES (Gm)

Horizontally stratified gravel is the dominant facies in the
depositional sequence, and occurs in nearly 25 percent of all
observed facies transitions.   In areas where channel margins
can be identified (Figure 7), individual bedding units are
tens of metres in lateral extent, spanning the channels

Figure 7. Truncated channel-fill cycles in a section roughly transverse
   to the paleoflow direction. Channel margins in the centre of the
   section are marked by thin lag gravel deposits, and channels contain
   multistorey sequences of Gm facies gravels, separated in places by
   thin sand lenses or by erosional surfaces. Moderate flow stage bar
   top deposits are preserved in a small channel at the left of the
   photo. The section is approximately 12 m thick.

Figure 8. Moderate and low flow stage deposits in an aggraded channel.
   Large-scale grouped sets of trough cross-stratified sand (facies St)
   are overlain by grouped sets of trough cross-stratified sandy gravel
   (facies Gt). These sets are in turn overlain by a complex alternating
   but generally fining upwards sequence of planar cross-stratified and
   trough cross-stratified sands (facies Sp and St), ripple laminated
   sand (facies Sr) and ripple laminated and massive fine sand and silt
   (facies Fl). The pick handle is approximately 1 m long.

and they may persist for more than 100 m in the down-stream direction. Set thickness varies from approximately 1 m to rarely more than 2 to 3 m. Multistorey sequences are common (Figure 7) and individual sets are separated by planar erosion surfaces or by lenses of fine-grained facies. The lower bounding surface of the sets may be transitional especially when overlying Gt facies (Figure 5), but is more commonly a planar erosion surface. Upper surfaces may be transitional to other coarse facies such as Gp and Gt; disconformably over-lain by finer facies; or scoured by succeeding Gm units.

The Gm facies has a crudely horizontally stratified structure, occasionally with alternating layers of openwork and matrix-rich gravel 10 to 25 cm thick. The facies is characterized by well developed imbricate fabric of the a(t), b(i) type (Harms et al. 1975; Rust 1975). In the lower portion of the sequence, isolated sets of horizontally stratified, matrix-rich gravel with poorly developed imbricate fabric often occur within Gm cosets. These units may represent the Gms facies, debris flood deposits which characterize the proximal alluvial fan depositional models of Miall (1977) and Rust (1978).

Planar Cross-Stratified Gravel Facies (Gp)

The Gp facies consists of large-scale, solitary sets of alpha-type cross-stratified coarse gravel (Allen, 1963). In the study area, Gp sets occur almost exclusively within multi-storey Gm sequences and occur in less than 5 percent of observed facies transitions (Figure 4). The sets have a lateral extent of more than 10 m and a down-stream extent of more than 20 m. Set thickness is usually 0.5 to 1 m, although one set, which developed in a 'bar front' association similar to that described by Eynon and Walker (1974), had a thickness of approximately 3 m.

The lower bounding surface of the sets is planar and non-erosional, although in cases a weakly developed lag gravel may be present. Upper bounding surfaces are transitional or slightly truncated when overlain by Gm facies (Figure 4). Foresets alternate between clast and framework-supported layers 10 to 20 cm thick, thickening towards their base and merging into a matrix-rich bottomset layer at the lower bounding surface.

Trough Cross-Stratified Gravel Facies (Gt)

This is the finest-grained of the gravel facies and is common in the sequence, making up 13 percent of the assemblage. It consists of grouped sets of pi type cross-stratified gravel (Allen, 1963). Solitary sets are less common. Gt facies cosets occur either in association with Gm sets (Figure 3) or as part of alternating sequences with finer-grained trough cross-stratified units (Figure 8). Cosets often consist of 10 or more sets with a total thickness of 3 to 5 m (Figure 5). Individual sets are 1 to 5 m in lateral extent and several times that length in the downstream direction. Set thickness ranges from 0.5 to 1.5 m at the maximum scour point. Within-set cross-strata are homogeneous and consist of graded layers of gravel and medium to coarse sand 5 to 15 cm thick. Sets are usually truncated on their upper surfaces by an overlying Gt set, often in an upwards fining sequence (Figure 8).

Horizontally Stratified Sand Facies (Sh)

Horizontally stratified sand is common in the sequence (17 percent of observed transitions) and is found in two associations, related to the flow regime at the time of deposition. It most frequently occurs as thin lenses within multistorey Gm sequences where sets are usually 10 to 25 cm thick and vary in lateral and downstream extent from several to tens of metres (Figure 7). The sets are characterized by poorly developed horizontal stratification and some contain appreciable amounts of gravel (Table 1). These sets may reflect deposition in the upper flow regime (Harms et al. 1975). The Sh facies deposited in the lower flow regime is found in vertical sequences with other fine-grained sediments such as small-scale St, and Sr facies. The lower bounding surfaces of these sets are planar erosion surfaces. Strata are thin (1 to 5 mm) and are usually well defined, often marked by heavy mineral concentrations (Figure 4).

Planar Cross-Stratified Sand Facies (Sp)

Planar cross-stratified sand is relatively uncommon, occurring in only 5 percent of observed facies transitions. It occurs as relatively thin (less than 20 cm) solitary sets of alpha-type cross-stratification (Allen, 1963) in association with Sh facies, or in thicker solitary sets (up to 50 cm) of hetero-geneous pebbly sand (Table 1). The latter type are more common. The lower bounding surface of these sets is usually planar and erosional. Foresets are planar to slightly concave in the downstream direction and consist of alternating layers of fine and coarse material. Concave foresets are typically marked by an asymptotic toe and together with bottomset sand and silt, form a thickened foreset base. Some of the foresets are cut by reactivation surfaces.

Trough Cross-Stratified Sand Facies (St)

Trough cross-stratified sand is common in the sequence and constitutes 20 percent of the observed transitions. It occurs as grouped sets of pi-type cross-stratification (Allen, 1963). Sets range in lateral extent from tens of centimetres to more than 1 m, and in the downstream direction more than 10 m (Figure 8). Set thickness at the maximum scour point is 20 cm to 1 m. Cosets often comprise more than 10 sets, sometimes having a fining upwards sequence. In transverse sections, cross-strata generally appear to be symmetrical and concordant with the lower bounding surface. The cross-strata are tan-gential to the lower surface in longitudinal sections. Upper bounding surfaces are usually truncated by overlying St sets, but in places they either grade upwards into finer-grained trough cross-stratified sediments or are truncated by Gt facies sets. Some large-scale solitary sets of theta-type cross-stratification occur and are similar to the Ss facies of Miall (1977).

185

Glacio-fluvial sedimentation and processes

Ripple Laminated Sand Facies (Sr)

This facies makes up approximately 8 percent of the facies
assemblage and includes fine to medium sand characterized by
a wide variety of cross-laminated structures. By definition,
primary structures in this facies have vertical dimensions of
less than 5 cm (Miall, 1977). The sediments may form units
up to 0.5 m thick, usually in association with other fine-
grained sediments.

Fine Laminated Sand and Silt Facies (Fl)

The Fl facies makes up approximately 6 percent of the facies
assemblage. It is the finest-grained of the facies (Table 1)
and like Sr facies, is characterized by a range of cross-
laminated structures (Figure 6). Sets often display A and B
type ripple lamination (Jopling and Walker, 1968), made up
of alternating laminae of fine sand, silt and some clay,
approximately 1 mm thick. Some occurrences are massive and
have no apparent structure. The latter type may be related
to the Fm facies of Miall (1977) but no organic material was
noted in any of the occurrences in the Caledon Area. The
facies usually forms layers 5 to 25 cm thick and may form
persistent marker horizons (Figure 8). Fl facies sediments
were also found as lateral equivalents of the till in many of
the sections, and may be a flow till deposit.

MARKOV CHAIN ANALYSIS

Markov processes occupy a portion of the continuum of causal
relationships which ranges from deterministic to purely random.
Markov chain analysis has been used in the study of coal
measure cyclothems (Read, 1969), meandering streams (Allen,
1970) and recently in the study of braided stream deposits
(Miall, 1973; Cant and Walker, 1976). Theoretical descriptions
of Markov processes are given by Krumbein and Dacey (1969),
Schwarczacher (1969), Agterberg (1974) and Harbaugh and
Bonham-Carter (1970). The methods outlined in this section
are based on the above studies.

A simple (single dependency) Markov process may be
defined as:

> 'a stochastic process in which knowledge about the
> state of the process at a given time t_2 can be
> deduced from the knowledge of its state at any earlier
> time t_1, and is independent of the history of the
> system before t_1. A Markov chain is a process for
> which development in time can be treated as a series
> of transitions between distinct states (eg. litho-
> logies).' (Agterberg, 1974, p.420).

Several types of Markov processes may be identified with
respect to the nature of the dependency relationship between
successive states in the sequence. When a given state is
dependent only on the immediately preceding state, the
relationship is termed a 'first-order' Markov chain (Harbaugh
and Bonham-Carter 1970). Those sequences in which several

preceding states influence the appearance of a given state are of higher order. Such sequences are also said to exhibit multiple dependence. In some sequences, the nature or magnitude of a dependency relationship may change with time and is thus said to be 'non-stationary' (Harbaugh and Bonham-Carter, 1970).

In order to simplify the present analysis, the transition data are assumed to constitute a first-order, single dependence stationary Markov chain. Similar assumptions have been made in other applications of the technique (Miall, 1973; Cant and Walker, 1976; Krumbein, 1967) and it is probable that they approximate real conditions in the braided stream environment.

Derivation of the Transition Probability Matrix

The transition frequency sums for all possible pairs of facies states in the measured vertical profiles are summarized in matrix form in Table 2. Each element (f_{ij}) of the Transition Frequency Matrix records the number of upward transitions from facies state 'i' on the matrix rows to an overlying different facies state 'j' on the matrix columns. Since a nominal scale observation interval was used, there are no entries on the main diagonal of the matrix. This form of the matrix is the 'embedded Markov chain' of Krumbein and Dacey(1969). A discussion of the characteristics of this matrix type is given by Harbaugh and Bonham-Carter, 1970) and Krumbein (1967).

Table 2. Transition Frequency Matrix

Facies	Gm	Gp	Gt	Sp	St	Sh	Sr	Fl	Row
Gm	0	5	4	1	14	19	1	1	45
Gp	6	0	0	0	0	3	0	0	9
Gt	14	3	0	0	7	1	0	1	26
Sp	0	0	1	0	5	4	0	0	10
St	5	2	9	2	0	4	5	2	29
Sh	15	2	8	4	5	0	5	1	40
Sr	2	0	1	2	1	2	0	6	14
Fl	2	0	2	0	2	3	4	0	14

Total transitions 186

The probability of occurrence of each upward transition (p_{ij}) recorded in the Transition Frequency Matrix (f_{ij}) derived according to the relation:

$$p_{ij} = f_{ij} / s_i \qquad (1)$$

where s_i is the sum of all upward transitions from the ith facies state.

187

Glacio-fluvial sedimentation and processes

Table 3. Transition Probability Matrix p_{ij}

Facies	Gm	Gp	Gt	Sp	St	Sh	Sr	Fl	Row sum
Gm	0.0	.111	.089	.022	.311	.422	.022	.022	.999
Gp	.667	0.0	0.0	0.0	0.0	.333	0.0	0.0	1.0
Gt	.538	.115	0.0	0.0	.269	.038	0.0	.038	.999
Sp	0.0	0.0	.100	0.0	.500	.400	0.0	0.0	1.0
St	.172	.069	.301	.069	0.0	.138	.172	.069	.997
Sh	.375	.050	.200	.100	.125	0.0	.125	.250	1.0
Sr	.143	0.0	.071	.143	.071	.143	0.0	.428	.999
Fl	.154	0.0	.154	0.0	.154	.230	.301	0.0	.999
Marginal probability	.237	.064	.134	.048	.182	.193	.080	.059	

The Transition Probability Matrix (p_{ij}) derived in this manner
is shown in Table 3. Large values in the matrix indicate
those transitions which occur with the greatest statistical
probability. Since the row totals in the matrix represent all
possible transitions for any given facies, the row probabilities
sum to unity.

The significance of the (p_{ij}) values may be enhanced by
the removal of that component of the probability which results
from purely random processes. The Random Probability Matrix
(r_{ij}) is shown in Table 4 and is derived according to the
relation:

Table 4. Independent Trials Probability Matrix r_{ij}

	Gm	Gp	Gt	Sp	St	Sh	Sr	Fl
Gm	0.0	.085	.177	.064	.241	.255	.106	.078
Gp	.248	0.0	.141	.051	.129	.203	.085	.062
Gt	.275	.075	0.0	.056	.212	.225	.093	.069
Sp	.250	.068	.142	0.0	.193	.204	.087	.062
St	.280	.076	.159	.057	0.0	.229	.095	.070
Sh	.301	.082	.171	.061	.238	0.0	.102	.075
Sr	.256	.070	.145	.052	.198	.209	0.0	.064
Fl	.254	.069	.144	.052	.196	.208	.087	0.0

$$r_{ij} = s_j / n \atop \underset{ij}{f_{ij} - s_i} \tag{2}$$

where s_j is the sum of all transitions into
facies state j.
s_i is the sum of all transtiions out of
facies state i.
n is the total number of transitions in
$\underset{ij}{f_{ij}}$ the sequence.

The Random Probability Matrix values may then be sub-
tracted from their equivalent transition probability values
to obtain the Difference Matrix (d_{ij}), shown in Table 5.
Positive values in this matrix indicate those transitions
which occur with greater than random probability, and identify
transition pairs with a significant dependency relationship.

Table 5. Difference Matrix d_{ij}

Facies	Gm	Gp	Gt	Sp	St	Sh	Sr	Fl
Gm	0.0	.026	-.088	-.042	.070	.167	-.084	.056
Gp	.418	0.0	-.141	-.051	-.129	.130	-.085	-.062
Gt	.263	.040	0.0	-.056	.057	-.186	-.094	-.030
Sp	-.250	-.068	-.042	0.0	.307	.195	-.087	-.062
St	-.108	.007	.253	.012	0.0	-.091	.077	-.001
Sh	.075	.032	.138	.038	-.107	0.0	.022	-.050
Sr	-.011	-.070	.019	.090	-.126	-.066	0.0	.365
Fl	-.100	-.069	.102	-.052	-.043	.023	.221	0.0

The significance of the (d_{ij}) values may be statistically
tested using a version of the Chi-Square Test (Harbaugh and
Bonham-Carter, 1970). The null hypothesis considered is that
the sequence represents only random variation in the environment of deposition. Rejection of the null hypothesis indicates the existence of non-random depositional patterns. The
test statistic for each transition pair is derived according
to the relation:

$$X^2 = 2 \underset{ij}{\overset{n}{}} f_{ij} \cdot \log_e (p_{ij}/p_j) \tag{3}$$

where p_j is the marginal probability for the jth
column of the Transition Probability Matrix.

The degrees of freedom in the system are determined according
to the relation:
$$V = (m - 1)^2 - m \tag{4}$$
where m is the rank of the matrix.

Glacio-fluvial sedimentation and processes

The total test value for the matrix according to equation (3) is 180.7, which greatly exceeds the limiting value for the system (X^2 = 55.8 at the .05 level for V = 41) and indicates that the null hypothesis may be rejected. Non-random depositional patterns thus are shown to exist in the facies sequence. The statistical validity of Chi-square tests for Markov processes has been inadequately defined (Harbaugh and Bonham-Carter, 1970) and should not be taken as definitive.

DERIVATION AND INTERPRETATION OF THE SUMMARY SEQUENCE

The Difference Matrix (d_{ij}) values in Table 5 identify explicit dependency relationships for single transition pairs while the interrelationships among larger groups of facies states are only indirectly indicated. Two methods have been used for the interpretation of transition probability data in terms of the entire sequence. The first involves the mathematical simulation of the depositional sequence. Harbaugh and Bonham-Carter (1970), Read (1969), Krumbein (1967) and others discuss algorithms for the simulation of sequences based on transition probabilities. Simulated sequences may be compared to actual sections and inferences made about the general depositional processes (Krumbein, 1967).

The derivation of an idealized summary sequence is more commonly based on construction of a path diagram for the transition data, in the context of field observation of special sequences or marker beds which may not be identified in the transition data, and which may not be included in simulated sequences. Diagrammatic display methods based on such an approach have been developed in studies by De Raaf *et al*.1965; Allen, 1970; Miall, 1973; Cant and Walker, 1976, and the current methodology is summarized by Walker (1979).

The Facies Relationship Diagram shown in Figure 9 constitutes a summary of the most probable depositional sequences for the deposit. The facies have been arranged in vertical sequence, on the basis of dependency relationships and field observations. The direction of transitions is given by an arrow, the width of which indicates the relative probability of that transition. The d_{ij} value for each transition is also shown beside the arrow: only those transitions with a d_{ij} value greater than 0.02 have been included. The facies states are represented by circles, the diameter of which represents their relative proportion of the total facies assemblage based on the determination of the fixed probability vector for the matrix (Harbaugh and Bonham-Carter, 1970).

Figure 9 summarizes depositional processes in several different sub-environments, ranging from the floors of channels at high flow stage to bar tops and aggraded channels during waning floods and at low flow stage. Since the diversity of these processes cannot be completely specified in one sequence, Figure 9 must be seen as a composite, indicating the overall depositional pattern. It shows that within-channel depositional processes predominate and that the basic cycle is the scour of a channel into the flood plain and its subsequent

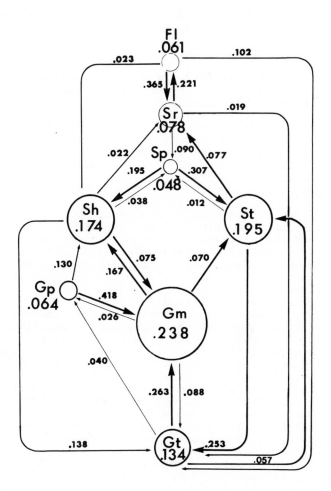

Figure 9.   Facies relationship diagram showing the
idealized depositional sequence for the Caledon
Outwash.   Numbers with the facies code designations
refer to their relative proportion in the assemblage in terms of number of occurrences.   Numbers
on facies transition arrows are Difference Matrix
probability values.

Glacio-fluvial sedimentation and processes

aggradation by successive high flow stage episodes. The
deposition of fine-grained sediments over the coarse facies
represents waning flow and the filling of the channel. Three
subsequences have been identified in the channel-fill cycle
and have been related on a qualitative basis to high,
moderate and low flow stages.

High Flow Stage Sub-sequence

The scour of underlying fine-grained sediments at high flow
stage and the deposition of trough cross-stratified gravels
define the base of the channel-fill cycle (Figures 2, 3, and
5). High probability values for upwards transitions from
fine-grained facies into Gt facies confirm this relationship.
The large-scale grouped sets of Gt facies represent the
migration of large sinuous-crested, transverse bedforms in a
pre-existing aggraded channel or by avulsion over disused
portions of the flood plain at the initiation of a high flow
stage event.

Upward transitions from Gt facies are of three types:
a dominant, weakly reciprocal transition to Gm facies; a well
developed reciprocal transition to St facies; and a unidirectional transition of relatively low significance to Gp
facies. The Gt to Gm transition is seen throughout the study
area and represents the initiation of longitudinal bedform
movement along the floors of the scoured channels. The contact
may be erosional or transitional as shown in Figures 3 and 5
respectively, and a crude coarsening upwards sequence may be
found in places. The Gt to St reciprocal transition is the
product of moderate flow stage deposition. In places, the
base of the channel-fill sequence is defined by a planar
erosion surface which truncates underlying sediments and may
be marked by a gravel lag. The erosion surface is overlain
by horizontally stratified Gm facies gravel, deposited by
migrating longitudinal bedforms. The Gm gravels dominate the
high flow stage sub-sequence, and usually occur in multistorey
sequences which result from aggradation during repeated high
flow episodes. Individual units are separated by Sh facies
which represent discharge fluctuations, or by planar erosion
surfaces and gravel lags (Figure 7). Occasionally there are
reciprocal transitions with Gp sets within the multistorey
sequences, representing deposition of large-scale transverse
bedforms or lateral modification of longitudinal bars during
falling stage flows. A general fining upwards trend in both
the thickness and the texture of the Gm units is often seen
in these sequences (Figure 7).

Moderate Flow Stage Sub-sequence

Upward transitions from Gm facies are generally into the
trough cross-stratified sands of St facies, wich some transition
to Gt facies. The strong Gm to Sh reciprocal transition
reflects the presence of thin sand lenses deposited between
successive Gm units during high flow stage. The Gm to St and
Gm to Gt transitions mark the onset of the moderate flow sub-
sequence, which consists of Gt, St, Sh, and minor Sp facies,
and reflects the migration of sinuous and straight crested

dunes and sand waves during flow conditions generally insufficient for the transport of coarse gravel. As in the high
flow stage sub-sequence, planar cross-stratification is of
characteristically rare occurrence. The moderate flow stage
sub-sequence may be found in three spatial associations.

  i) Overlying Gm facies sediments (Figures 2 and 7). This
     association results from the progradation of transverse
     bedforms in shallow water over the topographically higher
     portions of the system. The sequence represents falling
     flow stage in the system, although the frequent occurrence
     of upper flow regime Sh facies in this association
     indicates high flow velocity.

 ii) Fining upward sequences in smaller channels, similar to
     the 'Side Channel' facies of Eynon and Walker (1974).
     The channel in Figure 8 is dominated by a sequence of St
     and sandy Gt facies in alternating sequence. At the
     base of the sequence large-scale troughs consisting of
     unimodal sand are overlain by smaller-scale but coarser-
     textured sets, which in turn fine upwards both in grain
     size and scale, and near the top of the section grade
     into a low flow stage sequence of Sr and Fl facies.

iii) Alternating associations with high flow stage deposits.
     similar to the 'Sandy Braided' facies of Eynon and
     Walker (1974). This association is dominated by St
     structures which vary in scale and represent the migration
     of dunes in wide, shallow channels, usually in topo-
     graphically high parts of the system. The channels are
     in alternating sequence with thin units of horizontally
     stratified gravels of Gm facies, which represent the
     migration of small longitudinal bars or sheet flooding
     of gravel layers during brief periods of high flow. The
     gravel layers are in turn scoured by overlying cross-
     stratified deposits in shallow channels which migrated
     over the aggraded flood plain during moderate flow stage.
     Planar cross-stratified facies are rare in this
     association.

Low Flow Stage Sub-sequence

This sub-sequence comprises smaller-scale St sets, lower flow
regime Sh facies and predominantly, Sr and Fl facies. It is
the result of deposition in shallow water at low flow velocity
and corresponds to the low water accretion processes of Miall
(1977) and the vertical accretion sequence of Cant and Walker
(1976). In the summary sequence the strongest transition
probabilities are for the fining upwards St to Sr transition
and for the reciprocal transitions between Sr and Fl facies.
Low flow stage deposits are rarely found as thin drape deposits
in scour hollows or depressions on bar surfaces, or more often,
as fining upward sequences in the aggraded upper part of minor
channels. A typical occurrence of the latter association is
shown in Figure 8.

DISCUSSIONS AND CONCLUSIONS

An important process in the development of a facies model for a given depositional environment is its validation and refinement through comparison with numerous local examples (Walker, 1979). The main characteristics of the Caledon Outwash, based on interpretation of the summary sequence can thus be compared with descriptions of other local examples and with proposed facies models to support the following general conclusions.

1) The basic cycle in the Caledon Outwash is the scour of channels into the floodplain and their subsequent aggradation. The initiation of channel-fill sequences by the scour of large-scale trough cross-stratified gravels is the fundamental boundary between successive cycles, and has been discussed by Rust for the Donjet River (1972, 1979) and for the Carboniferous Cannes de Roche Formation (1978). A similar sequence is described for Pleistocene outwash gravels by Costello and Walker (1972).

   Above the scoured surface, a non-erosional transition from trough cross-stratified gravel to Gm gravels was often observed in the Caledon Outwash sequence and also characterizes some parts of the Donjek and Cannes de Roche sequences. Cant and Walker (1976) define the base of the channel-fill cycle for the Devonian Battery Point Formation by a scoured erosion surface overlain by trough cross-stratified sands. The Battery Point Formation is predominantly sandy however and there are no equivalents to the Gm facies.

2) The dominant depositional process in the Caledon channel-fill cycle is the aggradation of low relief longitudinal primary bedforms during high flow stage. The horizontally stratified Gm facies gravels produced by these bedforms are characteristic of the proximal braided stream environment (Smith, 1970, 1974; Williams and Rust, 1969; Church, 1972; Rust, 1972; Boothroyd and Ashley, 1975; Duckworth, 1979).

3) A significant proportion of the channel-fill cycle in the Caledon sequence results from the superposition of longitudinal bar gravels during repeated or interrupted high flow stage episodes. This process forms multistorey sequences of Gm facies separated by sand lenses or erosion surfaces. Multistorey sequences are diagnostic of the 'Scott Type' general model of Miall (1977, 1978), which is equivalent to the G_{II} facies assemblage of Rust (1978). Thick vertical sections are rare for the deposits upon which these models are based but an alternating sequence of horizontally stratified gravel separated by sand lenses has been described for the proximal portions of the Scott Fan (Boothroyd and Ashley, 1975, p. 218).

   More evidence is available from ancient deposits. Eynon and Walker (1974) describe a 9 metre section of 'bar core' facies which consists of Gm gravels with interlayered sand lenses. Rust (1978) notes that the Scott Type sequence is similar to sequences in the Malbaie Formation of the Gaspe region which consist of '... alternations of facies Gm and various sand facies interpreted as formed under progressively decreasing energy levels during flood cycles.... most flood cycles are interrupted so that gravel units commonly occur in erosional contact with the underlying gravel unit.'

4. Planar cross-stratified gravel is rare in the Caledon sequence and in the proximal braided stream environment in general (Smith, 1970, 1974; Miall, 1977; Rust, 1972, 1979). This reflects the low bedform relief, shallow depth of flow and lack of slip face development which characterize longitudinal bar forms in the proximal environment (Harms *et al.* 1975; Hein and Walker, 1979). Large-scale Gp structures have been described in association with high-relief bars which may have formed in deep, stable reaches of proximal streams (Eynon and Walker, 1974; Costello and Walker, 1972). One such example was observed in the lower part of the section in the Caledon deposits and may have formed in an incised alluvial fan channel. Rust (1978) describes the common occurrence of Gp facies in the Malbaie Formation. They may have resulted from climatic conditions which gave rise to deeper flow depths than in modern streams. Smith (1970) and Miall (1977) note that the down-stream increase in planar cross-stratification is one of the most prominent proximal-distal trends in the braided stream environment.

5) Although the Caledon sequence is dominated by the deposits of high flow stage, is also displays considerable variation in grain size and the scale of primary structures, and contains depositional cycles produced at moderate and low flow stages. In these respects the sequence resembles the Donjek Type model of Miall (1977) which is based on the mid and distal reaches of the Donjek River (Rust, 1972) and is equivalent to the G₁₁₁ facies model of Rust (1978). Rust (1979) summarizes the moderate flow stage depositional process based on the Donjek River and Cannes de Roche Formation sequences. Flow diversion around bars during waning flow scours minor channels at the bar margins through which sinuous crested dunes migrate depositing thick, fining upwards sequences of trough cross-stratified gravel and sand. Duckworth (1979) describes a similar association in glacio-fluvial deposits of the Oak Ridges Moraine in southern Ontario. Eynon and Walker (1974) describe a similar mode of formation for a thick sequence of cross-stratified sand in their 'Side Channel' facies, which developed on the flank of a large longitudinal bar.

6) In comparison to many published descriptions, the Caledon sequence has a low proportion of planar cross-stratified sand. Sp facies, which is deposited by the migration of straight crested transverse bedforms (sand waves and lingoid bars), is characteristic of sand-dominant braided streams (Rust, 1978). Walker and Cant (1979) note that in sandy braided streams sinuous-crested dunes migrated in the deeper channels and that the trough sequences are

overlain by the deposits of straight crested bedorms only in the upper portions of the aggraded channels. Moody-Stuart (1966) describes a Devonian fluvial sequence in which Sp facies is absent and in which St facies (in fining upwards sequence with Sr and Fl) is dominant. The sequence is interpreted to have been deposited in low sinuosity channels with few high relief bedforms or obstructions.

7) Low flow stage deposits are uncommon in the Caledon sequence, which may reflect their low preservation potential at the initiation of high flow periods (Rust, 1972; Miall, 1977). The low flow stage occurrence of Sr and Fl facies on bar surfaces, in cut-off channels and in overbank areas has been widely observed for modern braided streams (Church, 1972; Rust, 1972; Smith, 1974; Boothroyd and Ashley, 1975). Bar surface deposits in the Donjek and Scott systems consist of a veneer of ripple laminated sand and silt deposited in shallow water directly on the coarse grained bar surface. This association is rare in the Caledon sequence but again this material would have low preservation potential. The fact that modern streams are best observed at low flow stage may increase the chance of observing these fine grained sequences.

Overbank deposits, characterized by massive unstratified silt and clay and the inclusion of organic remains (Rust, 1972; Boothroyd and Ashley, 1975), were not observed. This may result from the restricted lateral extent of the Caledon floodplain and the frequency of high flow stage events in the system.

Comparison of the Caledon Outwash depositional sequence with local and generalized models for the braided stream environment indicates that it lies somewhere along a continuum of depositional types, the end-members of which can be defined by the G_{II} and G_{III} facies assemblages of Rust (1978). These assemblages are equivalent to the Scott and Donjek Type models of Miall (1977). The models summarize the depositional style in gravel-dominant braided streams ranging from low slope proximal reaches to low slope distal reaches. Although the Caledon sequence resembles the G_{II} assemblage with respect to the predominance of Gm facies gravel deposited by longitudinal bedforms, moderate and low flow stage deposits are common and give the sequence the variability and cyclicity characteristic of the G_{III} assemblage. The classification of the Caledon sequence as one model type or another is finally less important than the identification of those patterns in the local example that are found in other sequences. From these patterns the depositional mechanisms which characterize the braided stream environment in a range of specific conditions may be identified.

ACKNOWLEDGEMENTS

This paper is based on post-graduate research conducted in the Department of Geography, University of Toronto, under the supervision of Dr. A.V.Jopling. I am indebted to Dr. A.D.Miall for suggested improvements to the manuscript and to D.R.Sharpe and M.L.T.Crosbie of the Ontario Geological Survey who critically read the text.

REFERENCES CITED

Agterberg, F.P. 1974, *Geomathematics*,(Elsevier Publishing), 596 pp.

Allen, J.R.L. 1963, The classification of cross-stratified units, with notes on their origin. *Sedimentology*, 2, 93-114

Allen, J.R.L. 1970, Studies in fluviatile sedimentation: a comparison of fining upwards cyclothems, with special reference to coarse member composition and interpretation. *Journal of Sedimentary Petrology*, 40, 298-323

Boothroyd, J.C. and G.M.Ashley, 1975, Processes, bar morphology and sedimentary structures on braided outwash fans, northeastern gulf of Alaska, in *Glaciofluvial and glaciolacustrine sedimentation,* ed A.V.Jopling and B.C.MacDonald, (Society of Economic Paleontologists and Mineralogists, Special Publication No.23), 193-222

Cant, D.J. 1978, Development of a facies model for sandy braided river sedimentation: comparison of the South Saskatchewan River and the Battery Point Formation. in *Fluvial Sedimentology*, ed A.D.Miall, (Canadian Society of Petroleum Geologists, Memoir 5), 627-639

Cant, D.J. and R.G.Walker, 1976, Development of a braided fluvial facies model for the Devonian Battery Point Sandstone, Quebec. *Canadian Journal of Earth Sciences*, 13, 102-119

Chapman, L.J. and D.F.Putnam, 1966, *The physiography of Southern Ontario,* (Ontario Research Foundation, University of Toronto Press), 366 pp.

Church, M. 1972, Baffin Island Sandurs: a study of Arctic fluvial processes. *Geological Survey of Canada, Bulletin*, 216, 208 pp.

Costello, W.R. and R.G.Walker, 1972, Pleistocene sedimentology, Credit River, Southern Ontario: a new component of the braided river model. *Journal of Sedimentary Petrology*, 42, 389-400

Cowan, W.R. 1976, Quaternary geology of the Orangeville area, Southern Ontario. *Ontario Division of Mines, Geoscience Report*, 141, 98 pp. Accompanied by Maps 2326, 2327 and 2328 at a scale of 1:50 000

De Raaf, J.F.M., Reading, H.G. and R.G.Walker, 1965, Cyclic sedimentation in the Lower Westphalian of North Devon, England. *Sedimentology*, 4, 1-52

Duckworth, P.B. 1979, The late depositional history of the western end of the Oak Ridges Moraine, Ontario. *Canadian Journal of Earth Sciences*, 16, 1094-1107

Eynon, G. and R.G.Walker, 1974, Facies relationships of Pleistocene outwash gravels, Southern Ontario: a model for bar growth in braided rivers. *Sedimentology*, 21, 43-70

Fahnestock, R.K. 1963, Morphology and hydrology of a glacial stream - White River, Mount Ranier, Washington. *United States Geological Survey, Professional Paper,* 422-A, 70 pp.

Fraser, J.Z. 1976, Recommendations for sand and gravel extractive areas, Caledon Township, Southern Ontario. *Ontario Division of Mines, Open File Report,* 5202, 4 pp. Accompanied by one map, scale 1:50 000

Harbaugh, J.W. and G. Bonham-Carter, 1970, *Computer simulation in geology,* (Wiley Interscience, New York), 575 pp.

Harms, J.C., Southard, J.B., Spearing, D.R. and R.G.Walker, 1975, *Depositional environments as interpreted from primary structures and stratification sequences,* (Society of Economic Paleontologists and Mineralogists, Short Course 2 - Dallas), 161 pp.

Hein, F.J. and R.G.Walker, 1977, Bar evolution and development of stratification in the gravelly braided, Kicking Horse River, British Columbia. *Canadian Journal of Earth Sciences,* 14, 562-570

Hewitt, D.F. and P.F.Karrow, 1963, Sand and gravel in Southern Ontario. *Ontario Department of Mines, Industrial Mineral Report,* 11, 151 pp.

Jopling, A.V. and R.G.Walker, 1968, Morphology and origin of ripple-drift cross lamination, with examples from the Pleistocene of Massachussets. *Journal of Sedimentary Petrology,* 38, 971-984

Karrow, P.F. 1963, Pleistocene geology of the Hamilton-Galt area, Ontario. *Ontario Department of Mines, Geological Report,* 61, 68 pp.

Krigstrom, A. 1962, Geomorphological studies of sandur plains and their braided rivers in Iceland. *Geographiska Annaler,* 44, 328-345

Krumbein, W.C. 1967, Fortran IV computer programs for Markov chain experiments in geology. *Kansas Geological Survey, Computer Contribution,* 13, 38 pp.

Krumbein, W.C. and M.F.Dacey, 1969, Markov chains and embedded Markov chains in geology. *Mathematical Geology,* 1, 79-96

Leopold, L.B. and M.G.Wolman, River channel patterns: braided, meandering and straight. *United States Geological Survey, Professional Paper,* 282-B, 85 pp.

Miall, A.D. 1973, Markov chain analysis applied to an ancient alluvial plain succession. *Sedimentology,* 20, 347-364

Miall, A.D. 1977, A review of the braided stream depositional environment. *Earth Science Reviews,* 13, 1-62

Miall, A.D. 1978, Lithofacies types and vertical profile models in braided river deposits: a summary, in *Fluvial Sedimentology,* ed A.D.Miall, (Canadian Society of Petroleum Geologists, Memoir 5), 597-604

Moody-Stuart, M. 1966, High and low sinuosity stream deposits with examples from the Devonian of Spitsbergen. *Journal of Sedimentary Petrology,* 36, 1102-1117

Read, W.A. 1969, Analysis and simulation of Namurian sediments in central Scotland using a Markov process model. *Mathematical Geology,* 1, 199-219

Rust, B.R. 1972, Structure and process in a braided river. *Sedimentology,* 18, 221-245

Rust, B.R. 1975, Fabric and structure in glacifluvial gravels, in *Glaciofluvial and glaciolacustrine sedimentation,* ed A.V.Jopling and B.C.MacDonald, (Society of Economic Paleontologists and Mineralogists, Special Publication No.23), 238-249

Rust, B.R. 1978, Depositional models for braided alluvium. in *Fluvial sedimentology,* ed A.D.Miall, (Canadian Society of Petroleum Geologists, Memoir 5), 605-625

Rust, B.R. 1979, Coarse alluvial deposits, in *Facies models,* ed R.G.Walker, (Geoscience Canada, Reprint Series 1), 9-23

Schwarzacher, W. 1969, The use of Markov chains in the study of sedimentary cycles. *Mathematical Geology,* 1, 17-39

Smith, N.D. 1970, The braided stream depositional environment: comparison of the Platte River with some Silurian rocks, north-central Appalachians. *Geological Society of America Bulletin,* 81, 2993-3014

Smith, N.D. 1974, Sedimentology and bar formation in the upper Kicking Horse River, a braided outwash stream. *Journal of Geology,* 82, 205-223

Swan, D., Clague, J.J. and J.L.Luternauer, 1978, Grain size statistics I; evaluation of the Folk and Ward graphic measures. *Journal of Sedimentary Petrology,* 48, 863-878

Taylor, F.B. 1912, Pleistocene deposits of southwestern Ontario. *Summary Report of the Geological Survey Branch of the Department of Mines,* 1911, 262-272

Walker, R.G. 1979, Facies and facies models. General introduction, in *Facies models,* ed R.G.Walker, (Geoscience Canada, Reprint Series 1), 1-9

Walker, R.G. and D.J.Cant, 1979, Sandy fluvial systems, in *Facies models,* (Geoscience Canada, Reprint Series 1), 23-33

White, O.L. 1975, Quaternary geology of the Bolton area, NTS 30m/13, southern Ontario. *Ontario Division of Mines, Geological Report,* 117, 119 pp. Accompanied by Maps 2275 and 2276, scale 1:50 000.

Williams, P.F. and B.R.Rust, 1969, The sedimentology of a braided river. *Journal of Sedimentary Petrology,* 39, 649-679

PART 3

GLACIO-LACUSTRINE
AND
MARINE SEDIMENTATION

10 Comparison of sedimentation regimes in four glacier-fed lakes of western Alberta

Norman D. Smith, Mark A. Venol & Stephen K. Kennedy

ABSTRACT

Physical characteristics and sedimentation regimes of 4 river-dominated lakes fed by glacial meltwater are described and compared. The 4 lakes (Lower Waterfowl, Peyto, Hector, and Bow) are all located in intermontane valleys in the eastern Canadian Rocky Mountains.

Sedimentation patterns are strongly influenced by the type of initial mixing between inflow and lake water. Each of the 4 lakes is characterized by one of three kinds of inflow pattern: homopycnal, underflow, or overflow-interflow. Lower Waterfowl Lake is shallow and unstratified, and inflow carries uniformly low suspended sediment concentrations. Inflow mixing is homopycnal, and fine sediment is dispersed homogeneously through the lake, yielding negligible cross-lake and only weak downlake trends in sedimentation (grain size, deposition rates). In Peyto Lake, high inflowing suspended sediment concentrations result in predominantly underflows, and sediment transport and deposition patterns are largely controlled by bottom topography. Hector and Bow Lakes are both deep and thermally stratified during summer. Inflowing river water, carrying only moderate suspended loads, is less dense than the deep (hypolimnial) lake water and therefore enters the lakes as overflows and shallow interflows which are deflected rightward by the Coriolis effect. Pronounced crosslake as well as downlake sedimentation trends characterize both lakes.

Abundant fecal pellets of suspended-sediment-ingesting zooplankton, probably calanoid copepods, occur in Bow Lake. These may comprise an important, though previously unappreciated, mechanism in the dynamics of clay transport and deposition in similar lakes dominated by fine-grained clastic sediments.

Department of Geological Sciences, University of Illinois at Chicago Circle, Box 4348, Chicago, IL 60680

*Present Address: Department of Geology, University of South Carolina, Columbia, SC 29208

INTRODUCTION

In an effort to better understand processes and patterns of glacio-lacustrine sedimentation, a series of small, river-dominated, glacier-fed lakes were investigated in the Banff National Park region of western Alberta. A total of eight lakes were surveyed: Emerald (Yoho Park, B.C.), Louise, Moraine, Upper Waterfowl, Lower Waterfowl, Peyto, Hector, and Bow (all in Banff Park). The latter 4 lakes were studied the most closely and form the subject of this report. Most of the investigations were conducted in the summers of 1974-1976; supplementary data were obtained from Peyto and Lower Waterfowl in 1977, and a preliminary study of Bow Lake was made in 1973 (Kennedy, 1975).

The principal objective was to determine relationships between inflow properties, physical characteristics of the lakes, and lake sedimentation. The Banff lakes were well suited to this objective because of their small manageable sizes, accessibility, and variety. In this report, we describe the salient features of the 4 lakes (Lower Waterfowl, Peyto, Hector, Bow) and discuss some of the sedimentological consequences of these features. Each of the lakes occur near the Icefields Highway between Lake Louise and Jasper, Alberta, an area of rugged alpine topography in the eastern Canadian Rocky Mountains (Fig. 1). The lakes are each fed by overland streams supplied in part by glacial meltwater, the dominant source being the Wapta Icefield which straddles the continental divide between Alberta and British Columbia. Local bedrock consists of Precambrian argillites and quartzites in the lower slopes overlain by mainly Lower Paleozoic carbonates in the higher elevations where most erosion occurs. Sediment supplied to the lakes is composed of dominant dolomite and subordinate calcite, quartz, and clay minerals. The lakes are ice-covered about 5 or 6 months each year. All have formed in glacially steepened valleys following post-Wisconsinan recessions, and it is doubtful if any are more than 10 000 years old. For discussions of late Quaternary history, the reader is referred to the works of Heusser (1956), Shaw (1972), Rutter (1972), Harris and Waters (1977), and Luckman and Osborn (1979).

METHODS

Although their time spans varied, at least one summer field season was devoted to each of the 4 lakes, in each case preceded or followed by supplementary investigations in one or more additional field seasons.

For each lake, a bathymetry map was constructed from a combination of lead-line soundings and fathometer traverses. Temporary stream gaging stations were established

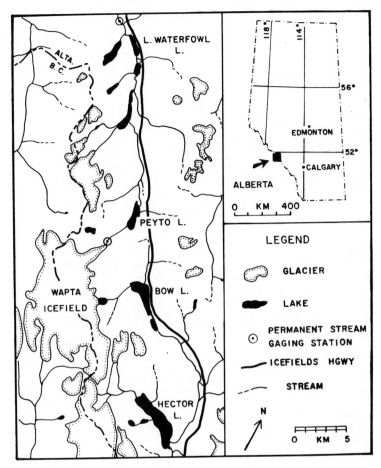

Figure 1.   Map showing locations of lakes in this study.

near the mouths of principal inflowing streams through one
(Peyto, Lower Waterfowl) or two (Hector, Bow) summers. Velocities for stream discharge computations were measured by a
cable-suspended current meter for Lower Waterfowl inflow
(Mistaya River) and by wading with a rod-mounted current
meter for the other streams. Resulting stage-discharge rating
curves were reasonably stable and provided for the only discharge records for Hector and Bow inflows (Balfour Stream
and Bow Outwash, respectively). The Water Survey of Canada
has maintained a gaging station on Peyto Creek near the
terminus of Peyto Glacier, 1.8 km upstream from our station,
since 1967, and another station on Mistaya River 5 km downstream from Lower Waterfowl Lake since 1950. Neither of
these stations, however, could serve our purpose for closely
monitoring inflow to the lakes.

Depth-integrated mid-stream samples were collected to
measure suspended sediment concentrations. Water conductivity
and temperature were measured in the field whenever stream

samples were taken. Lake water samples were collected with
a Van Dorn bottle and measured for conductivity and suspended
sediment concentration to assess the patterns of water and
sediment movement within the lake. Suspended sediment was
removed by vacuum through 0.8 μ Millepore filters in a field
laboratory within a few hours after collection. Conductivities of both stream and lake water were related to total
dissolved ion concentrations by plots of conductivity against
evaporation residues. Plots varied only slightly between
locations, yielding an overall relationship: dissolved concentration (mg/ℓ)$\stackrel{\sim}{\sim}$ 0.6 conductivity (μmho/cm). Lake temperature profiles were determined by thermistor probe. Transmissivity surveys were occasionally conducted with a Hydro
Products Model 612-S system to identify paths of suspended
sediment transport through the lakes. In each lake, sedimentation rates were measured directly by traps constructed
of weighted refrigerator containers with cross-sectional
areas of 95 cm^2. The traps, placed on the bottom and marked
by attached string and floats, were retrieved and reset
every one to two weeks, the contents filtered and weighed
in the field laboratory. Drogues, constructed of 60 x 45 cm
sheet aluminum and suspended at various depths, were occasionally used to observe lake current directions and estimate
current velocities by ascertaining successive drogue positions relative to shore features and surveyed buoys. An
Interocean Systems Model 135R current meter with a continuous recording option was used for lake current measurements
near stream mouths where inflow velocities were strong enough
to activate the instrument. This was done mainly in Peyto
Lake. Gravity cores 3.7 cm in diameter were obtained from
each lake. Grain size distributions were determined from
the top 3 or 4 cm of each core using standard sieve and
pipette techniques, and carbonate mineralogy was analyzed
in Hector and Bow cores (Kennedy and Smith, 1977). All lake
work was done from rowboats.

LAKE DESCRIPTIONS

Introduction

A large number of variables interact to determine the
sedimentation regime of glacier-fed lakes. The more important of these include quantity and caliber of inflowing
sediment, discharge and density of inflow, vertical density
distribution of lake water, bathymetry of the basin, basin
size and shape, wind regime, and possibly biological factors
such as burrowing and sediment-ingesting organisms. A major
process which subsequently affects sediment transport and
deposition patterns is the type of entrance mixing at the
stream mouth. This is governed both by density differences
between inflow and lake water and by density stratification
in the lake. The stream may enter as an overflow if its
density is less than the lake water, or an underflow if it
is more dense. Bates (1953) refers to these respectively
as hypopycnal and hyperpycnal inflow types and further des-

cribes resulting flow patterns away from the stream mouths to be plane jets. As discussed by Harleman (1961) and reviewed by Axelsson (1967), the greater the density difference between adjoining inflow and basin water, the lower the rate of turbulent exchange between the two masses, restricting inflow expansion and enhancing the tendency for inflowing river water to be maintained as a discrete density current through the lake. Overflows and underflows may occur in either stratified or unstratified lakes. If a lake is stratified, however, inflow density may be intermediate between high-density bottom and low-density surface water. In such cases, interflows may occur; in thermally stratified lakes, these typically move near the base of the epilimnion (low-density surface layer). A fourth type of inflow pattern, termed homopycnal by Bates (1953), occurs in weakly stratified or unstratified lakes in which densities of inflow and lake water are virtually equal. Mixing is three-dimensional and inflow patterns resemble axial jets. Inflowing water quickly loses its identity as it readily mixes with basin water.

Assuming negligible effects of pressure, three factors interact to determine the density of inflow: temperature, salinity, and suspended sediment concentration. Of these, the latter usually dominates in glacial rivers because it varies more widely and more rapidly than the other two factors and thus is almost always different from the lake water. Only in cases where inflowing suspended sediment concentrations are uniformly low and steady do river temperature and salinity become important in mixing processes.

All four types of entrance mixing were observed in our investigations. Typically, one or two types dominate in a given lake, and the principal sediment transport and deposition patterns within the lake invariably reflect the roles of these all-important entrance effects. The following discussions therefore center around the main inflow types in each lake: Lower Waterfowl is dominated by homopycnal inflow, Peyto by underflows, and Hector and Bow by overflows and interflows. Characteristics of river inflow to each lake are given in Table 1, and Table 2 lists physical features of the lakes. All 4 lakes are fresh and receive mainly inorganic detritus; biological (except for pelletization; see later discussion) and chemical effects on sedimentation are relatively unimportant.

Lower Waterfowl Lake

Of the 4 lakes, Lower Waterfowl is the only one not fed directly by glacial meltwater. Its principal source, Mistaya River, drains outflow from three glacier-fed lakes (Peyto, Mistaya, Cirque) and includes a large proportion of nonglacial runoff, most of which passes through Upper Waterfowl Lake one kilometer upstream from Lower Waterfowl. Upper and Lower Waterfowl Lakes are separated by an alluvial fan formed by nonglacial Noyes Creek, a small tributary that provides the only source to Lower Waterfowl not diluted by

Glacio-Lacustrine and marine sedimentation

Table 1. Characteristics of principal inflowing streams

	MISTAYA R.
Lake:	L. Waterfowl
Inflow Discharge (m^3/sec):	
1. Period of Record	6/20-8/30, 1976
2. Mean Daily	17.5
3. Mean Daily, Range	5.8-24.1
4. Maximum instantaneous	25.1 (7/10/76)
Water Temperature (^oC):	7.8-11.0
Conductivity (μmho/cm):	
1. Mean	158[b]
2. Range	135-184
Suspended Sed. Conc. (mg/ℓ):	
1. Mean	8.7[b]
2. Range	3.7-16.7
Total Susp. Discharge (m.t.)[a]	1.97 x 10^3 (summer 1976)
Drainage basin	
1. Area (km^2)	206
2. % glacierized	15
Dominant Inflow Type:	homopycnal

---

[a]Estimated from water discharge records and rating curves of susp. sed. conc. vs discharge   [c]n=58, 1976

[b]n = 51, 1974 - 1977   [d]average of two seasonal means, n = 117

---

upstream sinks. Noyes Creek supplies a small amount of bedload to the main stream (Mistaya) which is carried to the lake, but most inflowing sediment is very fine suspended material that escaped the upstream sinks. Inflowing suspended sediment concentrations are therefore low (ave. 8.7 mg/ℓ) with little variation (range 3.7-16.7 mg/ℓ) (Table 1).

Lower Waterfowl has the largest inflow (Table 1) and smallest volume, yielding by far the lowest mean residence time lake(volume/inflow discharge) of the 4 lakes (Table 2). This value, 7.2 days, is calculated from mean annual discharge derived from records of the permanent gage 5 km below the lake outlet. There records show that approximately 70% of the annual Mistaya flow occurs from June to August, thus, normal summer residence times are only about 2 or 3 days.

PEYTO CREEK	BALFOUR STREAM	BOW OUTWASH
Peyto	Hector	Bow
6/19-8/31, 1976	{6/23-9/16, 1974 {6/7-8/31, 1975	{7/20-9/1, 1973 {6/20-8/30, 1975
6.0	5.3	2.6
0.8 - 10.9	1.3 - 12.2	0.5 - 5.9
13.9 (8/15/76)	16.4 (7/11/75)	6.8 (7/13/75)
1.8 - 5.4	1.6 - 6.2	1.8 - 9.0
139[c] 80-201	84[d] 67-115	109[e] 84-152
720[c] 138-2156	225[d] 8-768	91[e] 4-1193
38.0×10^3 (summer 1976)	3.8×10^3 (summer 1974) 14.6×10^3 (summer 1975)	1.8×10^3 (summer 1975)
37 42	38 46	28 31
underflow	overflow/interflow	overflow/interflow

[e]average of two
seasonal means,
n = 94

This rapid exchange of lake water with inflow results in close similarity of their sediment concentration, salinity (conductivity), and temperature (Table 3), with consequently negligible differences in water density. Lower Waterfowl has an uncomplicated bottom topography (Fig. 2) and is the shallowest of the 4 lakes (Table 2), a factor which enhances vertical mixing by wind stresses. Unlike the other three lakes whose winds are mainly katabatic and downlake, wind directions at Lower Waterfowl are more multidirectional, a characteristic which probably aids the mixing process. Thorough mixing of the shallow lake water, together with similarity of inflow density, combine to prohibit development of stratification (Table 3): vertical profiles show the basin water to be nearly isothermal (mean $\Delta T = 0.5°$), isohaline (mean $\Delta C = 1.4$ μmho/cm), with suspended sediment homogeneously dispersed (mean $\Delta C_s = 1.9$ mg/ℓ). Typical profiles are shown in Figure 3.

Table 2. Physical parameters of lakes

	L. Waterfowl	Peyto	Hector	Bow
Area (km²)	0.72	1.4	5.9	2.8
Max. length (km)	1.8	2.4	5.8	2.4
Max. width (km)	0.6	0.8	1.3	1.1
Max. depth (m)	9.5	49	87	51
Mean depth (m)	5.3	27.8	48.5	22.9
Volume (m³)	4.0×10^6	39×10^6	286×10^6	64×10^6
Altitude (m)	1661	1844	1752	1940
Residence time (days)[a]				
Annual mean	7.2^b	200^b	$590^{d,e}$	--
Summer mean[c]	2.3	75	198^d	--
Thermal Stratification (mid-summer)	weak to none	weak to none	well developed	well developed

[a]Lake volume/inflow discharge

[b]Based on Water Survey Records adjusted to our gage records

[c]For dates of inflow records, see Table 1

[d]Combines inflows of Balfour Stream and Bow River. See Smith (1978)

[e]Assumes 75% of annual discharge occurs June-August.

Similarity of inflow and basin water, together with the absence of lake water stratification, results in homopycnal mixing at the stream mouth. Inflow combines quickly and effectively with lake water and moves through the basin as a more-or-less homogeneous mass -- the basin behaves essentially as a wide, deep river channel. Crosslake tranmissivity profiles (Fig. 4) show no significant tendency for preferred paths of sediment transport, unlike the other three lakes (see later). Drogue observations indicate that basin currents are generally downlake but complex in detail, a feature probably related to the polymodal wind patterns.

Sedimentation Patterns

The low sediment input and its homogeneous dispersal are reflected in principal sedimentation trends in Lower Waterfowl Lake. Ten sediment traps distributed evenly over the lake floor in summer 1976 yielded mean deposition rates ranging from 0.59 mg/cm²/day in the most proximal trap to 0.19 mg/cm²/day in the most distal trap. The average of all traps was 0.32 mg/cm²/day, comparable to but lower than the most distal locations in Hector (Smith, 1978) and Bow Lakes, and 15 times smaller than any location in Peyto (Vendl, 1978).

Table 3. Lower Waterfowl water characteristics*

WATER TEMPERATURE (T, °C)

No. of profiles	13
Range, all measurements	8.8-11.4
Inflow range (Table 1)	7.8-11.0
Mean ΔT, bottom to top	0.5
Max. observed ΔT	1.5
Min. observed ΔT	0

CONDUCTIVITY (C, μmho/cm)

No. of profiles	17
No. of samples	73
Mean of all samples	150
Inflow mean (Table 1)	158
Range of all samples	135-183
Max. ΔC, one profile	4
Min. ΔC, one profile	0
Mean ΔC, all profiles	1.4

SUSPENDED SEDIMENT CONCENTRATION (C_s, mg/ℓ)

No. of profiles	19
No. of samples	83
Mean of all samples	8.4
Inflow mean (Table 1)	8.7
Range of all samples	3.9-17.2
Max. ΔC_s, one profile	4.6
Min. ΔC_s, one profile	0.4
Mean ΔC_s, all profile	1.9

*Data collected in Summers 1975-1977

Assuming this figure to represent average summer 1976 deposition (not unreasonable because the traps were distributed evenly and inflowing sediment is mostly fine and homogeneously dispersed), a total of .16 x 10^3 metric tons of sediment deposition was calculated for the period June 20-August 31, 1976. Compared to calculated inflowing suspended load based on sediment discharge rating curves (.97 x 10^3 m.t., Table 1), this represents an effective sedimentation rate of 16.5% of the inflowing sediment, which is to say 83.5% of sediment supplied to the lake also escaped it. This estimate could be checked by comparing inflow and outflow suspended concentrations. Only 24 suspended sediment samples of outflow were collected in 1976; however, these were spread throughout the summer and showed remarkably little variation, averaging 8.03 mg/ℓ. Outflow and inflow water discharges are assumed to be similar because of no important intervening tributaries and the short residence time which minimizes evaporation losses. Calculations thus based on suspended sediment loss yielded an estimated .10 x 10^3 m.t. of deposition; this represents 9.8% of the inflowing suspended load, or, a 90.2%

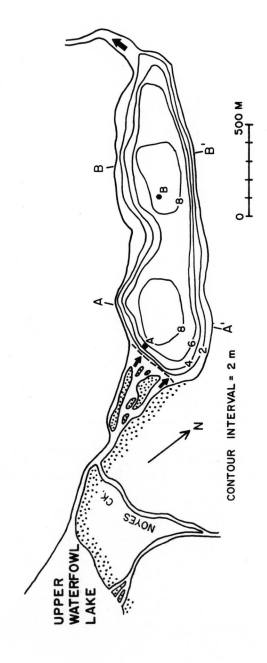

Figure 2.   Map showing Lower Waterfowl bathymetry and Noyes Creek fan. A-A' and B-B' indicate transmissivity cross sections in Fig. 4, and locations A and B are profile stations in Fig. 3.

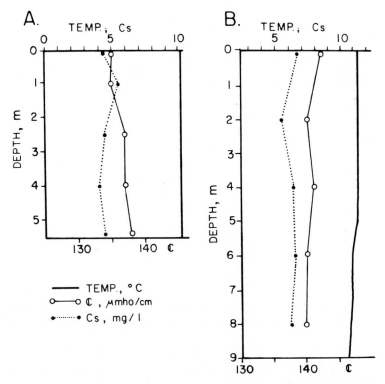

Figure 3. Two Lower Waterfowl profiles showing vertical distributions
of temperature (Temp.) conductivity (C), and suspended
sediment concentration (Cs), August 23, 1977.
Locations shown in Fig. 2.

escape rate. Considering the number of uncertainties in
these two estimates, they are in surprisingly good agreement,
yielding the same conclusion: Lower Waterfowl is not an
efficient sediment trap, i.e., most of what enters the lake
also leaves it.

Gravity cores typically show massive mud layers punc-
tuated by discrete layers of fine sand or silt up to one cm
thick. These coarse layers undoubtedly result from major
floods of Noyes Creek, as these sediments could not have
escaped the upstream sinks. Many of the layers are disrupted by burrowing activity. Surficial grain size distributions show a weak downlake fining trend but no prominent
crosslake trends (Fig. 5). All near-surface samples contained admixtures of coarse to fine silt in otherwise massive muds, probably the result of bioturbation in which thin
silt layers were destroyed and mixed with mud, the latter
of which comprises the normal sediment load in Lower Waterfowl Lake.

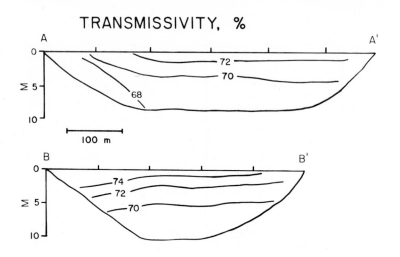

Figure 4.   Two Lower Waterfowl cross sections showing distribution of
light transmissivity, June 30, 1976. Values represent percent transmissivity through 10-cm path length and thus vary
inversely with suspended concentrations. Note little vertical or crosslake variation, especially when compared to
Figs. 10 (Peyto) and 17 (Bow). Locations of cross sections
shown in Fig. 2.

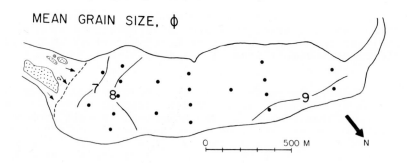

Figure 5.   Distribution of mean grain sizes of bottom sediment in
Lower Waterfowl. Dots indicate sample locations.

Peyto Lake

Although its inflow is intermediate in size, Peyto receives by far the most sediment of the 4 lakes (Table 1).

The lake is situated 3 km downvalley from Peyto Glacier, which has been studied extensively since 1966 by the Glaciology Division, Inland Waters Directorate, Environment Canada, in connection with the International Hydrological Decade program (Young and Stanley, 1976). Peyto Creek, the main source of inflow, originates at the glacier snout, flows in a single channel for 2 km, and debouches into a gravelly outwash plain 1 km upstream from the lake. The outwash plain is virtually devoid of vegetation and forms the topset of a classic Gilbert-type delta which is actively building into the lake. Inflow channels are mainly braided and unstable. Our temporary gaging station was operated in summer 1976 in a stable channel at the delta apex. Discharges at our station were about 30% higher than those at the permanent station near the glacier terminus because of intervening tributaries. Most of our study was conducted in 1976, with additional data obtained in 1975 and 1977.

Inflow discharge is weather-dependent and highly seasonal, with pronounced diurnal fluctuations during warm periods. Approximately 82% of the annual flow occurs in June, July, and August (Young, 1977). Of the 4 lakes, Peyto inflow contains the highest and most variable suspended sediment concentrations (ave. 720 mg/ℓ, range 138-2156 mg/ℓ; Table 1) and therefore has the highest density. Temperature and salinity also vary seasonally and diurnally, but their effects on inflow density variations are relatively small.

Bathymetrically, the lake consists of two basins, each with maximum depths of 49 m, separated by a mid-lake sill (Fig. 6). The sill slopes from east to west, reaching a maximum depth of 35 m on the west side and forming a notch that connects the two basins. The proximal basin is much flatter than the distal basin due to higher sedimentation near the delta. Acoustic profiles reveal a series of small mounds believed to be slumps occurring at and near the base of the delta foresets. These features are similar to those described by Gilbert (1975), Fulton and Pullen (1969), Smith (1978), and Pharo and Carmack (1979) for other deep intermontane lakes.

Although overflows, interflows, and underflows were all observed in Peyto Lake, underflows dominate lake sedimentation. These could usually be inferred visually by the nature of inflow plumes: underflowing plumes are small with distinct boundaries at plunge lines. Underflows were confirmed by 3 kinds of measurements: water profiles, velocity measurements, and transmissivity surveys.

Water profiles, consisting of temperature, conductivity, and suspended sediment measurements, were repeated 8 times at 3 locations (Fig. 6). Six of the profile series indicated

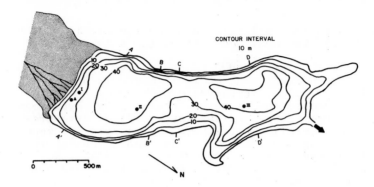

Figure 6. Bathymetry map of Peyto Lake showing locations of transmissivity cross sections (A-A' to D-D'; Fig. 10), velocity
measurement station (A; Figs. 8,9), and profile stations
(I-III; Fig. 7).

underflows, as shown by increased suspended concentrations
near the bottom (Fig. 7). During underflows, conductivity
decreases slightly with depth, reflecting the intrusion of
fresh glacial water. The lake is nearly isothermal, varying
between about 5 and 7.5°C through the summer, though a weak
thermal stratification may develop downlake on warm days
(Fig. 7B,C). Near-delta profiles show slight temperature
increases near the bottom (Fig. 7A), probably caused by
warmer surface water dragged down with the underflow.

Underflow velocities were measured directly by a recording current meter at a station 75 meters off the delta
shoreface. When anchored in place, the rotor of the meter
was situated 1.0 m off the bottom. Unfortunately, a continuous record for the whole season (1976) could not be obtained because of instrument problems and shifting stream
channels which caused the meter to be outside the main body
of underflow much of the time. The available records, however, indicated two main features of the underflows: (1)
velocities fluctuate widely within short time spans, and
(2) velocities generally increase with higher inflow. Similar observations were made in a Swiss lake by Lambert et. al.
(1976) and Lambert and Hsu (1979). Two sections of record
for July 17, 1976, are shown in Figure 8. The first section
(Fig. 8A) shows underflow velocities around noon when stream
discharge averaged 6.8 m³/s; maximum underflow velocity was
about 5 cm/s and major pulses were relatively infrequent.
Later in the day when discharge had increased to about
9.1 m³/s, maximum velocity increased to 13 cm/s and pulsations were more pronounced (Fig. 8B). The correlation
between underflow velocity and inflow discharge derives from
the higher inflow density conditioned by increased suspended
sediment concentrations, and probably also because a lower
proportion of inflow volume becomes mixed with lake water
(Harleman, 1961).

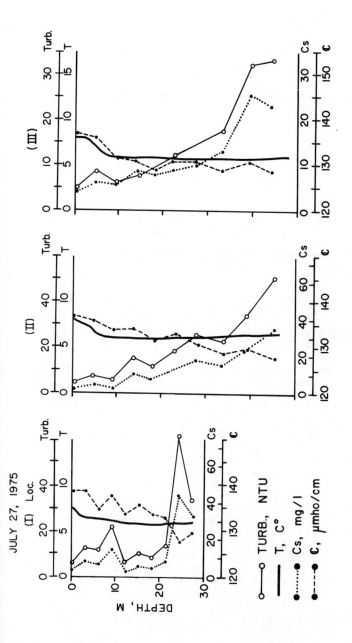

Figure 7. Peyto water profiles, July 27, 1975, showing underflow. For locations, see Fig. 6.
Symbols: Turb. = turbidity in nephalometric turbidity units (NTU), T = temperature,
Cs = suspended sediment concentration, C = conductivity.

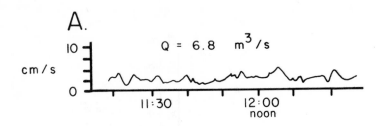

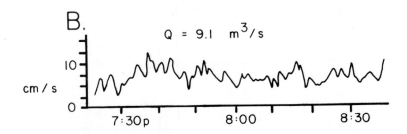

Figure 8. Underflow velocities recorded July 17, 1976, during midday (A) and early evening (B). See Fig. 6 for station location. Inflow discharge (Q) represents the average of each measurement period indicated.

The cause of the velocity pulsations is unknown, though they appear to be characteristic of underflows in those few cases where their velocities have been continuously recorded (Lambert et. al., 1976; Normark and Dickson, 1976; Lambert and Hsu, 1979). Lambert et. al., (1976) suggest that pulsating underflows result from supercritical velocities, that is, when densiometric Froude numbers exceed unity. At Fr=1, critical velocity is given by

$$U = \sqrt{g \frac{\Delta \rho}{\rho} h}$$

where $\Delta \rho$ is the density difference between underflow and lake water, ρ is lake water density, and h is underflow thickness. In those cases where our data permitted calculation of critical velocity, we found that measured velocities sometimes exceeded but often were less than critical velocity, yet the pulsations were always present. Normark and Dickson (1976) also found that Froude numbers were usually less than one for pulsating underflows in Lake Superior. Lambert et. al., (1976) also suggested that the pulsations may be caused by unsteady inflow, but neither their nor our stream records indicated inflow variations which correlated with the observed current meter fluctuations; however, the distance between our gaging station and the lake (1 km) may have been too great to permit such correlations, especially when the short frequency of underflow pulsations is noted. Periodic repacking of loose sediment on delta

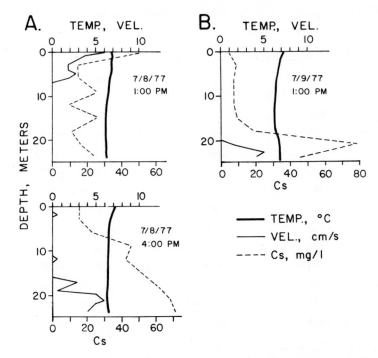

Figure 9. Station A profiles (Fig. 6) showing distributions of velocity, temperature, and suspended sediment concentrations for (A) July 8, 1977, and (B) July 9, 1977. Measurement times represent mid-points of approximately 45-minute periods required to obtain profiles.

slopes and internal waves at the upper boundary of the underflow were both suggested by Normark and Dickson (1976), but neither their nor our data were sufficient to evaluate either possibility.

Three underflow velocity profiles were obtained July 8-9, 1977, by measuring velocities at 1-meter vertical intervals 75 m offshore from the stream mouth. Because of pulsations, velocities were recorded from 3 to 5 minutes at each interval where they could be sensed; the average at each interval was then used to construct the profiles. Temperature and suspended sediment concentration were also measured in the 3 profiles. Two of the profiles were obtained July 8 which recorded a shift from overflow/interflow to underflow between 1:00 PM and 4:00 PM (Fig 9A). Apparently, the downward shift in inflow occurs in steps, as suggested by the small velocity peaks (interflows) well above the underflow body. The underflow itself was about 6 meters thick and comprised two velocity maxima, possibly representing a transitional stage between interflow and underflow. The profile on July 9 showed a well-developed underflow about 4 m thick with a maximum velocity of 5.0 cm/s occurring 2 meters off the bottom. All 3 profiles showed nearly iso-

Table 4. Relation between river suspended concentration and
          inflow type, Peyto Lake.

Date	Susp. Sed. Conc. (mg/l)	Inflow Type	Method
7/27/75	1566	underflow	water profile
7/29/75	715	underflow	drogue
8/18/75	411	interflow	transmissivity
8/23/75	40	overflow/interflow	water profile
6/20/76	1247	underflow	water profile
6/28/76	219	interflow	water profile
7/6/76	643	interflow	transmissivity
7/13/76	749	underflow	water profile
8/1/76	1298	underflow	transmissivity
8/18/76	135	interflow	transmissivity
8/30/76	295	interflow	water profile
7/8/77	696	overflow/interflow	current meter
7/8/77	1191	underflow	current meter
7/9/77	1465	underflow	current meter

thermal conditions and a correspondence between underflow
velocity and suspended sediment concentration. The generally
high suspended sediment content in the Figure 9B profile is
probably a residual effect of the downward shift from overflows to underflows.

Stream samples collected at the times of documented
underflows contained suspended sediment concentrations that
always exceeded 700 mg/ℓ (Table 4). Assuming 700 mg/ℓ to
be the critical concentration, the proportion of time that
underflows occur in Peyto Lake can be calculated from a computed flow duration curve and a rating curve of suspended
sediment concentration versus discharge (Vendl, 1978). We
thus estimate that underflows were present 68% of the time
during the summer of 1976. This estimate can only be considered approximate because (1) the correlation between suspended concentration and discharge is not good (r=.61, Vendl,
1978), and (2) other density-controlling factors such as
temperature, salinity, and suspended concentrations in the
lake are ignored.

Sedimentation Patterns

Because sedimentation in Peyto Lake is dominated by
underflows, bottom topography is an essential factor in controlling sedimentation trends. The preferred paths of sediment transport can be readily seen from transmissivity surveys (Fig. 10). After the inflow enters the lake as an
underflow, it spreads across the floor of the proximal basin

AUGUST 1, 1976   **TRANSMISSIVITY, %**

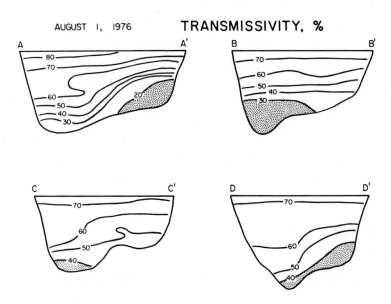

Figure 10.   Peyto transmissivity cross sections for August 1, 1976, showing underflow. Stippled pattern indicates zone of highest sediment concentrations (lowest transmissivity). Transect locations are shown in Fig. 6.

(A-A' and B-B', Fig. 10: Fig. 6), enters the distal basin through the notch around the subaqueous sill (C-C'), then shifts toward the east side of the lake as it proceeds to the outlet (D-D'). As the underflow moves across the lake floor, it gradually loses sediment as shown by progressively increasing values of transmissivity from proximal to distal locations (Fig. 10).

Sedimentation rates were directly measured in summer 1976 with 20 traps that were collected and reset every 10 to 16 days. Results showed that sedimentation rates varied considerably with time and location. The most proximal trap, situated 100 meters off the stream mouth, yielded a mean seasonal rate of 161 mg/cm^2/day compared to only 4.9 mg/cm^2/day for the most distal (northwest) location, a proximal-to-distal ratio of 33. In one collection, the ratio between the two locations exceeded 100. Overall, however, changes in lakewide mean rates for each collection interval correspond quite well to Peyto Creek discharge variations (Fig. 11).

The mean sedimentation rate for all 20 traps was 44.6 mg/cm^2/day for the period June 19-September 1. Assuming this value is representative for the entire lake, a total of 46.8 x 10^3 metric tons of deposition is estimated for the 75-day period. This compares fairly well with the estimate calculated from inflow data, 38.0 x 10^3 m.t. (Table 1),

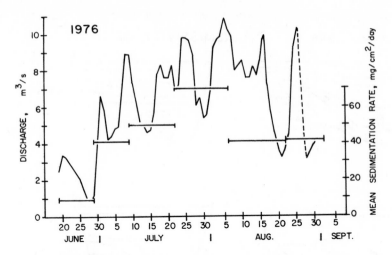

Figure 11. Relationship between mean sedimentation rate (horizontal bars) and mean daily inflow discharge for six sediment trap collection periods in Peyto Lake, 1976. Trap locations are shown in Fig. 12.

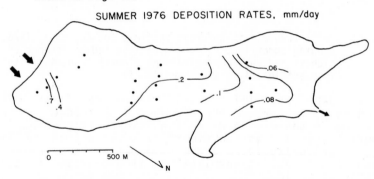

Figure 12. Map showing distribution of mean depositional rates in Peyto Lake, determined from sediment traps (dots) for the period June 19 to September 1, 1976. Note effect of bottom topography, especially the midlake sill (Fig. 6), on sedimentation pattern.

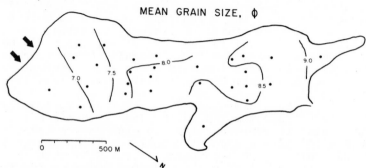

Figure 13. Map showing distribution of mean grain sizes of Peyto bottom sediments.

considering the uncertainties involved with both sets of measurements. The estimate based on trap data is likely too high because the area of the entire bottom was used in the calculation. The traps, however, were placed only in the deeper areas of the lake where deposition rates are certainly higher than in shallow areas. If, for example, deposition is considered to be negligible in depths of less than 10 meters, the trap estimate reduces to 40.0×10^3 m.t. In any case, the closeness of the two estimates indicates that Peyto Lake is an efficient sediment sink, especially when compared to Lower Waterfowl.

The areal distribution of mean deposition rates for summer 1976 is shown in Figure 12, converted to accumulated thickness (sediment bulk density = 2.1 g/cm^3). Deposition is quite even across the proximal basin, but preferred movement around the sill to the west is clearly indicated. In the distal basin, maximum deposition moves toward the east side toward the outlet, essentially in agreement with transmissivity data (Fig. 10). Contours of surficial grain size distributions show the same pattern: a general proximal-to-distal decrease in mean size with a preferred path around the sill and closure toward the outlet (Fig. 13).

Nearly all cores (26 total) contained well-developed horizontal laminations reflecting variations in texture and color. Current structures resulting from strong underflows were not found. Individual laminations vary considerably in thickness, from fractions of millimeters to over one centimeter. Comparison of summer accumulation rates (Fig. 12) with laminae thicknesses in cores from the same locations indicate that in most cores a number of distinct laminae are deposited in a year. These laminae are thought to represent inflow variations caused by short-term changes in weather. Annual deposits (varves) could not be confidently identified. Two cores collected in isolated embayments consisted of faintly laminated to massive clays. These areas were shallow (< 15 m) and isolated from the underflows.

Hector and Bow Lakes

These two lakes are similar in that they are deep, thermally stratified, and receive moderate sediment loads. Unlike Lower Waterfowl and Peyto, inflow and sediment dispersal patterns are dominated by overflows and shallow interflows. The survey of Hector Lake was completed in 1974 and 1975. Most of the Bow study was done in 1975, with a preliminary investigation undertaken in 1973 (Kennedy, 1975).

Sediment to both lakes is derived mainly from overland streams draining small outlet glaciers. Both primary inflows, Balfour Stream (Hector) and Bow Outwash (Bow) have formed steep, gravel-topped, Gilbert deltas at their mouths. Like Peyto, channels are braided and generally unstable, though the main inflow channels have remained in more-or-less stationary positions over the past few years. In addition, both lakes have important secondary stream sources.

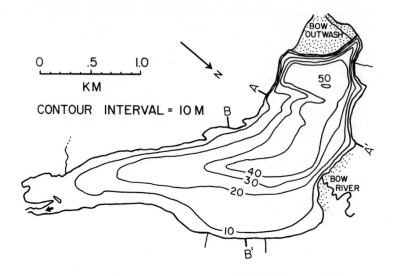

Figure 14. Bow Lake bathymetry. A-A' and B-B' mark transmissivity
cross sections in Fig. 17.

Nonglacial Bow River enters the north side of Bow Lake over
a largely inactive vegetated delta (Fig. 14). Though not
gaged, its discharge is somewhat smaller than glacial Bow
Outwash, and its sediment load is much smaller (ave. susp.
sed. conc. of 32 samples = 7.2 mg/ℓ compared to 91 mg/ℓ for
Bow Outwash; see Table 1). Bow Lake outflow (Bow River)
travels 15 km before entering the east end of Hector Lake
over a forested delta, opposite glacial Balfour Stream at
the west end of the lake (Fig. 15). We obtained discharge
records and stream samples for both inflowing streams during
the 1974 and 1975 field seasons. Balfour Stream, though the
smaller of the two, dominates sedimentation in Hector Lake
for two reasons: (1) it has a larger sediment load, and (2)
the lake outlet is very close to the Bow River inlet, quickly
drawing off Bow inflow before it spreads far into the lake.
Bow River suspended sediment concentration averaged only
about 11 mg/ℓ over the two summers, and its effect on Hector
sedimentation is largely confined to the delta region at the
lake's eastern end (Smith, 1978).

Hector, the largest of the 4 lakes, consists of 2 basins
each over 75 m deep separated by a broad sill over which
depths shallow to about 40 m (Fig. 15). Bow Lake is shallower than Hector and lacks a prominent mid-lake sill. The
lake consists of a deep, flat proximal basin which grades
into a trough-like central basin that gradually shallows to
the east (Fig. 14). Both lakes are regularly swept by downlake katabatic winds flowing off the Wapta Icefield.

Compared to Peyto Lake, Hector and Bow inflows contain
only moderate sediment loads (Table 1). Like Peyto Creek,
both glacial streams (Balfour Stream and Bow Outwash) are
highly seasonal and show strong diurnal variations during

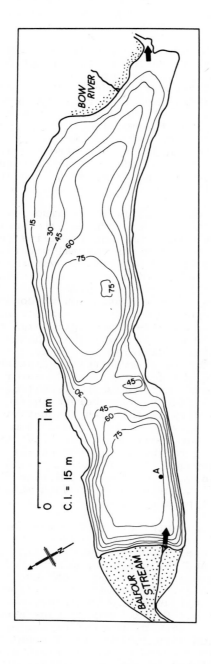

Figure 15.   Hector Lake bathymetry.   Station A shows location of sediment trap
represented in Fig. 21.

225

warm weather. In recent years, the supply of glacial sediment to Bow Lake via Bow Outwash has been greatly reduced by development of a pond at the terminus of the receding Bow Glacier (Smith, in press).

Thermal structures of the two lakes are similar; both are dimictic with well-developed stratification during the summer months. Bottom temperatures remain below 5°C and reach as high as 14° at the surface. Summer temperature profiles commonly define smooth curves that grade from the surface down to the top of the hypolimnion without a well-defined metalimnion, or thermocline. Exceptions occur during strong winds when the top 1-3 m become nearly isothermal from turbulent mixing, and near the stream mouth where inflow may completely disrupt the thermal structure of the epilimnion. Highest suspended sediment concentrations tend to occur in the epilimnion several meters below the surface.

A slight chemical stratification also develops during summer. Shortly after ice breakup in late spring, the two lakes are virtually isothermal and isohaline (uniform vertical conductivity). Later, as thermal stratification develops, low-conductivity inflow spreads over the hypolimnion, charging the warmer epilimnion with a consistently lower dissolved concentration than the colder, more saline hypolimnial water below. Average hypolimnial conductivities are about 143 and 147 μmho/cm for Hector and Bow Lakes, respectively. In both lakes, mid-summer epilimnial conductivities are approximately 10 μmho/cm lower than the hypolimnion, representing a salinity difference of 6 mg/ℓ. This corresponds to a difference in water density comparable to only a 0.5°C temperature change in initial 4° water. The chemical differences thus contribute to overall density stratification, but the effects are subordinate to temperature variations. The source of the high conductivity hypolimnial water is uncertain in view of the fact that most inflow is provided by low conductivity meltwater. Although this problem was not investigated by us, three sources seem plausible: (1) groundwater seepage; (2) nonglacial inflowing streams, all of which have higher conductivities than the two glacial streams, and (3) dissolution of suspended material as it falls through the hypolimnion.

Inflowing stream water enters Bow and Hector Lakes as overflows and shallow interflows. Underflows were not detected in either Lake. Upon entrance, inflow velocity rapidly decreases and the coarser sediment begins to settle, much of it carried downward by turbulent eddies. After mixing and dilution near the mouth, the inflow becomes established most commonly as a shallow interflow within the epilimnion (Fig. 16). Comparisons of mid-summer epilimnial conductivities with those of the inflow suggest that inflow is typically diluted with ambient water about 3- to 5-fold near the mouth before becoming an interflow further downlake. Once established, there is apparently little further dilution of the interflow by vertical diffusion as it spreads over the hypolimnion and moves downlake.

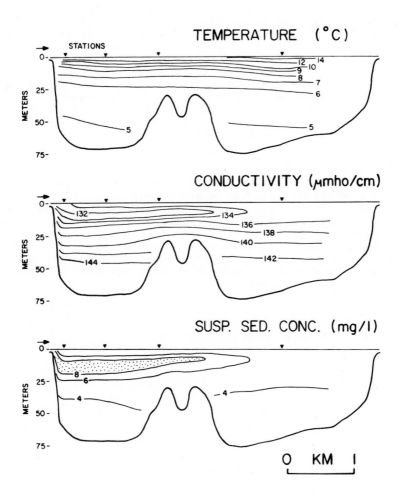

Figure 16. Longitudinal cross sections of Hector Lake, August 3, 1974, showing vertical distribution of temperature, conductivity, and suspended sediment concentration. Stipled pattern shows area of highest suspended sediment content. Cross section extends from mouth of Balfour Stream to Bow River delta (Fig. 15).

Glacio-Lacustrine and marine sedimentation

Sedimentation Patterns

Inflowing plumes show prominent right-hand deflections in both lakes. This is likely an effect of the earth's rotation (Coriolis force) as has been demonstrated (Hamblin and Carmack, 1978) or inferred (Sturm and Matter, 1978; Pharo and Carmack, 1979; Wright and Nydegger, in press) in other deep river-dominated lakes where major transport occurs in the epilimnion. This tendency was frequently shown by drogue movements and transmissivity surveys (Fig. 17): shortly after entering the lake, the inflow plume moves toward the right side and continues to hug that shoreline as it moves toward the outlet. Plume positions vary somewhat with inflow discharge and wind conditions, but the right-hand tendency is always present.

Longer-term persistence of rotational effects is demonstrated by sediment trap data and areal grain size distributions. In Hector Lake, contours of both bottom grain size and summer sedimentation rates are mainly parallel to the lake's long axis, with crosslake trends more prominent than downlake trends (Fig. 18). Similar trends are shown by distributions of detrital carbonate (Smith, 1978). Note in Figure 18 the negligible effect of the mid-lake sill (Fig. 14) on grain-size trends and only minor influence on sedimentation rates, both the consequence of dominant sediment transport in the epilimnion.

TRANSMISSIVITY, %

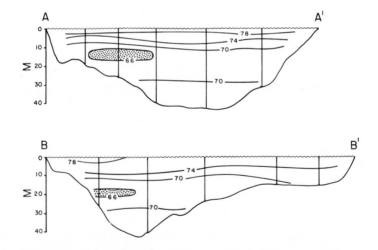

Figure 17. Transmissivity cross sections in Bow Lake, August 14, 1975. Locations shown in Fig. 14. Note zone of highest suspended sediment concentration (lowest transmissivity, stipled) occurs as interflow hugging south side of lake.

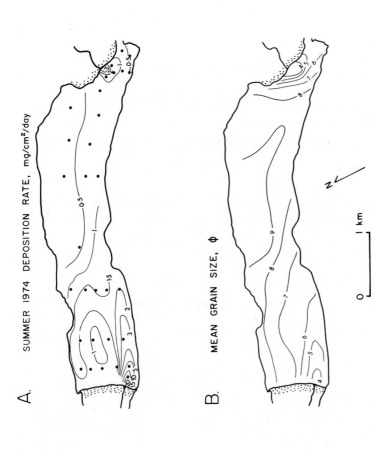

Figure 18. Areal sedimentation patterns in Hector Lake. (A) Mean sedimentation rates measured from sediment traps in summer 1974. (B) Mean grain size of bottom sediment.

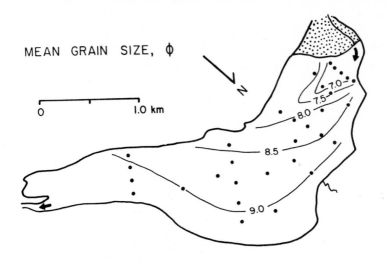

MEAN GRAIN SIZE, φ

0   1.0 km

7.0
7.5
8.0
8.5
9.0

Figure 19. Distribution of mean bottom-sediment grain sizes in
Bow Lake.

    In Bow Lake, a right-hand tendency in bottom grain
size is present though less pronounced, possibly because of
the lake's irregular shape and the left hand entrance of
Bow Outwash; however, left-to-right coarsening is apparent
in all but the most proximal cross sections (Fig. 19). The
areal pattern of mean depositional rates measured by 19
sediment traps in summer 1975 shows a plume-like distribution with a rightward-deflected axis, particularly in the
distal half of the lake (Fig. 20A). Separate maps representing individual collection intervals ranging from 6 to
13 days, however, show more variation in pattern and magnitude of short-term deposition (Fig. 20B). Most deposition
occurred between July 2 and July 29 (Fig. 20B, b-d), em-
bracing the two intervals of maximum inflow with peaks on
July 12 and July 28, 1975 (Fig. 20C). Following the second
inflow peak, sedimentation rates were low for the remainder
of the season (Fig. 20B, e-g), indicating that the lake
clears up rather quickly after the passage of a major sediment input event. Kennedy (1975), using fewer traps over
a shorter time span in 1973, likewise showed that most depositional pulsations could be correlated with specific peaks
and troughs in inflow discharge. Between the most proximal
and most distal trap locations, a greater than 20-fold decrease in mean daily sedimentation rates is indicated in
Figure 20A. This difference is probably greater than their
differences in mean annual rates because deposition, though
much reduced, tends to be more uniformly distributed during
low inflow periods (e.g., Fig. 20B, g), which comprise most
of any year. A more than 40-fold decrease in sedimentation
rates occurred between the most proximal and distal traps
in Hector Lake (Fig. 18A).

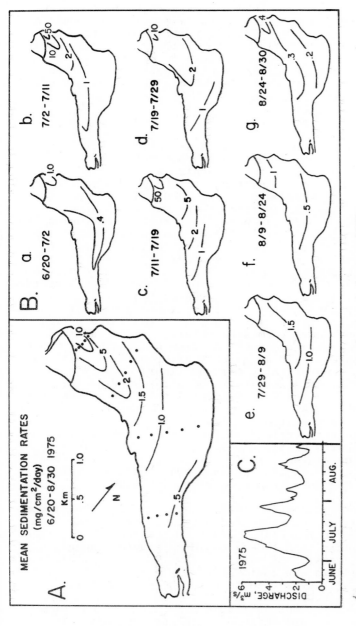

Figure 20. Bow Lake sedimentation rates measured from traps in summer 1975.
(A) Mean rates for whole season; dots show trap locations. (B) Rates for
individual collection intervals. (C) Hydrograph of Bow Outwash for summer
1975. Note discharge peaks on July 12 and 28 correspond to periods of high
lake sedimentation (B. b,c,d,; above).

Except in distal locations and in depths less than 15 meters, bottom sediments from both lakes are laminated, often containing well-defined classical varves. Both downlake and crosslake trends in varve thickness are well developed in Hector Lake, and the thicker summer layers usually contain sub-laminations formed by inflow variations of different time scales (Smith, 1978). Bow Lake varves record a recent shift (since the 1950's) from dominantly underflows to interflows in response to an abrupt reduction of sediment supply following the formation of a pond at the margin of Bow Glacier (Smith, in press).

The Problem of Clay Deposition

For deep stratified lakes such as Bow and Hector in which fine sediment is dispersed by epilimnial currents, a question arises regarding the mechanism and rates of clay deposition in the overall pattern of lake sedimentation. Our transmissivity surveys and suspended sediment measurements indicate that the epilimnion in both lakes acts as a sort of trap for the finest particles, while water below the thermocline maintains relatively low concentrations of suspended particles that escaped the turbulent surface layers. Similar observations were made by Sturm and Matter (1978) and Pharo and Carmack (1979). Under those conditions, the finest particles (clay) would be expected to remain suspended in the epilimnion and eventually transported out of the lake, whereas coarser suspensates (silt) would be more inclined to settle through the thermocline to the bottom. The correspondence between short-term sedimentation rates and inflow (Fig. 20) suggests that deposition from suspension is rapid, and that the lake clears up quickly after passage of a major inflow event. However, clay (8ϕ and finer) comprises major components of bottom sediments in both lakes (Fig. 18B, 19). Much of this clay resides in 'winter layers' of varves, but even so, calculations of Stokes settling rates for different clay diameters show that particles finer than 9ϕ and especially 10ϕ could not settle from the base of the epilimnion to the deeper parts of the two lakes within a single season. Yet, the average content of clay finer than 10ϕ (1 micron) in all Hector cores excluding those near the Bow River delta is 24.5%. In Bow Lake, the proportion is 27.9%.

Both Sturm and Matter (1978) and Matthews (1956) recognized this problem and suggested seasonal overturning as a mechanism for bringing clays closer to the lake floor; thus, settling distances (and times) could be reduced enough to permit annual deposits of 'winter clay' in varved sediments. We have observed in our sediment traps, however, that significant amounts of clay settle to even the deepest parts of the lake floor throughout the summer during maximum stratification. Furthermore, our available data suggest that summer clay settling rates are quite uniform and apparently independent of total sedimentation rates in proximal areas dominated by silt deposition (Fig. 21). It thus appears that some mechanism scavenges clay and brings it to the lake floor at a uniform rate much faster than predicted by calculated settling velocities of individual clay particles.

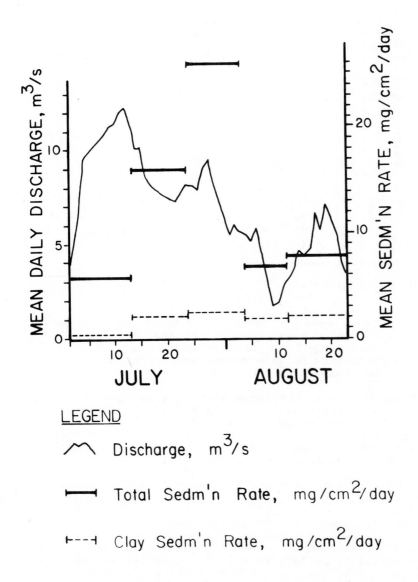

LEGEND

⌒ Discharge, m^3/s

▬ Total Sedm'n Rate, mg/cm^2/day

⊢--⊣ Clay Sedm'n Rate, mg/cm^2/day

Figure 21. Relationship between total sedimentation rate, clay
sedimentation rate, and inflow discharge at station A
sediment trap (Fig. 15), Hector Lake, 1975. Note that
while total sedimentation rates vary considerably, clay
sedimentation rates after 7/13 are quite steady.

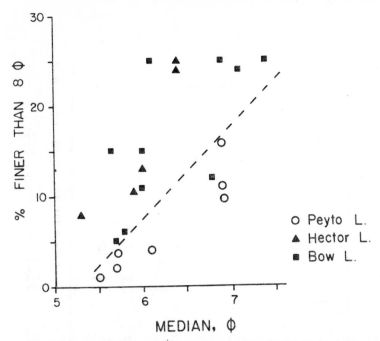

Figure 22.   Median grain size versus % finer than 8 phi (clay) for
sediment recovered from sediment traps in 3 lakes. Note
samples from Peyto, an underflow lake, have lower clay
percentages for given median diameters than Bow or Hector,
both overflow-interflow lakes.

Flocculation is not a probable mechanism because of the low
sediment concentrations and salinities of the lake water
(Kranck, 1973; Whitehouse et. al., 1960).   Furthermore, a
correlation between the settling rates of clay and total
sediment would be expected if flocculation were important;
such is not the case, however (Fig. 21).

     A plausible explanation for the observed settling be-
havior is the aggregation of clay as fecal pellets produced
by zooplankton, especially calanoid copepods.   These free-
swimming organisms were frequently caught with water samples
in both Hector and Bow Lakes and were found in Lower Waterfowl and Peyto Lakes as well.   Such downward transport of
fine detritus by pellets is well known in marine environments
(Schrader, 1971; Honjo and Roman, 1978; Syvitski and Murray,
in press) but has only recently been demonstrated to be
important in freshwater lakes (Ferrante and Parker, 1977).
The possible role of pelletization did not occur to us until
after the main part of the field program was completed, so
we did not investigate this when the timing would have been
best.   In August 1979, however, we set 4 sediment traps at
2 stations in Bow Lake; one station was mid-lake, the other
distal.   At each station, one trap was set on the bottom and
the other suspended at mid-depth.   Each trap was sampled

twice over an eleven-day period (August 20-31), the trap contents examined by microscope the same day in a field laboratory. In each sampling, the sediment was found to contain abundant fecal pellets, slightly ovoidal and ranging from about 1/8 to 1/4 mm in long diameter. We estimated that between one-third and two-thirds of the sediment in the traps were pelletized.

These results, though suggestive, are crude and pre-liminary. To better assess the role of pelletization in such lakes, information is needed about pellet settling be-havior, size and composition of pelletized constituents, and the spatial and seasonal activities of pellet-producing organisms. The discovery of abundant fecal pellets in Bow Lake, however, lends an interpretation to the relationships in Figure 22 which shows that for a given median grain size in summer sediment trap samples, the percentage of clay is higher in underflow-dominated Peyto Lake than in either Hector or Bow. One might ordinarily expect the opposite relationship, i.e., more summer clay in Peyto because clay is brought directly to the bottom by underflows instead of being transported out of the lake by epilimnial currents as envisaged for Bow and Hector. Fecal pellets, however, pro-vide a means for bringing clay suspended in the epilimnion quickly to the lake floor. Presumably, though not yet demonstrated, Peyto's turbid underflows are inhospitable environments for pelletizing zooplankton, so clay particles remain discrete and settle more slowly.

CONCLUSIONS

We have described the salient characteristics of 4 glacier-fed lakes and presented some of their main sedimen-tological features. In particular, we stress the importance of the type of entrance mixing, as this ultimately affects the principal sediment transport and depositional patterns within each lake. To summarize:

1. Lower Waterfowl Lake is shallow, unstratified, and well mixed. Inflowing river water, having passed through upstream lakes, contains low suspended sediment concen-trations and has virtually the same density as the lake water. Entrance mixing is therefore homopycnal, and sediment is dispersed homogeneously away from the stream mouth through the lake. Neither bottom topography nor Coriolis force significantly affect sedimentation. Crosslake sedimentation trends are absent, and only weak proximal-distal trends occur.

2. Peyto Lake, fed directly by an active glacier, is dom-inated by underflows arising from high suspended sedi-ment concentrations in inflowing Peyto Creek. Although the lake is deep, thermal stratification is weak to absent due to disruption of the thermal structure by underflowing river water. Sedimentation trends are greatly affected by bottom topography as sediment-laden

underflows seek the lowest areas of the lake floor.
Strong proximal-distal trends and topography-controlled
crosslake trends are reflected in bottom sediment distributions.

3. Hector and Bow Lakes are deep, thermally stratified,
and receive intermediate suspended loads. Inflowing
river water enters each lake as overflows and shallow
interflows which remain within the epilimnion as they
disperse over the lake. These near-surface currents
are deflected rightward by the earth's rotational
(Coriolis) effect, a process that is reflected in both
short and long-term sedimentation trends. Strong
right-to-left (looking downlake) as well as proximal-
distal trends occur in both lakes. Bottom topography
assumes a relatively minor role in sedimentation.

A heretofore unrecognized, but possibly major, factor
in the transport and deposition of clays in glacier-fed lakes
may be fecal pellets formed by sediment-ingesting zooplankton, especially calanoid copepods. These provide mechanisms
for bringing clay to the bottoms of deep lakes much faster
than would be possible if the clays settled as nonaggregated
particles. Pelletization may be especially important in
overflow/interflow lakes such as Bow and Hector where clay
trapped in the epilimnion might otherwise be transported out
of the system. Free-swimming copepods were discovered in
all 4 lakes, but their relative importance to sedimentation
processes is unknown at this time. Of particular interest
may be the possible role of pelletization in the formation
of laminated sediments.

REFERENCES

Axelsson, V., 1967, The Laitaure Delta: a study of deltaic
    morphology and processes. *Geografiska Annaler,* 49,
    1-127.

Bates, C.C., 1953, Rational theory of delta formation.
    Amer. Assoc. Petrol. Geol. Bull., 37, 2119-2162.

Ferrante, J.G., and Parker, J.I., 1977, Transport of diatom
    frustules by copepod fecal pellets to the sediments
    of Lake Michigan. *Limnol. Oceanog.,* 22, 92-98.

Fulton, R.J., and Pullen, M.J.L.T., 1969, Sedimentation in
    Upper Arrow Lake, British Columbia. *Canad. Jour.
    Earth Sci.,* 6, 785-791.

Gilbert, R., 1975, Sedimentation in Lillooet Lake, British
    Columbia. *Canad. Jour. Earth Sci.,* 12, 1697-1711.

Hamblin, P.F., and Carmack, E.C., 1978, River-induced
    currents in a fjord lake. *Jour. Geophys. Res.,* 83,
    885-899.

Harleman, D.R.F., 1961, Stratified flow. in: Streeter, V.L.
    (ed.) *Handbook of Fluid Dynamics,* McGraw-Hill,
    New York, 26 p.

Harris, S.A., and Waters, R.R., 1977, Late Quaternary history of southwest Alberta: a progress report. *Bull. Canad. Petrol. Geol.*, 25, 35-62.

Heusser, C.J., 1956, Postglacial environments in the Canadian Rocky Mountains. *Ecol. Monographs*, 26, 253-302.

Honjo, S., and Roman, M.R., 1978, Marine copepod fecal pellets: production, preservation and sedimentation. *Jour. Mar. Res.*, 26, 45-57.

Kennedy, S.K., 1975, Sedimentation in a glacier-fed lake. Unpubl. M.Sc. Thesis, Univ. Illinois Chicago Circle, 55 p.

Kennedy, S.K., and Smith, N.D., 1977, The relationship between carbonate mineralogy and grain size in two alpine lakes. *Jour. Sed. Petrol.*, 47, 411-418.

Kranck, K., 1973, Flocculation of suspended sediment in the sea. *Nature*, 246, 348-350.

Lambert, A.M., and Hsu, K.J., 1979, Non-annual cycles of varve-like sedimentation in Walensee, Switzerland. *Sedimentology*, 26, 453-461.

Lambert, A.M., Kelts, K.R., and Marshall, N.F., 1976, Measurements of density underflows from Walensee, Switzerland. *Sedimentology*, 23, 87-105.

Luckman, B.H., and Osborn, G.D., 1979, Holocene glacier fluctuations in the middle Canadian Rocky Mountains. *Quaternary Res.*, 11, 52-77.

Mathews, W.H., 1956, Physical limnology and sedimentation in a glacial lake. *Geol. Soc. Amer. Bull.*, 67, 537-552.

Normark, W.R., and Dickson, F.H., 1976, Man-made turbidity currents in Lake Superior. *Sedimentology*, 23, 815-832.

Pharo, C.H., and Carmack, E.C., 1979, Sedimentation processes in a short residence-time intermontane lake, Kamloops Lake, British Columbia. *Sedimentology*, 26, 523-541.

Rutter, N.W., 1972, Geomorphology and multiple glaciation, Banff area, Alberta. *Geol. Surv. Canada Bull.* 206.

Schrader, H.J., 1971, Fecal pellets in sedimentation of pelagic diatoms. *Science*, 174, 55-57.

Shaw, J., 1972, Pleistocene chronology and geomorphology of the Rocky Mountains in south and central Alberta. in: Slaymaker, H.O., and McPherson, H.J. (eds.) *Mountain Geomorphology*, Tantalus Press, Vancouver, 37-46.

Smith, N.D., 1978, Sedimentation processes and patterns in a glacier-fed lake with low sediment input. *Canad. Jour. Earth Sci.*, 15, 741-756.

Smith, N.D., in press, The effect of changing sediment supply on recent sedimentation in a glacier-fed lake. *Arctic and Alpine Res.*

Sturm, M., and Matter, A., 1978, Turbidites and varves in
    Lake Brienz (Switzerland): deposition of clastic
    detritus by density currents. in: Matter, M., and
    Tucker, M.E. (eds.), *Modern and Ancient Lake Sedi-
    ments,* Internat. Assoc. Sedimentologists Spec. Publ.
    2, 147-168.

Syvitski, J.P., and Murray, J.W., in press. Particle inter-
    action of suspended sediment in a fjord receiving
    glacial meltwater. *Marine Geology.*

Vendl, M.A., 1978, Sedimentation in glacier-fed Peyto Lake,
    Alberta. Unpubl. M.Sc. Thesis, Univ. Illinois
    Chicago Circle, 96 p.

Whitehouse, U.G., Jeffrey, L.M., and Debrecht, J.D., 1960,
    Differential settling tendencies of clay minerals
    in saline waters. *Natl. Conf. Clays and Clay Minerals,*
    7, 1-76.

Wright, R.F., and Nydegger, P., in press. Sedimentation
    of detrital particulate matter in lakes: influence
    of currents produced by inflowing rivers. *Water
    Resources Research.*

Young, G.J., 1977, The seasonal and diurnal regime of a
    glacier-fed stream; Peyto Glacier, Alberta. *Alberta
    Watershed Research Program Symposium,* Edmonton,
    16 p.

Young, G.J., and Stanley, A.D., 1976, Canadian glaciers in
    the International Hydrological Decade Program,
    1965-1974: No. 4, Peyto Glacier, Alberta, summary
    of measurements. *Scientific Series 71,* Inland Waters
    Directorate, Environment Canada, 65 p.

11 Site location and instrumentation aspects of a study of sedimentation processes in a proglacial lake in southeastern British Columbia,Canada

Frank H. Weirich

ABSTRACT

The paper examines research conducted on a small, unnamed proglacial lake in southeast British Columbia, Canada. The study concentrates on continuous monitoring of sediment concentration, currents and temperature in the lake and correlates changes in these parameters with the nature of the sediments being deposited. Specifically, the work is a process study of lake bottom sediments deposited by density currents. A secondary goal is to analyse the entire meso-scale glacial-hydrologic system of which the lake is only a component. The present discussion outlines the characteristics of the site, the general nature of the study, and in particular, describes the instrumentation involved.

INTRODUCTION

Glacial varves and rhythmites are the subject of a vast literature, but actual on-site studies of the sedimentation processes governing the formation of such deposits are relatively few. Despite early pioneering work by Johnson (1922) and Kindle (1930) most research has been restricted to field correlation between different sites, or to laboratory and statistical analysis of recovered cores. Similarly, although the existence of density flows was recognized in Lake Geneva by Forel as early as 1885, it was not until after the interest generated by the early Lake Mead studies that Kuenan (1951) suggested density flows as a mechanism for varve (more properly rhythmite) formation. Moreover, not until the latter 1950's did writers such as Matthews (1956) begin to advocate integrated studies of glaciohydrological systems in order to better understand both glacial sediments and associated density flows.

Recent work (see Smith, this volume) reflects a growing interest in sedimentation processes in glacial lakes. To date, however, few detailed, quantitative, integrated, on-site studies have been carried out on the process of sediment

---

* Frank H. Weirich
  Formerly of Department of Geography, University of Toronto
  Currently of Department of Geography, U.C.L.A.,
  Los Angeles, CA 90024, U.S.A.

deposition resulting from the passage of density flows (including turbidity currents) in proglacial lakes. It was determined therefore to attempt such a study. Specifically, the primary goals were to: a) continuously monitor density flows in a proglacial lake for temperature, sediment concentration, velocity; and b) correlate the characteristics of the flow with the nature of the depositing sediment and the hydroclimatic parameters affecting the transport process in an effort to provide an empirical basis for the testing of theoretical models. A secondary aim was to relate the present processes to the glacial and climatic history of the site.

The above ·goals necessitated, in effect, the study of an entire climatic-hydrologic system, for although the focus of the work was upon the lake and the sediment processes at work in the lake, an effort was also required to monitor and assess the effects of both present and past climatic and hydrologic processes underway in the research basin. The secondary goal of determining the glacial and climatic history of the site, while involving considerable field work for the collection of palynological, dendrochronological, soil and vegetation data, was a relatively straightforward operation. The primary goal of studying the actual processes of sedimentation in a glacial lake and in particular the motion of turbidity currents within the context of a broad study of an entire glaciolacustrine system however necessitated a rather extensive and somewhat complex instrumentation network. Unfortunately, this need for instrumentation was in direct conflict with both the limitations of the research funds which were available and the major logistical constraints on remote field research. The result was the need for careful planning of the field operations and an extensive search for equipment which might be borrowed from within the university, from other universities, and from government departments. Moreover, in cases where the required instrumentation was not available or could not be purchased because of budgetary limitations, it became necessary to design and build appropriate equipment and facilities. The discussion which follows deals with the site selection, site characteristics, and instrumentation aspects of the work.

THE QUESTION OF A SUITABLE RESEARCH SITE

The first step in any field research is the selection of an appropriate research site. Because of the desire to establish and operate a remote research station and a complex instrumentation network on a very limited budget the need to find a site with both the correct scientific and logistical characteristics assumed an added significance. In effect, the aim was to find a natural laboratory for such research. It therefore became necessary from the outset to define the required site characteristics in quite rigorous terms and to then conduct an extensive search for a suitable location. The following criteria for a site were established:

1. The hydrological boundaries of the site should be

distinct and the basin of manageable size (on the order of a few tens of km.sq.) in order to enable adequate instrumentation of the watershed.

2. The glaciolacustrine system should be a relatively simple one with preferably only a single inlet stream carrying meltwater from the glacier and entering the lake and one main outlet stream draining the lake.

3. The glacier should be on the order of a few square kilometers in size in order to facilitate instrumentation and reduce the length of signal cables required.

4. The depth of the lake is a major consideration as well. The lake should be only shallow to moderate in depth (on the order of 5 to 15 meters). This is desirable not only as a means of reducing cable and line lengths but perhaps more significantly to enable high altitude cold water scuba diving to be carried out. The capability of checking and servicing the underwater instrumentation while the equipment was in position was regarded as a virtual necessity because of the complexity of the instrument array. The limitations imposed by high altitude decompression requirements in the cold glacial lake waters would have introduced severe constraints on such underwater work. Hence, the desirability of a lake only 5 to 15 meters in depth where the decompression requirements would not become a major consideration.

5. Sediment input into the lake from the glacial stream should be large and preferably subject to frequent and considerable variations. This would enhance the distinctive character of turbidity currents and reduce the resolution capabilities required of the instrumentation.

6. The presence of subsurface channels is desirable both as an indication of the occurrence of density underflows as well as offering the possibility that such flows would be concentrated in the channels thereby increasing the likelihood of their detection.

7. The geology of the area should not be excessively complex in nature (either in terms of unusual lithologic associations or complex fault structures). A complex geology could make the study of the water chemistry of the system a very difficult undertaking through the introduction of many different components into the dissolved load. From a hydrologic viewpoint a simple geological situation is also desirable. Complex faulting or unusual geological characteristics could make it very difficult to determine the water budget for the system as a result of subsurface movement of the water in the system and especially groundwater movements into and out of the lake.

8. Road access is preferred. Alternatively, economical

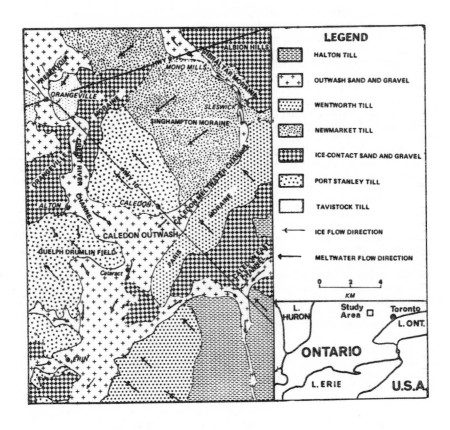

Figure 1. Location and surficial geology of the Caledon
Outwash study area (after Cowan unpublished)

(short ferry time and short lift distance) helicopter
access is acceptable. Reasonable accessibility is of
course needed for moving large amounts of equipment as
well as personnel into and out of the site at the
beginning and end of each field season. More importantly
perhaps is the need to have good lines of communication
and supply established in order to facilitate the repair
and servicing of the complex equipment.

9. A history of previous work on the site is desirable.

Consultation with various federal government agencies
indicated clearly that no other suitable site with a record
of previous work was available. It was therefore determined
that an entirely new research site would have to be found.
A careful study of the topographic sheets of all areas of
British Columbia, Alberta, the Yukon, and the western portion
of the Northwest Territories where glaciers are present was
undertaken. On the basis of this analysis a list of some
250 sites was assembled. This list was reduced to 40 possible
sites through careful study of aerial photographs. A summer's
field reconnaissance narrowed the selection down initially
to 6 and finally a single site emerged as clearly the most
suitable.

DESCRIPTION OF THE RESEARCH SITE

The site chosen was an unnamed lake and glacier in the Eastern
Purcell Mountains of British Columbia at latitude 51 N and
longitude 116 W. The general location of the site is indicated in Figure 1. The topography of the valley is shown in
Figure 2a and the general character of the basin is clearly
indicated in the photo in Figure 3. There are two glaciers,
five lakes, and several perennial snowpacks in this upper
valley. Both of the glaciers are cirque types. A large
portion of the valley floor is occupied by the five lakes.
The two larger lakes are glacial, two of the others are nonglacial, and the fifth is of an intermediate nature receiving
its input largely from the perennial snowpacks.

All the research activity was confined to the upper
valley and in particular, the sub-basin occupied by the larger
glacier and one of the glacial lakes. The boundaries of
this area are indicated by the dashed lines in Figure 2b.
The sub-basin consists of five major physiographic components:
1) an extensive area of bare rock and unvegetated slopes;
2) the glacier itself; 3) a large depression extending from
the glacier terminus down valley some distance; 4) a vegetated zone surrounding part of the lake; and 5) the lake.
The extent of each of these areas as well as the general
character of the study area is indicated in Figures 2 and 3.

The lake itself is of particular interest. Figure 4 is
a simplified bathymetric map of the lake. The maximum depth
is 6 meters while the average depth is approximately 5 meters.
Essentially, the lake is a shallow depression with a relatively
uniform bottom. A classic Gilbert type delta with three main

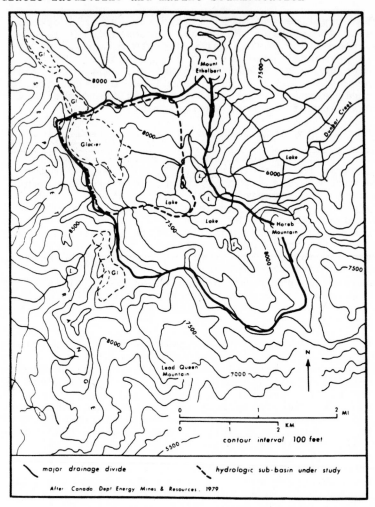

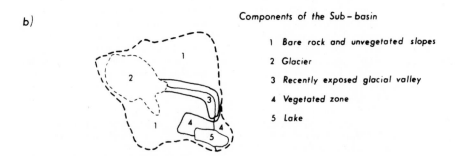

Figure 2(a). Topographic map of the research site. The
           drainage boundaries of the upper valley and
           the study sub-basin are clearly indicated.
     2(b). The major components of the sub-basin.

Figure 3. The study sub-basin. The glacier supply the bulk
of the meltwater is partially visible in the upper left
of the photo. Also apparent is the relatively simple
hydrologic setting of the site - only a single major
input stream and a single outlet stream for the lake.

stream branches crossing its surface is being built out into
the lake. Also present are several shallow bottom depressions
which may be channels. The major water input into the lake
is the single glacial meltwater stream from the large glacier.
There is however, some input at the northwest end to the
lake from a small glacier remnant high up on the rock wall as
well as some runoff from the vegetated zone and the broken
rock along the south and western sides of the lake. Surface
runoff from the bare rock areas and the depression above the
settling basin all enters the lake via the glacial meltwater
stream. Only a single outlet stream drains the lake.

The detailed geology of the area is described in Reesor
(1973). The bulk of the sediment deposited in the lakes is
from the Mt. Nelson formation. This consists of thick, cliff-
forming, competent successions of dolomite and dolomitic
limestone in beds varying from a few millimeters to a meter
in thickness. The Dutch Creek formation is also of importance
as it is this unit which underlies the lake bottom. It
consists of basal quartzite grading into slates.

The climatic conditions of the site tend to the extremes.
Precipitation, largely in the form of snow, exceeds 1000 mm.
annually. The average annual temperature is less than 2°C.

Bathymetry

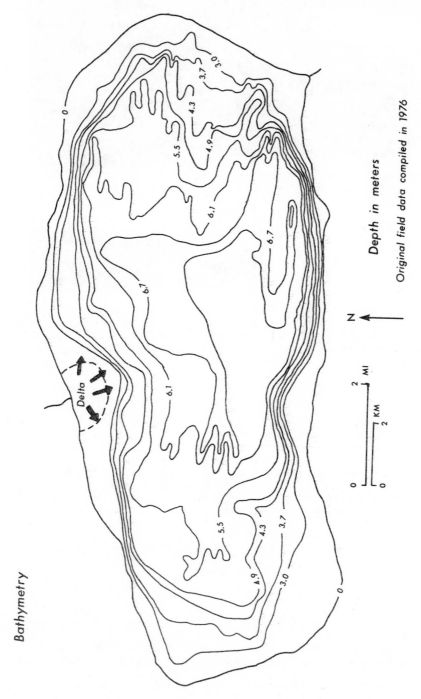

Depth in meters

Original field data compiled in 1976

Figure 4. Bathymetric map of the lake

The vegetation and soils of the research basin clearly reflect these rigorous climatic conditions. In terms of the biogeographic classification scheme developed by Krajina (1969) the research basin falls within two zones: the Alpine Tundra (AT) zone and the Engelmann Spruce-Subalpine Fir (ESSF) zone.

In summary, the site chosen was a relatively small and easily isolated component of the upper valley containing a lake which receives the vast majority of its input from a single glacial meltwater stream fed by a nearby glacier and drained by a single outlet. Moreover, the relatively straightforward geological setting, the rapidly changing and often extreme climatic conditions and the open alpine vegetation present provide, in effect, an outdoor laboratory in which many of the processes to be studied are both relatively intense and quite distinct.

THE GENERAL INSTRUMENTATION SCHEME

As initially envisioned the project required the use of climatic, hydrologic, and sedimentologic instrumentation located at specific key locations throughout the study basin. The conceptual distribution of the equipment is indicated in Figure 5. Climatic equipment would be concentrated in three locations. On the glacier surface a climate station would be established to monitor wind, radiation, precipitation, temperature, and relative humidity. At a point between the glacier and the lake and approximately in the centre of the study basin a second climate station would be established to monitor parameters similar to those measured on the glacier. This would provide an indication of the conditions in the study basin as a whole. On the delta and extending out into the lake a third concentration of climatic equipment would be deployed to provide information on the climatic conditions of the lake. In addition to these three concentrations of climatic instrumentation an array of precipitation gauges and anemometers would be installed around the lake and in different areas of the basin. Data derived from these would provide a more complete understanding of the variations in climatic conditions in the study basin.

The hydrologic equipment, as in the case of the climatic network, would be concentrated in several areas. Specifically, water level gauges would be required on the inlet stream, on the lake itself, and on the outlet stream. In addition, a systematic collection of water samples for suspended sediment and water chemistry analysis would be undertaken at three sample stations: one located near the input stream gauge; one near the gauge on the outlet stream; and a third near the midpoint of the lake. Finally, any other streams entering or leaving the lake would also be monitored in some manner (ie. staff gauges). Such a program of collecting stream discharge and lake level data, in conjunction with the climatic data described earlier, should enable the determination of the water balance of the lake and in general terms of the entire sub-basin. Moreover, the water balance data, when

Components of the Study

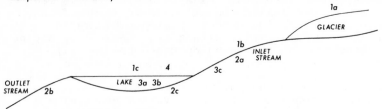

1. Climate Monitoring System
   a) glacier climate station
   b) basin climate station
   c) lake climate station

2. Hydrologic, Sediment and Water Chemistry System
   a) inlet station
   b) outlet station
   c) lake station

3. Underwater Network
   a) sensor grid
   b) distal station
   c) recording station

4. Coring and Sampling System
   boat and coring equipment

Figure 5.   Conceptual scheme for the components of the study.

combined with the water sampling program, were intended to enable the determination of a sediment and chemical budget for the lake.

The climatic, hydrologic and water chemical networks described above, although of major significance in the research, are technically and logistically quite straightforward. The sedimentation instrumentation network proposed for monitoring the sedimentary processes in the lake, however, was much more complex and somewhat unconventional in character. It entailed a detailed and multi-stage program. At the beginning of a season systematic coring and depth recording would be done. By conducting a preliminary inspection of the cores and preparing a bathymetric map of the lake floor it would be possible to determine the (or a) major subsurface flow channel(s) followed by input waters after they enter the lake. Once the major subsurface channel had been isolated, the next step would involve the installation of a three-dimensional grid of sensors to monitor the passage of the flows in such a channel. The sensors, located so as to bracket the flow area, would provide a continuous record of both turbidity and temperature on several levels and at several different stations in the grid. In all there would be 9 stations and at each station measurements would be taken at 3 levels or depths.

Information from the sensors would be transmitted via cable to a multichannel recording system on the shore thus permitting the passage of a density flow to be monitored on an integrated recording system. In addition to the turbidity and temperature sensors, suspended sediment samplers would be located at each station and at each level. These would be operated remotely from the shore and it should be possible to analyse the samples and relate the results to the information collected by the recording system. Thus analysable samples would be available to support the instrument readings. At the end of the season the pattern coring and depth recording of the lake would be repeated, thereby enabling the record of the season's sediment input to be evaluated. Moreover, the results of studying the cores could be related to specific flow events recorded during the season.

THE BASIN INSTRUMENTATION NETWORK

The actual deployment of instrumentation in the basin is shown in Figure 6a. The glacier climate station, consisting of: a Belfort snow and rain gauge; a Casella anemometer, a Swissteco net radiometer with an accompanying single pen Mosley recorder; and a Stevenson screen with maximum and minimum thermometers and a hygrothermograph, was established on the lower level area of the glacier. Access to the station was via a route up the moraine on the left side of the glacier and then directly out onto the ice surface. The central climate station for the entire sub-basin was located in a clearing behind the living quarters. It consisted of a 5 meter square grid layout with: a tipping bucket rain gauge; a Kipp solarimeter; and Stevenson screen (at standard height) containing maximum and minimum thermometers, a hygrothermograph, and a precision thermistor temperature probe. A standard rain gauge was located in the centre of the square. Data from the tipping bucket, the radiometer and the temperature probe was transmitted via cable down to the main recording system located along the shore of the lake. The climate instrumentation located on the delta and forming the lake station consisted of: a Thornthwaite 3 level wind system (with sensors at 2.5, 5.0 and 10.0 meters height), a class A evaporation pan, a standard Casella anemometer (at 1.5 meters); a Belfort snow and rain gauge; a Swissteco net radiometer; and a Stevenson screen containing maximum and minimum thermometers, a hygrothermograph, and a precision thermistor temperature probe; a wind direction sensor (consisting of a modified ocean engineering underwater current direction sensor); and several standard rain gauges distributed over the delta surface. A concerted effort was made to place this equipment as far out into the lake as possible. The Thornthwaite wind system stood in approximately 1 meter of water. The Stevenson screen was located in 0.75 meters water and the net radiometer was mounted on the end of a 2 meter pipe which was bolted to the base of the Stevenson screen and extended out beyond the end of the delta surface to operate in water ranging from 2.0 to 2.5 meters depth. All sensor output from the lake-delta climate instrumentation was transmitted via cable to the instrument recording system located in a cabin beside the delta. The data collected at the lake-delta climate station was supplemented by information obtained from several standard rain gauges and Cassella anemometers situated around the periphery of the lake and by a Casella anemometer placed near mid-lake on a raft.

a)

Location of Instrumentation
and Support Facilities

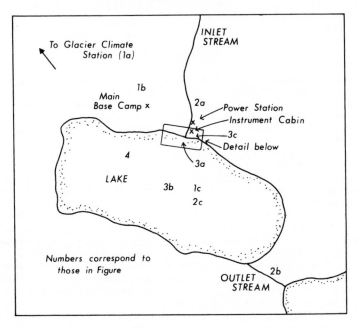

b)

Underwater Instrumentation Network

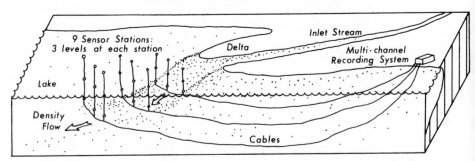

Figure 6(a). Actual deployment of the instrumentation in
the basin.
6(b). A detailed view of the underwater instrumentation network.

As intended, three water level recorders were installed. At both the inlet and outlet of the lake a Leopold and Stevens A-71 clock driven water level recorder was installed and a rated section established. On the lake itself a simple custom made potentiometric recorder with output directly to the main recording system was used to monitor lake levels. Water sampling stations were also established. Samples were initially taken with a DH-48 water sampler but a direct method of filling 500 ml. plastic bottles was soon adopted because of the large number of samples involved. Water samples were collected at 8:00, 12:00, 16:00, 20:00 and when possible 23:00 hours each day. These sample collections coincided with instrument reading times of non-automated instruments such as the Cassella anemometers and time checks on various instruments such as the water level recorders.

THE UNDERWATER NETWORK

The underwater network, designed to monitor the passage of density currents down the delta foreslope and out into the lake consisted of 27 sensor packages organized in a 3 x 3 x 3 array. Each sensor package consisted of: a) a temperature sensor, b) a photo-optical turbidity sensor, and c) a suspended sediment sampler system. The temperature sensor was a precision thermilinear thermistor which was potted in a brass tube using an abrasion resistant resin. The temperature probes are accurate to within 0.05 C from -5 to 20 C. The turbidity sensors consist of a measuring photocell and a reference photocell. The tungsten light source is filtered before reaching the photocells by the use of band pass filters thereby reducing the operating range to a pre-selected 100 nanometer band. An optical path of only 10 centimeters was selected with high sediment loads in mind. The suspended sediment sampling unit consists of a bank of 2 solenoid operated samplers capable of taking a 100 cc. sample when remotely fired from the shore facilities.

Three sensor packages are mounted one above the other on a rectangular aluminum frame (see Figure 7). This arrangement allows the units to be raised and lowered to suit the flow conditions being studied. At the same time the rigid aluminum frame allows the three packages to be treated as a single rigid unit - a distinct advantage when working from a small boat on a windy lake. A simple suspension utilizing lead anchors and several polypropelyne lines was devised which enabled the samplers to be unloaded and the photo-optical system to be checked while still ensuring the locational and orientational integrity of the system. At the lake surface, in small sealed boxes mounted on the anchoring rafts, the electrical cables from the three sensor packages were connected to a main trunk cable running to shore. There were nine such raft-anchor stations in the network. Each could be moved to a different location to deal with changes in current flow patterns. The underwater network is shown in Figure 6b.

Figure 7.   One of the underwater instrument arrays.
The location of the samplers and their corresponding
temperature and photo-optical sensors may be adjusted
on the frame to accommodate differing turbidity
current thickness.

In addition to the sensor packages, three current meters were also incorporated into the grid. One, a Hydroproducts savonius rotor type unit was situated at the bottom beside the central station of the middle line. The remaining two units, both Marsh-McBirney electromagnetic sensors measuring velocity in the X and Y plane, were located at the bottom beside the forward and rear stations in the middle of the grid. A fourth current meter and sensor package was located well out into the lake, beyond the three dimensional sensor grid, in an attempt to detect the more distal activities of the currents. All told, some 90 channels of data of various kinds were transmitted by the underwater instrument network. They provided direct information on both the motion and character of the turbidity currents.

THE RECORDING SYSTEM

The 90 channels of data from the underwater network were brought to shore via some 7000 meters of signal cable. In addition, some 20 channels of data from the hydrologic and climatic networks also crossed the delta. All data was transmitted to the instrument cabin where the central recording system was housed. The cabin, strategically placed on the edge of the lake to minimize cable lengths, also afforded a good view of the processes taking place in the lake.

The actual recording system is shown in Figure 8. The incoming data cables are wired into four different boards. On these boards the 110 channels of incoming data, plus an additional 10 channels of signals monitoring different power supply and signal strength levels within the total instrument network are reorganized and distributed to the different recording devices. The data was recorded in several different ways:

1. All the data was scanned by a Fluke Summa II data logger and was then recorded on a Kennedy incremental tape recorder. The data logger scanned at 15 channels a second and the interval between scans was varied from a minimum of one scan every ten minutes up to a maximum of a continuous scan (one cycle every 9 seconds). The scan rate was varied in response to variations in the activity levels in the system.

2. Some of the data (usually every tenth scan) was also recorded on a Sedeco paper printer incorporated into the Fluke data logger.

3. Certain channels of data for which continuous records were desirable were recorded on single and dual pen analogue strip chart recorders. Radiation, wind, and current meter information were some of the data also recorded in this manner in addition to being recorded as interval data on the data logging system. This also afforded the opportunity for detailed analysis of short term events.

4. Finally, several multipoint chart recorders totalling

Figure 8. The recording system. Signal cables from the instruments terminated at the panels. From these panels, the signals were distrubuted to the array of recording devices.

30 channels capacity were operated in parallel with the data logging system to ensure the collection of designated key data in the eventuality of a failure of the main Fluke logging system.

In addition to the numerical recording system described above, an effort was also made to provide a visual record of the events taking place. This effort took the form of a time lapse movie camera system. The camera, located on the roof of the instrument cabin overlooking the delta and lake, was programmed to take a single frame photo of the lake surface once every minute. The timing of this system was closely monitored and related to the operation of the data logging system in order that the exact readings taken at a particular time could be related to a specific picture frame. This visual record of the processes taking place proved quite useful when the interpretation of the numerical data took place.

SUPPORT FACILITIES

Laboratory and support facilities

The amount and complexity of the recording system and need for adequate laboratory and instrument facilities resulted in the construction of a building specifically with these requirements in mind. The location of the instrument cabin and laboratory is indicated in Figure 6a. The structure consists of three distinct areas: a small laboratory for hydrologic and water quality work (containing a Mettler balance, a commercial turbidity meter, and facilities for titrations and microscope work on sediment and pollen samples); a second and larger room with one portion of the room devoted to the recording system and the other portion containing a workbench and a power supply facility.

The power system

It should be apparent at this point that the recording and instrumentation systems described above require considerable amounts of electrical power. As originally conceived, the plan to supply power involved the use of portable gasoline driven alternator units. Because of the demands for carefully regulated power by most of the recording equipment and especially the data logger, the following scheme was devised: 1) the unstable alternating 110 volt current from the gasoline driven alternator was converted to a 12 volt direct current and used to charge a bank of batteries; 2) a large inverter would then draw current from the batteries and convert it back to a stable 110 volt alternating current signal; 3) and finally, a voltage stabilizer would ensure the stability of the supply. The system, while in theory sound, encountered difficulties due to the tendency for the gasoline engines driving the alternators to overheat and shut down. This situation was attributed to the inability of the cooling systems of the gasoline engines to keep the units within operating temperatures in the thinner air at the elevation of 2300 meters.

Figure 9. The hydroelectric system. The use of a gate
value permitted careful regulation of flow rates to
the pelton wheel. The entire generating system was
housed in a simple plywood A-frame shelter

Figure 10. The boat
as modified for diving
and coring. Note
the stabilizing pontoons,
the winching system and
the three point anchoring
system.

These difficulties and the high operating costs incurred by having to fly in large volumes of gasoline prompted an alternative approach.   This entailed the construction of a simple hydro-electric facility on the glacial stream at the point where it drops rapidly through the escarpment down to the lake.   The unit, custom designed by the author, consisted of a twin bucket pelton wheel which was supplied water by a four inch line consisting of aluminum irrigation pipe.   A 4000 watt commercial alternator, connected to the pelton wheel by a pulley system generated the electrical power. The power station is shown in Figure 9.

The stability of the output, generally inherent in a hydro-electric system, was further ensured through the use of a voltage stabilizing system installed in the instrument cabin.   Transmission lines from the power station entered through the back wall of the instrument cabin into the voltage monitoring system.   From there the power went through a sola voltage stabilizer and then to the recording instruments.   In addition, a backup emergency power supply consisting of a large capacity charger, a bank of batteries, and a large capacity inverter system was available.   If a power failure occurred the emergency system would take over to ensure the continuity of the recording systems operations.   This system proved quite successful holding voltage to within one volt and frequency to within one cycle over the duration of a field season.   The result was minimal recording equipment failure.

The boat

The need to obtain cores, conduct surveys, install components of the underwater and other networks, and dive in the lake required a boat with special characteristics and capacities. The weight limitations imposed by the lifting capacity of the helicopter used to transport the equipment added to the difficulty of the problem.   The solution consisted of modifying a 4.3 meter aluminum boat as follows:

1. Reinforcement of the structure to withstand the added strains of winching when cores were extracted.
2. A well with a boom and an electric winch was installed to allow coring work to be done through the middle of the boat rather than over the sides.

3. Pontoons were added to the sides of the boat to increase stability and to enable easier access for divers emerging from the water.

4. A three point anchoring system was also added to enable more exact positioning of the boat and to improve station keeping ability.

The result was a versatile and stable working platform for the conduct of the lake work.   Figure 10 indicates the general character of the changes made to the boat.

THE FIELD PROGRAM

The actual field program spanned three field seasons. During the first field season (1976) the research station, consisting of two cabins containing a field laboratory, workshop, instrument and living areas was established. Mapping of the research basin, a detailed bathymetric survey of the lake and a detailed study of the delta were carried out. Numerous cores from both the delta area and the lake bottom were collected. Based on the data collected an underflow channel was located and designated as the focal point for future study. Field testing of the underwater instrumentation packages was carried out and major components of the climatological and hydrological systems were installed and operated. It should be noted that extremely poor weather conditions during the summer field season and the problems of establishing a research station in a fairly rigorous field area hampered to some extent the work which was accomplished during the summer of 1976. Nevertheless, the field work did establish the suitability of the site, the presence of density currents, the capability of the instrumentation to measure the flows, and the logistical and base facilities for future work. During the winter of 1976-77 laboratory and field studies were carried out in order to improve the design of the underwater sensor package.

The second field season during the summer of 1977 saw a fuller development and operation of the instrumentation. Climatological data on solar and net radiation, precipitation, temperature, humidity, evaporation and wind were collected for eight weeks at the three climate stations. The stage recorders were installed on the lake and on the inlet and outlet streams. Systematic collection of water samples was carried out and major components of the water chemistry analysis (pH, calcium, magnesium, and total hardness) were undertaken in the field laboratory. Samples for future dendrochronological and palynological analysis were also collected. The emphasis of the work in the 1977 season was, however, primarily sedimentological in nature. A major underflow channel was instrumented to monitor the passage of the turbid water as it flowed down the foreset slope of the delta onto the bottomset. The monitoring system consisted of a 2-dimensional array of 9 sensor packages located in a line down the underflow channel. Time-lapse photography was done on the lake surface to provide further information, and cores were taken from the lake bottom.

In the final field season, 1978, the climatic system was expanded to increase the gauge and sampler density and the quality of the water chemistry data was increased by more frequent measurements. However, the main effort was directed at expanding the size and sophistication of the underwater sensing grid deployed along the course of the main density underflow channel. The underwater system installed in 1977 was 2-dimensional rather than 3-dimensional. In 1978 the full 3-dimensional grid was established for the monitoring of the subsurface flow patterns. Lake bottom and delta coring was also carried out.

During the course of the three summer field seasons some 40,000,000 observations were collected. In addition over 1000 water and hundreds of sediment samples were also collected. Analysis of this data is currently underway.

CONCLUSION

Although the approach used in this work was clearly demanding in terms of instrumentation needs and logistical requirements it was felt that such an approach was necessary if a more thorough understanding of the sedimentation processes in the lake was to be achieved. Moreover, in addition to the utility of such an approach for studying glacio-lacustrine processes, studies of this type may well provide rather unique opportunities to gain a greater insight into the much broader question of the general mechanics of density and particularly turbidity current flow. Proglacial lakes can provide a somewhat 'ideal' natural site, in effect outdoor laboratories, to study the character of such flows. Finally, it is hoped that the instrumentation developed for this work, and the technical expertise gained in this somewhat ideal case could be readily applied to more general situations found in reservoirs, behind dams, and in harbours where it might be of practical use in dealing with silting and erosion problems.

ACKNOWLEDGEMENTS

This project was supported by funding from NSERC and the Department of Energy Mines and Resources. The project would not have been possible without the generous loan of equipment by Professors D.C. Ford, J.A. Davies, and W. Rouse at McMaster University, the Atmospheric Environment Service and the Institute of Environmental Studies at the University of Toronto. The work was done under the supervision of Professor A.V. Jopling in the Department of Geography at the University of Toronto.

BIBLIOGRAPHY

Kindle, E.M.   1930,   Sedimentation in a glacial lake. *Journal of Geology*, 38, 81-87

Krajina, V.J.   1969,   Ecology of forest trees in British Columbia. *Ecology of Western North America*, 2(1), 1-146

Kuenan, P.H.   1951,   Mechanics of varve formation and the action of turbidity currents. *Geol. Foren. Forhandl.*, 73, 69-84.

Matthews, W.H.   1956,   Physical limnology and sedimentation in a glacial lake. *Geological Society America Bulletin*, 67, 537-552

Reesor, J.E.   1973,   Geology of the Lardeau Map-Area, East-Half, British Columbia. *Geological Survey Canada, Memoir*, 369

Rowe, J.E.   1972,   *Forest regions of Canada*. (Canadian Forestry Service, Dept. of the Environment, Information   Canada, Ottawa), 172 pp

Smith, N.D.   (this volume),   *Recent developments in sedimentological studies of glacial lakes*

12 Glacio-lacustrine sedimentation on low slope prograding delta

D.A. Leckie & S.B. McCann

ABSTRACT

Well exposed sections of lacustrine sediments at Conne River, southern Newfoundland, provide a basis for the development of a model of glaciolacustrine sedimentation in a recessional, valley glacier environment. Three distinct lithological units occur: a lower unit of thin, parallel-bedded, very fine sands, silts and clays; a middle unit of ripple cross-laminated and massive sands interbedded with clayey-silts; and an upper unit of poorly sorted, structureless sands and gravels with crude horizontal stratification. The lower unit represents lake bottom sediments emplaced by two sets of processes. The finely laminated silts were deposited out of suspension from sediments introduced into the lake by inter- and over-flow currents, and the sharp-based, graded beds were deposited by turbidity currents. The sands of the middle unit were deposited on the front of a low slope, prograding delta, subject to slump-induced grain flows. During quiet intervals, finer material settled out of suspension, and a seasonal periodicity is inferred from the couplets of sand and clayey-silt which are present. The coarse upper unit represents the proximal, glaciofluvial, topset beds of the advancing delta. The depositional processes recognized in the sediments suggest a refinement of the existing models of glaciolacustrine sedimentation to incorporate situations where a low slope, prograding glaciofluvial delta advances over glaciolacustrine sediments.

INTRODUCTION

The Conne River bank is the best exposed and most complex section of a series of glaciolacustrine and glaciofluvial deposits preserved within a few metres of present sea level in coastal locations around the head of Bay d'Espoir in south-central Newfoundland (Figure 1). Taken together the deposits indicate the ponding of a large freshwater lake at the head of the bay by an ice dam near the entrance to Little River, during the late-Wisconsinan (Leckie, 1979). Because of the excellent exposure and readily observed stratigraphy and

* D.A.Leckie, Department of Geology, McMaster University, Hamilton, Ontario, L8S 4M1.
  S.B. McCann, Department of Geography, McMaster University, Hamilton, Ontario, L8N 4M1.

261

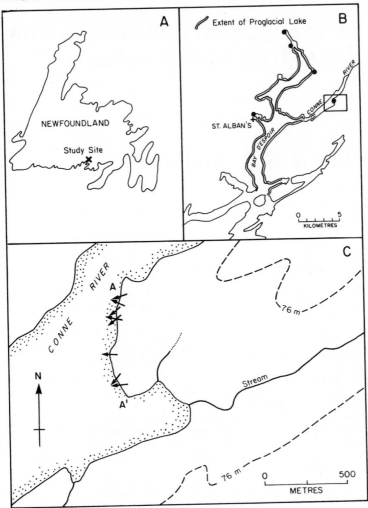

Figure 1. A & B: Location of Conne River bank at the head
   of the Bay d'Espoir in southern Newfoundland.   Dots on
   1B indicate sites where glaciolacustrine sediments are
   exposed. C: Map of study site. Vertical section of
   exposed face A-A' is given in figure 2. Paleocurrent
   arrows indicate flow to west and southwest.

sedimentary structures, the Conne River section was selected
as the site for a detailed examination of the deposits to
provide the basis for a paleoenvironmental interpretation of
sedimentary conditions in the proglacial lake. In 1978 the
outcrop was 600 m long and 15.4 m high. It lies between a
narrow inlet of the sea, known as Conne River, and a small
stream to the south, approximately 3.5 km northeast of the
settlement of Conne River. At high tides the sea reaches the
foot of outcrop and wave action causes periodic undercutting
and slumping, providing new, well exposed faces.

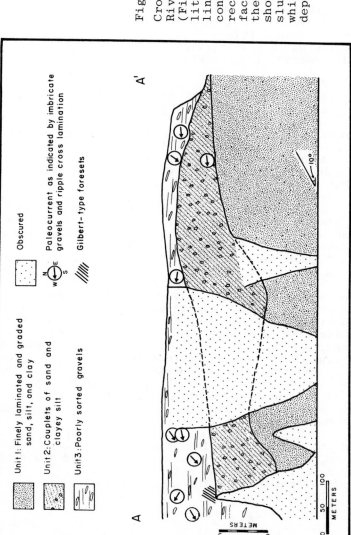

Figure 2.

Cross-section of Conne River bank, along line A-A' (Figure 1C), showing three lithologic units. Dashed lines indicate inferred contacts obscured by recent debris falls on the face. The solid line in the lower right corner shows the location of a slump scar within Unit 1, which developed during deposition.

Unit 1: Finely laminated and graded sand, silt, and clay

Unit 2: Couplets of sand and clayey silt

Unit 3: Poorly sorted gravels

Obscured

Paleocurrent as indicated by imbricate gravels and ripple cross lamination

Gilbert-type foresets

Glacio-lacustrine and marine sedimentation

The Conne River sediments were first described by Jewell (1939), who noted 'faintly varved' grey clays overlain by 'fluvial gravels' and proposed that the clays were deposited in an ice-dammed lake. Subsequently, Widmer (1950) counted more than 1600 'varves', again suggesting that they had been deposited in a freshwater proglacial lake. The deposits are more complex than either of these earlier descriptions indicate. In fact, there are three distinct lithologic units present (Figure 2), each characterized by variations in texture and sedimentary structure: a lower unit of thin, parallel-bedded, very fine sands, silts and clays; an intermediate unit of ripple cross-laminated and massive sands interbedded with clayey-silts; and an upper unit of poorly-sorted, structureless and crude horizontally stratified gravels. In the account which follows the sedimentary structures and textures of each unit are systematically described and mechanisms responsible for their deposition are deduced. In the conclusion, a palaeoenvironmental model of the depositional setting is presented.

UNIT 1: THINLY-BEDDED AND LAMINATED FINE SANDS, SILTS AND CLAYS

The lowermost and thickest unit consists of thin, gently dipping and sub-horizontally stratified very fine sands, silts and clays. Average mean grain size of several random samples is 6.8ϕ. The base of the unit rests on bedrock at one location but otherwise is not visible as it is continuous to below sea level. The upper contact is gradational over a very short vertical distance into the overlying unit and varies in elevation from 3.9 to 11 m asl (Figure 2). An unusual and deceptive feature of the unit is the marked colour difference between the lower (dark bluish grey, Munsell colour 10BG3/1) and upper (greyish olive, Munsell colour 5Y 5/3) portion. In places the greyish olive sediments extend downwards into the bluish grey sediments as what appear to be channels entrenched into the lower material. Close examination, however, shows that individual continuous laminae can be seen in every instance crossing the apparently erosive contact between the two different coloured materials. Textural analyses of five samples from each colour zone reveal no significant difference in grain size (Figure 3A). Average mean size of the dark grey sediments is 6.9ϕ and that of the dark olive is 6.6ϕ. The colour change is probably due to oxidation of the upper sediments or alternatively is diagenetic in origin, or related to groundwater seepage from the overlying coarser sandy unit.

Within the unit as a whole (both colours) there are two primary bedding types: finely laminated and graded bedding. The former is more common but both occur arbitrarily throughout the unit. In addition, the original bedding is deformed at several locations.

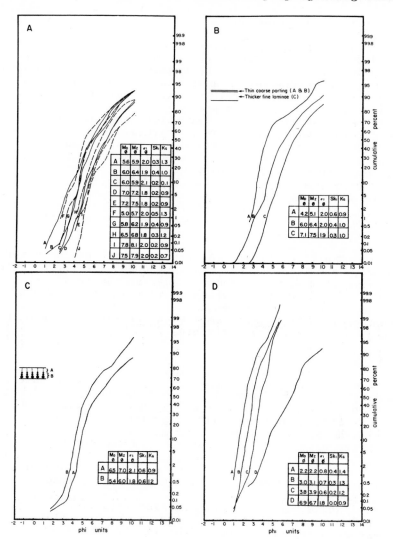

Figure 3.   Textural analyses of the Conne River sediments.
Folk (1974) statistical parameters are shown in boxes.
A.   Glaciolacustrine bottom sediments (Unit 1). Average
mean size of dark olive sediments (A to E, solid lines)
is very similar to that of dark grey sediments (F to J,
dashed lines).
B.   Single laminated couplet from finely laminated silts
in Unit 1: the thicker, fine silt layer (C) and the two
bounding, coarser silt partings (A and B).
C.   Upper (A) and lower (B) parts of a single graded bed
to Unit 1.   The lower part contains coarser grained sediment for all percentiles than the upper part.
D.   Three rippled, summer sand beds (A,B.C) and one
overlying winter fine layer (D), from Unit 2.

Glacio-lacustrine and marine sedimentation

Finely laminated sediments

These consist of dark, clayey-silt strata separated by thin
(0.5 to 2 mm) partings of slightly coarser silts and very
fine sands. The clayey-silt beds vary in thicknesses from a
fraction of a millimeter to more than 12 cm. Individual beds,
defined by the coarser partings, may contain several micro-
laminae. One 12.3 cm thick bed contained more than 70 micro-
laminae, each showing slight variations in tone and/or texture. Alternatively, there are also relatively thick (e.g.
2 cm) beds having a massive structure in which no micro-
laminae can be distinguished. Textural analysis of a single
laminated couplet (Figure 3B) gave a mean grain size of 7.5ϕ
for the clayey-silt layer and 5.1ϕ and 6.4ϕ for the two
bounding silt partings. Microscopically, some of the thicker
sand-silt partings have a sharp contact. The upper contact
grades over a relatively short vertical distance into the
finer overlying clayey silts.

Micro-faulting (Figure 4A) is common in the laminated
sediment, usually as normal faults and fault stepping with
occasional micro-graben. Some of the laminae terminate
abruptly as if broken or pulled apart (Figure 4B) and are
replaced by thoroughly mixed and disturbed sediment. Minute
fragments of the original laminae can be distinguished in the
otherwise now homogeneous mixture.

Graded beds

These are well graded, sharp based beds varying in thickness
from 0.5 to 2.0 cm (Figure 4C). Textural analyses of the
upper and lower parts of a single graded bed (Figure 3C) show
that the latter contained coarser grained sediment for all
percentiles than the former. The mean grain size difference
between the upper and lower portions is one phi unit. Occasionally the coarse portion of a graded bed will be interrupted by a 1 to 2 mm thick lamina of fine silt and clay
followed by coarser material, again grading up into the fine.

Small scale load structures, deformation features and
erosional surfaces abound in the graded bedding (Figure 4C),
although none were observed in the finely laminated sediments.
Undisturbed oriented monoliths from Unit 1 were returned to
the laboratory for detailed inspection and micro-photography.
A sample of graded bedding was dried and pried apart along its
bedding planes. At the base of one plane a series of several
parallel, coarse grained ridges, 1 to 2 mm deep, 1 to 2 mm
wide and more than 7 cm long protruded into the underlying
clayey-silts. The grooves were oriented northwest-southeast.
The lower portion of another graded bed contained several
small pebbles up to 6 mm across. This was the only noted
occurrence of material larger than sand size in this unit.
The pebbles were not ice-rafted as there was no indication of
disturbance or warping by the pebbles of overlying and underlying beds. Large scale erosional surfaces, although not
abundant, do occur. At one location a broad shallow channel
cutting down through several centimeters of laminae could be
seen.

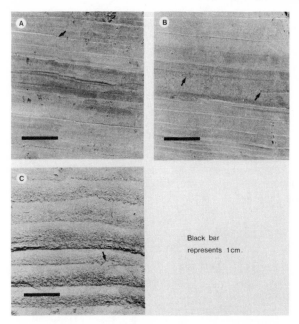

Black bar
represents 1 cm.

Figure 4.   Details of bedding and structures in Unit 1 sedi-
    ments.   Bar represents 1 cm in each case.
    A.   Finely laminated beds showing microfaulting.
    B.   Finely laminated beds showing sudden termination of
    laminae within the 1 cm thick massive bed in the centre
    of the photograph due to tension or liquefaction.   Frag-
    ments of the original bedding are still preserved in the
    massive mixture.
    C.   Sharp based graded beds, showing micro-erosional
    structures and silt rip-ups.   The difference in grain
    size between the upper and lower parts of a single
    graded bed is shown in Figure 3C.

Deformed bedding

There are several instances of continuous deformed beds, 4 cm-
2 m thick, overlain and underlain by undisturbed parallel
strata (Figure 5).   In a few instances the tops of convolu-
tions have been truncated by overlying horizontal beds. One
particular, 20 cm thick, convoluted zone, dipping along strike
to the north, could be followed for more than 150 m. The folds
vary from open anticlinal and synclinal forms to very tight
extremely involuted features.   Faulting and minor thrusting
is common in extremely contorted structures. The frequency and
magnitude of disturbance is greatest near the central portion

Figure 5. Two examples of deformed (convolute) bedding
overlying and underlying undisturbed parallel strata
within Unit 1.

of the outcrop where Unit 1 is also thinnest. With the exception of very small zones of convolute bedding there is very little secondary deformation at the southern end of the exposure.

Interpretation

The occurrence of two distinct types of bedding (finely laminated and graded) indicates that two independent processes contributed to the deposition of Unit 1.

The finely laminated sediments settled out of suspension having been introduced into the lake as interflow and overflow currents. Recent process studies of glaciolacustrine sedimentation have demonstrated the existence (Gustavson, 1975 a,b; Gilbert, 1975) and predominance (Smith, 1978) of these currents. The density of the inflowing water is insufficient to create an underflow current but there is enough sediment in suspension to construct visible laminations (Smith, 1978). Harms (1974) theorized that coarse to fine silt introduced into a density stratified basin as an interflow current would settle out of suspension creating thin parallel strata, less than 1 to 2 mm thick, of alternating light coloured coarse silt laminae and dark, finer sediments. In his model, density stratification was the result of differences in salinity and temperature between inflowing and basin water; the lake studied by Smith was thermally stratified. Theakstone (1976) and Shaw (1977) interpreted very finely laminated silts with a base of 'minor sand laminae' as having been deposited out of suspension in glacial lakes.

The consistent lack of flow structures or erosional features in the finely laminated sediments strongly confirms that current action did not play a significant role. Some of the thicker, slightly coarser sand partings (up to 2 mm) however, may have been transported by weak, sluggish underflow currents which stagnated in the immediate area producing the overlying massive non-laminated clayey-silt beds. Although the micro-laminae undoubtedly represent periodic variations in sediment supply or rate of sedimentation, the time cycle involved (diurnal to annual) cannot be distinguished.

The micro-faulting of the finely laminated material (Figure 4A) occurred as the result of consolidation and dewatering. Consolidation may also have been responsible for the suddenly terminated laminae in Figure 4B. As compaction and consolidation progressed water would have been released from the finer grained laminae increasing pore water pressure in the slightly coarser material and decreasing its shear strength to the point where liquefaction occurred, creating a homogeneous medium with occasional preserved fragments of the original bedding.

A turbidity current origin is proposed to account for the graded bedding and related features. The idea is not new to glaciolacustrine sedimentation, having been suggested as a (partial) mechanism of 'varve' formation by several authors (e.g., Kuenen, 1951; Jopling and Walker, 1968; Banerjee, 1973;

Ashley, 1975; Gustavson, 1975b; Harrison, 1975; Shaw, 1977).
The best documented mechanism for generating lacustrine
turbidity currents is one where sediment laden incoming water,
having a higher density than ambient lake water, sinks and
flows as a density underflow current capable of erosion and
deposition (Houboult and Jonker, 1968; Gilbert, 1975;
Gustavson, 1975a,b; Lambert et al 1976). The result is a
series of graded beds formed by a pulsating turbidity current
(representing diurnal, subseasonal, seasonal and/or possibly
annual cycles). Another possible generating mechanism is
subaqueous slumping of the prodeltaic slope. When slumping
does not create turbidity currents the displaced sediment
often accumulates at the foot of the delta slope as slump
mounds (Mathews, 1956; Fulton and Pullen, 1969; Gilbert, 1972,
1975; Gustavson, 1975b; Smith, 1978).

The lack of cross-bedding in the graded beds, suggests
that most of the deposition from the turbidity currents was
from suspension, there being no, or little, bedload transport.
The thin laminae (~1 mm) of clayey silt which occasionally
interrupt the coarse portions of the graded beds suggest that
there were short pauses in the density underflow currents
which permitted fines to settle out of suspension.

The deformed bedding is probably a result of subaqueous
slumping, though other processes such as plastic deformation
at the time of deposition or shearing due to the overriding
turbidity current, cannot be ruled out. Slumping can occur
on lake bottom slopes as low as 1° (Morgenstern, 1967), and
Shaw (1977) has presented an argument for slumps occurring on
very low slope angles as the result of compaction of lake
bottom sediment. Sediment shifting a short distance over a
bed of detachment will maintain its plasticity, contorting
and deforming the displaced bedding. The slump scar shown
on Figure 2 is considered to represent a disturbance which
occurred on the lake floor during sedimentation, as only the
lower part of Unit 1 has been disrupted. The upper beds of
the unit are continuous, curving gently over the top of the
scar.

An annual period of deposition sometimes characterizes
finely laminated couplets settling out of suspension from
inter- and overflows (Smith, 1978) and from density underflow
generated graded bedding (Gilbert, 1975; Gustavson et al,
1975; Gustavson, 1975b), but in Unit 1 at the Conne River
bank there is no good evidence of an annual periodicity. A
distinct clay drape would be expected (Agterberg and Banerjee,
1969; Ashley, 1975) but was not observed, nor was an over-
abundance of clay noted. The uniform dark grey colour of
Unit 1 indicates deposition of the sediments occurred under
anaerobic reducing conditions suggesting stagnant bottom
water having a low oxygen content (Theakstone, 1976).

UNIT 2. RHYTHMICALLY BEDDED RIPPLE CROSS-LAMINATED SANDS AND CLAYEY SILTS

The middle unit consists of rhythmically bedded, medium to fine grained sands and clayey-silts. It varies in thickness from 1 to 8 m (Figure 2). The lower contact is gradational into Unit 1, the change being defined by an upwards thickening and coarsening of sand layers between alternating clayey-silts. The upper contact is erosive, having been scoured by the overlying unit. The sands generally exhibit small-scale cross-laminations; palaeoflow at one location was towards 255° (Figure 1). Sand in any one bed is moderately well to well sorted and mean grain size varies slightly from bed to bed (Figure 3D). There are occasionally, relatively thick, massive structureless beds of sand with a wavy upper contact and a planar lower contact.

Alternating with the sands are beds of poorly sorted clayey-silts (Figure 3D) of relatively uniform thickness (1 to 2 cm). The contacts between the sand and overlying silt were either sharp or transitional, the latter especially in the lower portion of the unit. The lower contact of the sand is always sharp. Couplets of sand and clayey-silt near the base of the unit have an overall higher proportion of silt to sand than those higher up towards the middle or at the top. There were several instances where sequences of couplets showed thinning and fining upwards tendencies over a vertical distance of 0.3 to 0.5 m (i.e., within a given sequence the thickness of the sand portion of a couplet decreases upwards although the silt-clay remained relatively constant).

Load, flow and flame structures are common in several sets of beds. Normal faults also occur, although infrequently.

Interpretation

The alternation of sand and clayey-silt beds is typical of deposition in proximal glaciolacustrine environments (Gustavson *et al*, 1975; Gustavson, 1975). The cross-laminated sands were transported as bedload by density underflow currents on gently sloping deltaic foresets during the summer melt season, whereas the overlying clayey-silts settled out of suspension in quiet water during the following winter. Although it was not possible to measure the foreset slope angle it probably had a dip of ~5°, based on similarities with a kame delta measured by Jopling and Walker (1968). Any given couplet of sand and clayey-silt is a varve representing a year's deposition. The lower couplets with a high silt to sand ratio, represent deposition on the distal prodelta slope immediately over-lying the lake bottom sediments; couplets higher in the unit, with a much lower silt to sand ratio are a more proximal pro-graded facies. The thinning and fining upwards of some sequences of couplets is due to the thinning of the summer sand layer. This may be due to channel abandonment as distri-butaries on the delta top gradually shifted in position from year to year. Alternatively, increasing distance from the ice-front may have been responsible but this is highly improbable as the sequences are recurrent and appear to have occurred over short periods of time.

The beds of structureless sands, with a planar lower and undulatory upper contact, are similar to features described by Shaw (1977) as grain flows. Grain flows can occur on delta fronts as the result of drawdown of the lake late in the melt season. They occur on slopes as low as 3 to 6^0 and may be accelerated to a point where transformation into a low concentration turbidity current occurs.

The deformation features (flame, flow and load structures) occur as the result of relatively heavy, high porosity sands being deposited onto a lower porosity somewhat plastic clayey silt layer which is very malleable and easily deformed. The features are characteristic of several environments and not diagnostic by themselves (Potter and Pettijohn, 1963).

UNIT 3: POORLY-SORTED SAND AND GRAVEL

The uppermost unit consists of poorly-sorted, structureless and crude horizontally stratified gravels with occasional pockets and pinchouts of better sorted pebbles and sands. Individual clasts are generally less than 8 cm long although the largest clast observed had a long axis of 20 cm. The base of the unit is sharp and erosive, with occasional small channels ~1 m across and less than 0.5 m deep incised into the underlying unit. Its thickness varies; at one location it changes from 1.8 to 3.6 m thick over a horizontal distance of 9 m.

The gravels are moderately imbricated. Results of pebble fabric analysis (resultant vector mean) at 8 locations (Figures 1 and 2) indicate that flows responsible for the gravel transport and deposition, ranged from between 230^0 to 275^0. The gravels are thickest at the north end of the section and at one location (Figure 1) there is 1.5 m of poorly exposed angle of respose gravel foresets dipping to the south-southwest. (The foresets are probably more extensive but the face is badly slumped.)

Interpretation

These sands and gravels are glaciofluvial, braided outwash. The imbricate clasts, crude horizontal stratification and general lack of cross-bedding suggest deposition at a location fairly proximal to the source (Boothroyd and Ashley, 1975, figure 25). This material formed the delta surface over which sediment and meltwater were transported to the prodelta slope from the glacier. It appears, based on paleocurrent data (Figures 1 and 2), that two meltwater systems may have been operative, occupying the Conne River valley and the valley of the smaller stream to the south. The southwest oriented paleoflow directions, especially at the north end of the section, the southwest dipping foresets and the much thicker gravels of what may have been a major channel distributary represent flow coming out of the Conne River valley.

SUMMARY AND CONCLUSIONS

On the basis of sedimentary structures and textures the sequence of deposits exposed at the Conne River bank is interpreted as a low slope (~5°), prograding, glaciofluvial delta which advanced over glaciolacustrine bottom sediments. Figures 6 and 7 are diagrammatic models illustrating the processes and depositional environments of the three distinct lithologic units which are present.

Unit 1 was deposited on the glacial lake floor by two different processes. The finely laminated strata settled out of suspension from sediments introduced into the lake as interflow or underflow currents and the series of multiple graded beds are the result of turbidity current deposition. The best understood mechanism for generating lacustrine turbidity currents is density underflows where density differences between incoming meltwater having a relatively high silt/clay content and ambient lake water cause the inflow to plunge to the lake bottom as a continuous turbidity current (Gustavson, 1975a,b; Gilbert, 1972; Lambert et al,1976). Significance of the density underflow varies from year to year as they may occur for only a few hours one or two times during the melt season in one year, and for at least half the season in the next (Church and Gilbert, 1975). Contorted bedding (Unit 1), faulting (Unit 1) and grain flows (Unit 2) indicate that slumping occurred on the lake floor and delta front and may have been a second mechanism for generating the turbidity currents. Deposition on the lake floor apparently alternated between episodes of turbidity current generation and sedimentation by suspension from above. Deposition from suspension of the interflow and overflow introduced material occurred throughout the melt season but was only preserved when turbidity currents were not active. It is not possible to assign any periodicity to the bedding in Unit 1. Agterberg and Banerjee (1969) and Banerjee (1973, figure 2) suggested that the upper portion of a single turbidite, or the top of a sequence of turbidites will be capped by a winter clay layer. This could not be discerned in the graded bedding, nor anything similar in the laminated material.

Unit 2, consisting of alternating cross-laminated sands and clayey silts, was deposited as a low slope, prograding delta. Episodic slumping caused massive grain flows which occasionally developed into turbidity currents. The repetitive couplets of sands and clayey silts represent the summer melt and winter freeze-up, respectively. Why seasonal effects can be seen in Unit 2 but not in Unit 1 cannot be explained at this point. The upper unit represents the glaciofluvial, or topset, portion of the delta. The sands and gravels were probably deposited in a fairly proximal location relative to the ice front. Paleocurrent data and other evidence suggests the influence and convergence of two outwash systems.

The mean grain size of the sediments increases upwards through the three units from silts and clays to alternating sands and silts, to sands and gravels. A similar coarsening trend of sediments has been observed in samples from a modern lacustrine environment where a fluvial supplied delta is prograding out onto the lake floor (Gilbert, 1972, figure 6).

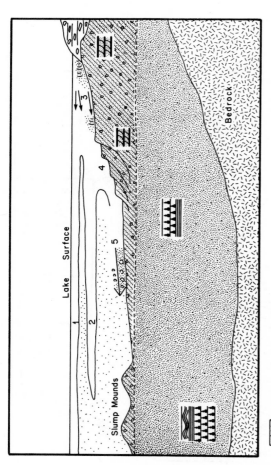

Figure 6. Sedimentary character and inferred depositional processes at the Conne River bank: 1 – Overflow; 2 – Interflow; 3 – Underflow; 4 – Subaqueous Slumping; 5 – Turbidity current.

UNIT 1. Lake bottom sediments.

UNIT 2. Low slope prograding delta.

UNIT 3. Glacio-fluvial gravels.

Deformed bedding.

Parallel laminations.

Graded bedding.

Alternating couplets of clayey silt and rippled or massive sand.

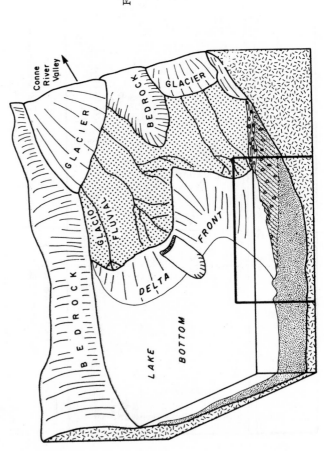

Figure 7. Diagrammatic model demonstrating the depositional environment of the Conne River sediments.

ACKNOWLEDGEMENTS

The research was funded by NRC Operating Grant A5082, and Department of Energy, Mines and Resources Agreement No.2239-4-154-77 to S. B. McCann.

REFERENCES

Agterberg, F.P. and I. Banerjee, 1969, Stochastic model for the deposition of varves in glacial Lake Barlow-Ojibway, Ontario, Canada. *Canadian Journal of Earth Sciences*, 6, 625-652

Ashley, G.M. 1975, Rhythmic sedimentation in glacial lake Hitchcock, Massachusetts - Connecticut, in *Glacio-fluvial and glaciolacustrine sedimentation*, ed A.V. Jopling and B.C.McDonald, (Society of Economic Paleontologists and Mineralogists, Special Publication No.23), 304-320

Banerjee, I. 1973, Sedimentology of Pleistocene glacial varves in Ontario, Canada. *Geological Survey of Canada, Bulletin,* 226, 1-44

Boothroyd, J.C. and G.M.Ashley, 1975, Processes, bar morphology, and sedimentary structures on braided outwash fans, Northeastern Gulf of Alaska, in *Glaciofluvial and glaciolacustrine sedimentation,* ed A.V.Jopling and B.C.McDonald, (Society of Economic Paleontologists and Mineralogists, Special Publication No.23), 193-222

Church, M. and R. Gilbert, 1975, Proglacial fluvial and lacustrine environments, in *Glaciofluvial and glacio-lacustrine sedimentation,* ed A.V.Jopling and B.C. McDonald, (Society of Economic Paleontologists and Mineralogists, Special Publication, No.23), 22-100

Folk, R.L. 1974, *Petrology of sedimentary rocks.* (Hemphill's Austin, Texas), 170 pp.

Fulton, R.J. and M.J.L.T.Pullen, 1969, Sedimentation in Upper Arrow Lake, British Columbia. *Canadian Journal of Earth Sciences,* 6, 785-791

Gilbert, R. 1972, Observations on sedimentation at Lillooet Delta, British Columbia, in *Mountain geomorphology,* ed O. Slaymaker and H.J.McPherson, (Tantalus Press, Vancouver), 187-194

Gilbert, R. 1975, Sedimentation in Lillooet Lake, British Columbia, *Canadian Journal of Earth Sciences,* 12, 1697-1711

Gustavson, T.C. 1975a, Bathymetry and sediment distribution in proglacial Malaspina Lake, Alaska. *Journal of Sedimentary Petrology,* 45, 450-461

Gustavson, T.C. 1975b, Sedimentation and physical limnology in proglacial Malaspina Lake, southeastern Alaska, in *Glaciofluvial and glaciolacustrine sedimentation,* ed A.V.Jopling and B.C.McDonald, (Society of Economic Paleontologists and Mineralogists, Special Publication, No.23), 249-263

Gustavson, T.C., Ashley, G.M. and J.C.Boothroyd, 1975, Depositional sequences in glaciolacustrine deltas, in *Glaciofluvial and glaciolacustrine sedimentation*, ed A.V.Jopling and B.C.McDonald, (Society of Economic Paleontologists and Mineralogists, Special Publication, No.23), 264-280

Harms, J.C. 1974, Brushy Canyon Formation, Texas: a deep water density current deposit. *Geological Society of America, Bulletin*, 85, 1763-1784

Harrison, S.S. 1975, Turbidite origin of glaciolacustrine sediments, Woodcock Lake, Pennsylvania. *Journal of Sedimentary Petrology*, 45, 738-744

Houboult, J.J.H.C. and J.B.M.Jonker, 1968, Recent sediments in the eastern part of the Lake of Geneva (Lac Leman). *Geologie en Mijnbouw*, 47, 131-148

Jewell, W.B. 1939, Geology and mineral deposits of the Baie d'Espoir Area. *Newfoundland Geological Survey, Bulletin*, 17

Jopling, A.V. and R.G.Walker, 1968, Morphology and origin of ripple-drift cross-lamination, with examples from the Pleistocene of Massachusetts. *Journal of Sedimentary Petrology*, 38, 971-984

Kuenen, P.H. 1951, Mechanics of varve formation and the action of turbidity currents. *Geologiska Foreningens i Stockholm Fordhandlingar*, 73, 69-84

Lambert, A.M., K.R.Kelts and W.F.Marshall, 1976, Measurements of density underflows from Walensee, Switzerland. *Sedimentology*, 23, 87-105

Leckie, D.A. 1979, *Late Quaternary history of the Hermitage Bay area, Newfoundland*. (M.Sc. thesis, McMaster University, Hamilton, Ontario), 188 pp.

Mathews, W.H. 1956, Physical limnology and sedimentation in a glacial lake. *Geological Society of America, Bulletin*, 67, 537-552

Morgenstern, N.R. 1967, Submarine slumping and the initiation of turbidity currents, in *Marine geotechnique*, ed A.F.Richards, (University of Illinois Press), 189-220

Potter, P.E. and F.J.Pettijohn, 1963, *Paleocurrent and Basin Analysis*, (Academic Press, New York), 296 pp

Shaw, J. 1977, Sedimentation in an alpine lake during deglaciation, Okanagan Valley, British Columbia, Canada, *Geografiska Annaler*, 59A, 221-240

Smith, N.D. 1978, Sedimentation processes and patterns in a glacier-fed lake with low sediment input. *Canadian Journal of Earth Sciences*, 15, 741-756

Theakstone, W.H., 1976, Glacial lake sedimentation, Auslerdalsisen, Norway. *Sedimentology*, 23, 671-688

Widmer, K. 1950, *Geology of the Hermitage Bay area, Newfoundland*. (Unpublished Ph.D. thesis, Princeton University)

13 Coarse grained facies of glacio-marine deposits near Ottowa, Canada

Richard J. Cheel & Brian R. Rust

ABSTRACT

Some Late Quaternary sand and gravel ridges near Ottawa are
believed to have formed by coalescence of subaqueous outwash
fans deposited where glacial metlwater conduits emerged from
the Wisconsin ice front beneath the Champlain Sea. The ridges
are approximately parallel to the direction of ice transport,
and developed as the ice front retreated northward. Exposures in the ridges have allowed a detailed investigation of
coarse-grained glacio-marine deposits in relation to changing
ice front morphology.

Clast-supported cobble to boulder gravel was deposited on
the fan apex, near the mouth of the conduit. Clast long axes
are oriented either normal or parallel to the flow direction,
depending on current velocity and clast size. Downfan from
the gravel, cross-stratified sand accumulated, occasionally
interbedded with flow till. These deposits are cut by steep-
sided sand-filled channels that were eroded into the fan surface by cold, dense, sediment-laden currents issuing from
the conduit. Soft-sediment deformation structures are common
in silty fine sand on distal parts of the fan. They are preserved as thick units filling gravitational slumps, and above
buried blocks of ice.

All the above facies ideally are present in subaqueous
outwash deposits, although variations are known, and are
attributed to confinement of the depositional site within
inlets of the glacier front. Variations include: 1) Lower
incidence of cross-stratified sand due to extensive reworking
by channel migration within the inlet; 2) Absence of mud-
sized sediments, transported beyond the inlet; 3) Intense
deformation in response to the melting of ice walls and buried
glacial ice.

[1] Richard J. Cheel, Department of Geology, McMaster University,
Hamilton, Ontario, Canada, L8S 4M1
[2] Brian R. Rust, Department of Geology, University of Ottawa,
Ottawa, Ontario, Canada, K1N 6N5

INTRODUCTION

Between approximately 10 000 and 13 000 years BP the Ottawa
Valley was occupied by the Champlain Sea (Richard, 1978), an
arm of the Atlantic Ocean which flooded the then isostatically
depressed land surface as the Laurentide Ice Sheet retreated
northward (Rust and Romanelli, 1975). Sediments believed to
have been deposited in the submerged proglacial environment
are well exposed in excavations into linear ridges of sand
and gravel (Figure 1) which trend approximately parallel to
the last direction of ice advance, as indicated by local
striae and drumlin orientations (Gadd 1963, Richard *et al*,
1974). Access to these exposures has provided an excellent
opportunity to examine the sedimentology of coarse-grained
glacio-marine deposits. In the literature sediments of this
type have mostly been described in terms of ice-rafting or
shoreline processes, but in the present case unidirectional
meltwater currents were the main depositional agency.

This paper describes the sediments of those ridges which
were interpreted by Rust and Romanelli (1975) as deposits
from glacial meltwater on subaqueous fans at the ice front.
They termed such deposits 'subaqueous outwash' to distinguish
them from subaerial outwash and glaciofluvial channel deposits.
The subaqueous outwash environment is also distinct from the
esker delta environment (De Geer, 1940) which, by the
definition of the term 'delta' (Coleman, 1976; Miall, 1976),
includes both subaerial and subaqueous deposition where a
meltwater conduit terminates in a standing body of water.
Rust (1977) described the facies of subaqueous outwash and
their distribution on a single fan. Continued work in the
Ottawa area, particularly in new exposures along the Stittsville Ridge (Figure 1) has led to a better understanding of
subaqueous outwash deposits.

FACIES OF SUBAQUEOUS OUTWASH

Proximal gravel facies

Clast-supported gravel, ranging from cobbles and pebbles to
boulders several metres in diameter, make up the most proximal
facies of the subaqueous outwash fan. Clasts are generally
rounded to subrounded and composed of materials derived from
local Paleozoic carbonates and Precambrian rocks. Clasts
making up the framework of the gravel are poorly sorted at
any one location, as is the sandy gravel matrix.

Two preferred clast fabrics have been observed: 1) *a*-
axes oriented parallel to *ab* plane imbrication; and 2) *a*-
axes normal to *ab* imbrication. Johansson (1963) found that
a-axis parallel imbrication was indicative of transport by
saltation over the bed. *A*-axis normal to imbrication, however,
has been observed to develop in gravels which have been
transported by rolling on the bed (Rust, 1972).

The large clast size and evidence of transport by saltation is suggestive of deposition near the mouth of the

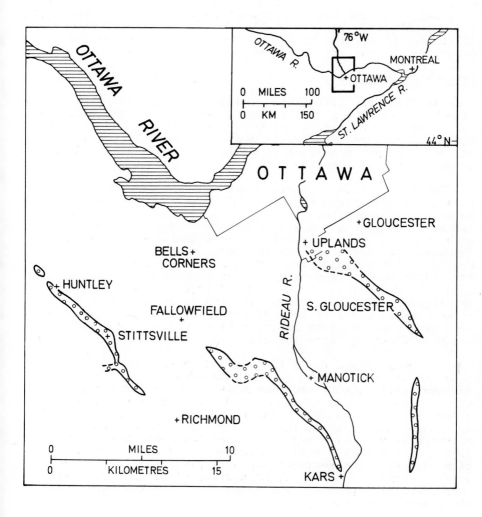

Figure 1. Location map for linear sand and gravel ridges in the vicinity of Ottawa (circle ornament)

meltwater conduit, where current velocities were greatest.
Rolling bed-load probably was deposited near the conduit when
flow was below the velocity required to induce saltation. One
would expect the mode of transport to vary, depending on clast
size and local meltwater discharge from the glacier. Although
not yet observed, it is probable that both types of clast
fabric may be present in any one gravel unit, reflecting
annual or seasonal variation in meltwater discharge.

Interchannel facies

Down-fan from the gravels the sediments are predominantly sand
sized, fining from granular sand to silty fine sand away from
the meltwater conduit. These deposits contain abundant primary
current structures and are termed 'interchannel facies' here
because they are preserved in areas between channels, described
below, which cut into the fan.

The most proximal interchannel deposits are planar
stratified granular sands and fine gravels. These are believed
to have been deposited quite near to the proximal gravel
facies although the transition between the two has not yet
been observed. Cross-stratified sands dominate the interchannel
deposits, including tabular and wedge-shaped planar and trough
cross-stratification (Blatt, Middleton and Murray, 1972).
The thickness of planar sets ranges from 10 to 25 cm, while
trough cross-sets are between 3 and 10 cm thick. Occasionally
interbedded with the cross-stratified sands are massive sands,
in some cases normally graded, which were probably deposited
from high concentration sediment flows during periods of high
sediment discharge from the glacier.

Climbing ripple drift (Joping and Walker, 1968) in fine
sand and silty fine sand occurs interstratified with the
coarser sands, but is predominantly preserved at the highest
stratigraphic levels exposed. Individual co-sets range from
a few centimetres to 75 cm thick and are commonly separated
by massive fine sand or thin silt strata. In general, the
climbing ripple units and associated sediments are interpreted as the most distal fan sediments, deposited from waning
high concentration sediment flows originating from the meltwater conduit. Silt units, separating climbing ripple sets,
were probably deposited from suspension when discharge from
the glacier was low.

Sparsely dispersed throughout the cross-stratified sands
are isolated clasts, commonly striated, that range in size
from pebbles to boulders (Figure 2). These are interpreted
as dropstones derived from glacier ice floating over the
active fan. Poorly sorted matrix-supported gravel, containing
large angular clasts, is locally observed interstratified with
cross-stratified deposits (Figure 3). It is interpreted as
subaquatic flow till which accumulated on the adjacent glacier
and subsequently slid onto the fan.

Channel facies

Three types of channels have been recognized in the subaqueous

Figure 2.   Angular boulder within cross-stratified sands
            below a Type A channel. Note the discontinuous gravel
            beds within the sands which fill the channel. (The
            exposure is approximately parallel to the trend of
            the channel.)

Figure 3.   Matrix-supported gravel interstratified with
            interchannel sands. Overlying clast-supported gravel is
            believed to have been deposited during the migration of
            the site of proximal gravel deposition near the fan
            apex. Stick for scale is 1.5 m long.

Figure 4. Massive sand-filled channel (Type B) with inverse
     to normal grading at the base, eroded into cross-
     stratified sands. Knife for scale is approximately
     25 cm long.

outwash deposits of the Ottawa area. These are: Type A
channels filled with horizontally stratified medium sand, with
imbricate gravel along the erosional channel base and along
bedding planes within the sands; Type B channels filled with
massive sands; and Type C channels filled with subhorizont-
ally laminated sands.

     Although sections cut at right angles to the channels are
rare, the channel form has been observed in some cases
(Figure 4). They are relatively steep-sided asymmetric forms
with erosional bases and height-to-width ratios of approximately 0.40. The largest channels are of Type A, which
generally occur in the lowest stratigraphic position of all
the channels. In general the size of the channels decreases
at higher stratigraphic levels.

     Type A channels contain rounded to well rounded pebbles,
cobbles and boulders with *a*-axes oriented normal to the
imbrication of the *ab* planes. An exposure parallel to the

axis of a Type A channel is shown in Figure 2. Note that
while gravel beds occur along particular bedding planes they
are not continuous along the length of the channel. It is
the discontinuous nature of the gravel beds within channels
which may cause confusion in differentiating between Type A
channels and Types B and C.

Type B and C channels are very similar, except for the
absence of internal stratification in the former. A notable
feature of both of these types is the occasional occurrence
of silt or clay laminae adjacent to the erosional boundary
of the channels. Angular clay intraclasts and rounded limestone pebbles were observed within some Type B channels, as
well as inverse to normal grading near their bases (Figure 4).

The imbricate pebbles and boulders at the bases of Type A
channels suggest that they were formed by erosive currents
transporting gravel as bed load. The gravel was probably
locally eroded from sediments cut by the channels and transported relatively short distances to be deposited in discontinuous beds along the base. Sand-size sediment, transported in suspension along the channels, was deposited on the
interchannel areas and at more distal positions on the fan.
From time to time these channels were apparently inactive,
depositing the silt and clay laminae observed above the
erosional boundary of some Type B and C channels. Imbricate
gravel along bedding planes within Type A channels indicates
that they were repeatedly occupied by strong, erosive currents
transporting gravel. The channels are believed to have
bifurcated and become smaller in the downfan direction, causing the vertical decrease in channel size seen in exposures
that preserve sediment deposited at increasingly distal
positions as the ice front retreated.

The mode of channel formation outlined required frequent
pulses of dense currents over the fan. The high density of
these currents, which resulted in underflows across the fan
rather than mixing with standing water at the ice front, may
have been due to high concentrations of suspended sediment
in the meltwater and/or its low temperature. The pulsating
nature of the currents is a typical feature of glacial meltwater streams (Sugden and John, 1976) in which summer discharge commonly doubles over 24 hour periods in response to
daily melting. More dramatic increases have been observed
in response to precipitation on the ice. One might expect,
therefore, that these high discharge events, of relatively
short duration, would provide pulses of cold, sediment-laden
water to the subaqueous outwash fan.

The sand-size sediment in the channels is believed to
have been deposited by mass flows, although the specific type
of flow (see Middleton and Hampton, 1976) could not be identified in all cases. For most of the channels there are
insufficient criteria for the exact determination of transport
mechanism, except for massive sand-filled channels with inverse
to normal grading at their bases. Sallenger (1979) found that
the heavy and light minerals in sediments which were inversely
graded had size distributions comparable to those calculated

Figure 5. Broad, channel-like structure filled with deformed silty-fine and fine sand, cutting into cross-stratified sands at site S-4. Shovel for scale (centre) is approximately 1 m high.

Figure 6. Thick unit of soft-sediment deformation structures immediately adjacent to climbing ripple beds. Shovel for scale is approximately 1 m high.

for sediments supported by dispersive pressure during transport (Bagnold, 1954). The presence of inverse grading in
some of the channels is interpreted, therefore, to indicate
sediment transport as grain flows (Middleton and Hampton,
1976). The grain flows may have been initiated by failure
of the upstream channel walls. Alternatively, sediment
derived directly from the meltwater conduit may have been
sufficiently concentrated that dispersive pressure became an
important support mechanism during downslope transport.

Slump facies

Rust (1977) described soft-sediment deformation structures
in subaqueous outwash deposits and included them in the channel
facies. However, more extensive exposures in new excavations
have shown that the deformed sediments occur in two different
situations: 1) in broad channel-like structures with erosional
bases (Figure 5), and 2) in a unit showing abrupt lateral
contact with a thick unit of climbing ripples (Figure 6), the
base of which has not been observed.

In both situations ball and pillow structures are overlain
by dish structures in a silty fine sand matrix. In the channel-
like situation the sequence often includes convolute stratification at the base. The genesis of the sequence of structures is believed to be essentially the same for both situations and has been attributed by Cheel and Rust (1980) to
rapid sediment dewatering. Each situation has a more specific
environmental implication, although both are included in the
'slump facies' because of their similar sedimentology.

The channel-like structures are interpreted as slump
scars (Figure 5), that developed on the subaqueous outwash
fan and were subsequently filled by sediments which also failed
in response to excess pore water pressures. The slumps are
much broader than the stratigraphically lower channels and
are analogous to slumps observed on the continental slope,
the surficial expression of which has been described by
Kelling and Stanley (1976, Figure 27). The possible causes
of slumping on the fan include: 1) shock from earthquakes or
icebergs impacting on the nearby bed; 2) the rapid deposition
of a sediment, causing a sharp increase in the pore water
pressure of the subjacent sediment; and 3) failure of silt and
fine sand which had been deposited on a surface sloping at 15°
or more (Lowe, 1976, p 295).

Where the deformation structures occur in abrupt lateral
contact with adjacent climbing ripples strata, the latter are
bent sharply upwards (Figure 6). Bending is attributed to
upward movement of fluidized sediment (see below), while the
abrupt contact is thought to represent the edge of a former
buried ice mass. Articulated valves of marine molluscs are
preserved in some of the uppermost ball and pillow structures
within the deformed unit. A radiocarbon date of 11 300 ± 120
years BP was obtained from these fossils by Gadd (1978), who
questioned Rust's (1977) interpretation of the deposit as
subaqueous outwash. The subaqueous outwash interpretation
requires proximity to the ice front, whereas the fossiliferous

sediments were deposited when the glacier front was perhaps 80 km north of the present site. We believe that the sediments in this unit were deformed in response to the release of water by melting of ice buried below impermeable distal interchannel deposits. The ice persisted, insulated by the overlying sediment, for some time after the glacier had retreated, and after the fan surface, no longer active, had been populated by a marine fauna. Gradual melting caused an increase in pore water pressure at the base of the sediment pile, which eventually was sufficient to induce local fluidization of the overlying sediment and its disruption by vertical fluidization channels. The fossiliferous beds at the top of the section were also disrupted, sinking downwards as fine material passed upward through the vertical channels as a water-rich slurry. This material accumulated at the surface, where it dewatered more slowly, to form dish structures (Cheel and Rust, 1980).

DISCUSSION

Continued investigation of subaqueous outwash deposits in the Ottawa area has warranted some revision of the depositional model postulated by Rust (1977). Figure 7 summarizes the facies that have been described here and shows their distribution on a single fan. Also shown is the paleocurrent distribution which would be expected from a large number of directional measurements in all the facies. However, ridges formed by the longitudinal overlap of fans as the ice front retreated predictably would have a different paleocurrent distribution. The topographic effect of the ridge would deflect currents symmetrically from the ridge axis.

As the ice front retreated, the resultant vertical succession would comprise a fining-upward sequence, with clast-supported gravel at the base and increasingly distal interchannel sediments at higher stratigraphic levels. Channels become smaller upward and are no longer present at levels where climbing ripple units dominate. Simple sequences are not always present, however, because the rate of ice retreat is probably sufficiently slow to allow a number of annual deposits to be superimposed at any one place on the fan. The sedimentology of each annual deposit would be strongly controlled by the hydrologic regime of the glacier. Furthermore, by analogy with deltas (Coleman, 1976) and submarine fans (Walker, 1978) one would expect the site of deposition on the fan to migrate laterally with time. An active lobe would develop in one place and then be abandoned as deposition decreased slopes on that part of the fan. The migration of an active lobe could accumulate a coarsening-upward sequence of proximal gravels over interchannel sediments.

Slump facies are preserved in distal parts of the fan where fine sediment is available to trap original pore water and meltwater from buried ice, rendering the sediment prone to deformation by rapid dewatering. Where coarser sediment overlies melting ice, faults develop at the border of the ice mass, as shown by Rust and Romanelli (1975, Figure 12). In

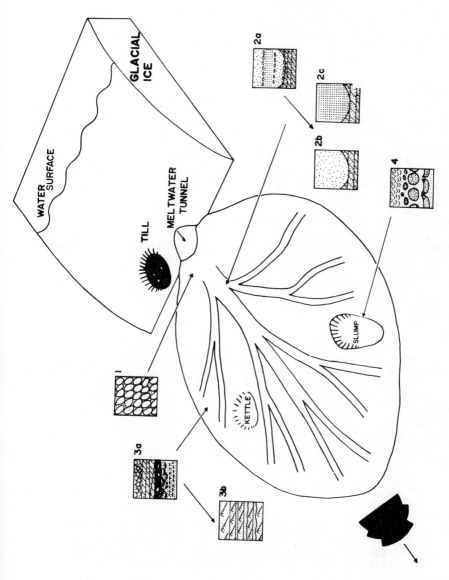

Figure 7.
Deposition model
for a single sub-
aqueous outwash
fan.
1) Proximal gravel
   facies,
2) Channel facies,
3) Interchannel
   facies, and
4) Slump facies.
Also shown is the
predicted paleo-
current distribu-
tion from all
facies of the fan.

either case the surficial expression of the ice-melt is a
kettle on the fan (Figure 7), later filled by marine sediments (Hayward and French, This volume).

The most common type of deposit overlying subaqueous outwash in the Ottawa area is wave-worked lag gravel, in most
cases unconformable on the fan sediment, and not part of the
fan itself. This gravel provides direct evidence that the
underlying fan sediments were deposited subaqueously, for it
was formed by reworking of the fan surface when raised to
wave base by isostatic uplift. At other locations a lag gravel
may not develop if the body of water had insufficient fetch
to allow the generation of effective waves, or gravel was
lacking in the underlying deposits. Furthermore, similar
deposits may develop in proglacial lakes, in which rapid
drainage could inhibit wave activity.

Variations from the model are attributed to variations in
the morphology of the ice front at the site of deposition.
Exposures in a relatively narrow, steep-sided portion of the
Stittsville Ridge (Figure 1) show a generally fining-upward
sequence of unfossiliferous sediments overlain by a coarsening-upward sequence of fossiliferous sands and gravels. The
deposit is interpreted as subaqueous outwash passing upward
into a regressive marine sequence. Sediments within the ridge
are intensely faulted in the central portion and along the
exposed flank where faults trend approximately parallel to
the ridge axis. It is postulated that a subaqueous outwash
fan was deposited within an inlet in the ice front which
restricted the lateral construction of the fan. The depositional environment and the sequence of events leading to the
observed stratigraphy are depicted in Figure 8. The inlet
may have been the ice frontal expression of a radial crevasse
system in the glacier or a flooded supraglacial valley. With
the melting of ice walls and buried ice the deposit was
intensely deformed, destroying much of the diagnostic criteria
for subaqueous outwash.

Further north along the Stittsville Ridge deposition in
an asymmetrical inlet is believed responsible for deflecting
paleocurrents to the west of the ridge axis, as indicated in
the depositional model (Figure 9). Channel deposits predominate in the sediments of the ridge, due to extensive
reworking of the fan surface by channel migration within the
confined area of the inlet. Silty fine sand beds of climbing
ripple drift are notably absent in the deposit due to the
flushing of fine sediment out of the inlet and beyond the
flanks of the ridge.

Figure 8.   (A) Depositional model for subaqueous outwash
      deposited in a narrow inlet into the glacier front.
          (B-E) The sequence of events leading to the
      formation of the ridge as it is preserved.

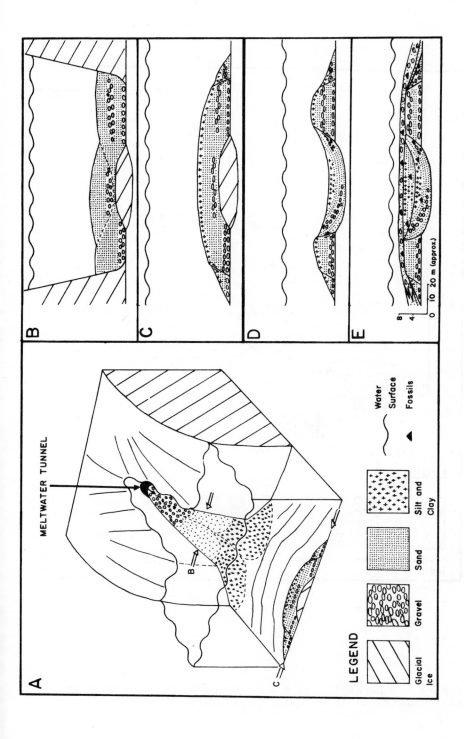

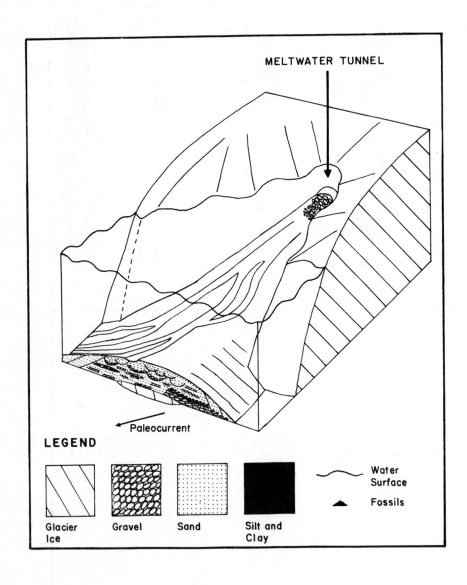

Figure 9. Depositional model for subaqueous outwash in an asymmetrical inlet into the glacier front.

CONCLUSIONS

Coarse-grained glacio-marine deposits are often attributed to ice-rafting or shoreline processes, but the deposits described here are predominantly formed by unidirectional meltwater currents. They superficially resemble subaerial outwash (fluvioglacial deposits), but accumulated beneath a column of standing water as subaqueous fans. The facies developed (channel, interchannel and slump facies) may be used for identification of similar deposits elsewhere, although facies inter-relationships may differ in some details.

Although not widely recognised, the deposits discussed in this paper must be a common feature of continental deglaciation, because isostatic depression commonly confines a water body against the ice front. Thus stratified outwash is deposited beneath standing water, which in the present case was marine. However, in mid-continental areas an equivalent situation would involve ponding of fresh water. In this case faunal evidence for submergence would generally be lacking, but the facies relationships discussed here should provide evidence for deposition as subaqueous outwash. It is concluded that this type of deposition should be anticipated as a common feature of successions formed during continental glaciation in the Pleistocene and earlier glacial periods.

ACKNOWLEDGEMENTS

We thank the Natural Science and Engineering Research Council of Canada and the Ontario Ministry of Colleges and Universities for funding; pit owners for access to their properties; Suzanne Meunier for typing and Jack Whorwood for photographic work.

REFERENCES CITED

Bagnold, R.A. 1954, Experiments on a gravity free dispersion of large solid spheres in a Newtonian fluid under shear. *Proceedings Royal Society of London (A)*, 225, 49-63

Blatt, H., Middleton, G.V. and R. Murray, 1972, *Origin of sedimentary rocks,* (Prentice-Hall, Inc., Englewood Cliffs, New Jersey), 634 pp.

Cheel, R.J. and B.R. Rust, 1980, A sequence of soft-sediment deformation structures in Late Quaternary subaqueous outwash near Ottawa, Ontario. *Geological Association of Canada, Program with Abstracts,* 5, 45

Coleman, J. M. 1976, *Deltas: processes of deposition and models for exploration,* (Continuing Education Publication Corp., Inc., Illinois), 102 pp.

De Geer, G. 1940, Geochronologia suecica principles. *K. svenska Vetensk-Akad. Handl., Ser.3,* 18, 6. Text and atlas.

Hayward, M. and H. M. French, 1980, Nearshore deposits of the Champlain Sea, near Ottawa, Canada. (This volume)

Gadd, N. R. 1963, Surficial geology of Ottawa map-area, Ontario and Quebec. *Geological Survey of Canada, Paper*, 62-16, 4 pp.

Gadd, N. R. 1978, Mass flow deposits in a Quaternary succession near Ottawa, Canada: diagnostic criteria for subaqueous outwash: discussion. *Canadian Journal of Earth Sciences*, 15, 327-328

Johansson, C. E. 1963, Orientation of pebbles in running water. A laboratory study. *Geografiska Annaler A*, 45, 85-112

Jopling, A. V. and R. G. Walker, 1968, Morphology and origin of ripple-drift cross-lamination with examples from the Pleistocene of Massachusetts. *Journal of Sedimentary Petrology*, 38, 971-984

Kelling, G. and D. J. Stanley, 1976, Sedimentation in canyon, slope and base-of-slope environments. in *Marine sediment transport and environmental management*, ed D. J. Stanley and D.J.P.Swift, (John Wiley) 379-435

Lowe, D. R. 1976, Subaqueous liquefied and fluidized sediment flows and their deposits. *Sedimentology*, 23, 285-308

Miall, A. D. 1976, Facies models - 4. Deltas. *Geoscience Canada*, 3, 215-227

Middleton, G.V. and M. A. Hampton, 1976, Subaqueous sediment transport and deposition by sediment gravity flows. in *Marine sediment transport and environmental management*, ed D.J.Stanley and D.J.P.Swift, (John Wiley), 197-218

Richard, S.H. 1978, Age of Champlain Sea and 'Lampsilis Lake' episode in the Ottawa-St. Lawrence Lowlands. *Geological Survey of Canada Paper*, 78-1C, 23-28

Richard, S.H., Gadd, N.R., and J.-S. Vincent, 1974, Surficial materials and terrain features, Ottawa-Hull, Ontario-Quebec. *Geological Survey of Canada, Map*, 1425A

Rust, B.R. 1972, Pebble orientation in fluvial sediments. *Journal of Sedimentary Petrology*, 42, 384-388

Rust, B.R. 1977, Mass flow deposits in a Quaternary succession near Ottawa, Canada: diagnostic criteria for subaqueous outwash. *Canadian Journal of Earth Sciences*, 14, 175-184

Rust, B.R. and R. Romanelli, 1975, Late Quaternary subaqueous outwash deposits near Ottawa, Canada. in *Glaciofluvial and glaciolacustrine sedimentation*, ed A.V.Jopling and B.C.McDonald, (Society of Economic Palaeontologists and Mineralogists, Special Publication 23), 177-192.

Sallenger, Jr., A. H.   1979,   Inverse grading and hydraulic equivalence in grain-flow deposits.   *Journal of Sedimentary Petrology,* 49, 553-562

Sugden, D. E. and B. S. John,   1976,   *Glaciers and landscape,* (Edward Arnold), 376 pp.

Walker, R. G.   1978,   Deep-water sandstone facies and ancient submarine fans: Models for exploration for stratigraphic traps.   *Bulletin of the American Association of Petroleum Geologists,* 62, 932-966

14 Nearshore deposits of the Champlain Sea, near Ottawa Canada

M. Hayward & H.M. French

ABSTRACT

The study of sections exposed in the Twin Elm and Herbert Corners commercial workings south of Ottawa permits the identification and classification of marine sediments derived from ridges of glacigenic deposits. The ridges formed during the retreat of Wisconsin ice and contemporaneously with the early stages of the Champlain Sea or a lacustrine predecessor. Subsequently, a progressively falling wave base resulted in their reworking. Deposition occurred either within kettle depressions, formed through the melt of buried ice bodies, or as sand sheets on ridge flanks. In addition, lag deposits, derived from the reworking of the ridge materials, in places rest unconformably upon earlier marine deposits. Boulder beaches and beach ridges are associated with these littoral deposits.

INTRODUCTION

The Champlain Sea inundated ice-free parts of the Ottawa-St Lawrence lowlands about 12 800[14]C years B.P. and existed for approximately 3000 years in the Ottawa region. The aim of this paper is to describe the nature and extent of marine reworking of glacigenic sediments during this period. Fieldwork, undertaken at a number of localities south of Ottawa where sand and gravel excavations were actively proceeding, took the form of the detailed drawing of sections. These now provide a basic body of sedimentological and stratigraphical data. In this paper, sections are described and interpreted from two localities referred to as (a) Twin Elm and (b) Herbert Corners (Figure 1).

[1]Department of Geography,
University of Reading, Reading RG6 2AU, United Kingdom

[2]Departments of Geography and Geology,
University of Ottawa, Ottawa, KIN 6N5, Canada

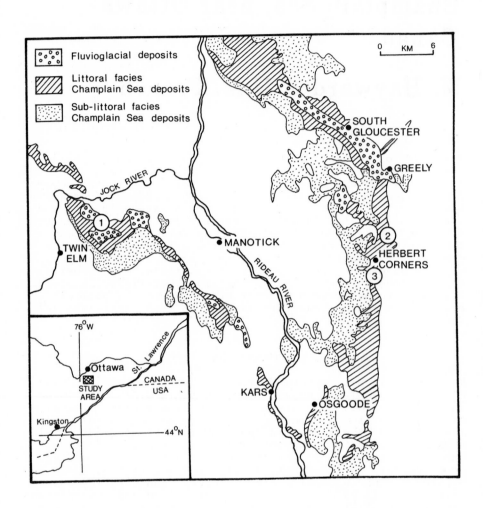

Figure 1. Map of study area showing location of sand and
gravel pits mentioned in the text, and the distribution
of major fluvioglacial and Champlain Sea nearshore deposits
as mapped by Richard *et al* (1977).
1 - Trail Road pit, near Twin Elm; 2 - Tierney's pit,
Herbert Corners; 3 - Pyper's pit, Herbert Corners.
As interpreted in this paper, the term fluvioglacial should
be regarded as subaqueous outwash (Rust and Romanelli,
1975).

NEARSHORE SEDIMENTATION IN THE CHAMPLAIN SEA

Isostatic uplift brought about the recession of the Champlain Sea, and this exposed a lowland with an extensive cover of marine and glacial deposits. These sediments have been mapped by the Geological Survey of Canada (e.g. Richard *et al,* 1977). To the south of Ottawa, sediments associated with the Wisconsin ice sheet include till and ridges of sand and gravel. The latter are interpreted as subaqueous outwash deposits by Rust and associates (e.g. Rust and Romanelli, 1975; Rust, 1977, 1978; Cheel and Rust, 1980a, 1980b), an interpretation with which we agree. Gadd (1978) raises some evidence which appears to conflict with this interpretation but Rust (1978) has responded to this. Areas of till usually occur as a veneer overlying faulted limestone bedrock which form elevations in the pre-marine relief.

The marine deposits which overlie unconformably the glacigenic sediments have been divided into three map units by Richard *et al,*(1977): 1) Champlain Sea bottom facies, mostly clays, 2) sub-littoral facies, notably sand, and 3) littoral facies, mostly gravels, up to cobble size. Lacking from this classification is consideration of the parentage of these materials and the degree of reworking to which they have been subjected. To this end, Table 1 illustrates the relationship between the various marine deposits and features present in the Ottawa area, and the nature of their reworking.

Table 1.   Classification of Champlain Sea nearshore
sediments and processes

Shoreline Foundation	Processes	Results		Features
1. Bedrock ridges	Reworking of till veneer	a)	Removal of fines to deeper water	Leda clay (in part)
		b)	Formation of lag deposits	Boulder beaches Beach ridges
2. Glacigenic ridges	Reworking of sand and gravel	a)	Redeposition of sand beside and on flanks of ridges	Sand sheets Sand bars and spits
		b)	Kettle-filling	Kettle-fills
		c)	Formation of lag deposits	Stittsville lag

The marine reworking of glacigenic sediments must be viewed within the context of a falling wave base associated with the marine regression. Clearly, topographic 'highs', constituting either bedrock or subaqueous outwash ridges, were the first to experience wave action and reworking. Fines were removed from till and deposited in deeper water. Similarly, sand was

Figure 2. Boulder beach near French Hill (grid reference
   672362) developed from till overlying limestone bed-
   rock at an elevation of 100 m a.s.l.
Figure 3. Beach ridges on the limestone plateau near south
   Gloucester, south of Ottawa. Elevation - 130 m a.s.l.
   (Part of A 23217-180)

removed from the outwash deposits and redeposited, sometimes
by currents, at shallower depths near the ridges. At the
same time, the melt-out of ice blocks buried within the
glacigenic ridges led to the formation of kettle-like submarine depressions. These became infilled with sediment
transported by slumping and slope instability together with
sediment gravity flows, induced by wave washing. Finally,
ice rafting, especially in the early stages of the Champlain
Sea, contributed dropstones and other coarse particles to
deep water sediments. Many exposures, including some to be
discussed, show an apparent threefold stratigraphic division
in the marine deposits, especially those in depressions on
the ridges. The basis for this division is the occurrence of
unconformities. The first member of the marine sequence
frequently comprises deformed, poorly sorted materials which
possibly were laid down before wave attack commenced on the
ridges. Erosion of the ridges due to the encroachment of
wave base is reflected in the second member, while the third
is thought to signify the operation of swash zone processes.

As wave base dropped, progressively larger tracts of the
sea bottom became subject to wave action. Attrition of till
and sand and gravel features led to the formation of extensive
lag deposits, with some reworking and redeposition on the
flanks, giving a coarse littoral facies which sometimes rests
unconformably upon older marine sediments.

Geomorphological evidence of these events in the Ottawa
area appears restricted mainly to littoral forms associated
with the final stages of the receding sea. However, in
comparison to other areas in the Ottawa-St Lawrence lowlands
(e.g. Terasmae, 1965; Gadd, 1971; Richard, 1976, 1977), there
is a relative paucity of such forms. This may be due to the
breaking up of the water body in this area either by bedrock
controlled relief or the glacigenic ridges. Most frequent
are lag deposits forming boulder beaches lying at elevations
between 114 m and 99 m a.s.l. (Figure 2). Less common are
beach ridges, which are best recognised from air photographs
(Figure 3). However, the range of forms, as described by
Gadd (1971) from the Bécancour area of the St Lawrence lowlands, and their considerable size and extent, as described
from the Cornwall area by Terasmae (1965), are lacking. It
follows therefore, that a stratigraphic, rather than a geomorphological, approach is most suited to the Ottawa area.
Moreover, the glacigenic ridges, which are subject to extensive commercial excavations, provide excellent opportunities
to observe the degree of reworking of glacial sediments.

CASE STUDIES

The description of sections from two localities in the study
area is intended to illustrate the relationship between glacial
and marine sediments, the nature and extent of reworking, and
the relative importance of littoral and sub-littoral deposits.
For the purposes of the present discussion it is intended to
draw a distinction between deposits inferred to have been
laid down and reworked in the swash zone, here referred to as

Table 2. List of fossil symbols and information
used in Figures 4, 5, 6, 9, and 10

STATE OF PRESERVATION

⊙   Pelecypod(s) in life position

✷   Pelecypods in various states of preservation

●   Single valves and pelecypod fragments

■   Barnacle(s) intact or in life position

∠   Barnacle fragments

FOSSIL NAMES

Hà   Hiatella arctica

Mb   Macoma balthica

Bh   Balanus hameri

Bc   Balanus crenatus

Bs   Balanus species

littoral, and arenaceous sediments of deeper water, designated sub-littoral. Fossil information is given in Table 2
and grain size classes are those of Wentworth. A complete
description of the following sections, and others, can be
found in Hayward (1979).

A. Twin Elm

Sections exposed in the Twin Elm workings along Trail Road
in Nepean Township (grid: 394091) during the summer of 1978
are regarded as a collective 'type locality' for Champlain
Sea nearshore sedimentation. The Twin Elm ridge is a shallow
feature located south and east of the Jock River and runs in
a southeast direction towards Kars (Figure 1). The origin
of the ridge has not been investigated but a variant of the
subaqueous outwash model (Rust, 1977; Cheel and Rust, 1980b)
seems likely. Since the maximum elevation of the ridge is only
110-120 m a.s.l., it probably came under wave attack fairly
late in the period of marine submergence. Beach ridges occur
on the surface of the ridge.

Three sections, located in an approximate south - north
transect across the northern flank of the ridge, illustrate
the range of marine sediments. Section 1 (Figure 4) reveals
three major stratigraphic units. The lowest comprises faulted,
fining upward, clast supported gravel, and a deformed sequence
of other sediments also affected by the same faults. The
second member includes a fossiliferous diamicton and a silty
shell bed overlain by a fossiliferous bed of stratified sand.
Hiatella arctica and *Balanus hameri* are present in the sand

302

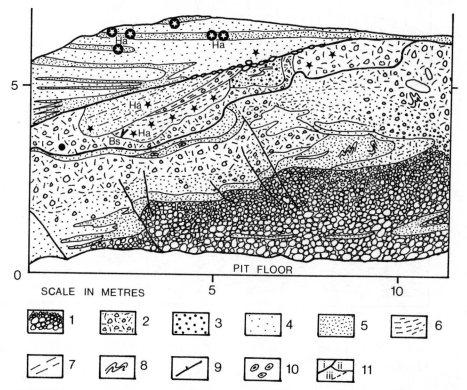

Figure 4. Section I in Trail Road pit at Twin Elm, July 1978.
Aspect of exposure 260°. Fossil information as in Table
2. Key: 1 - Gravel and boulders; 2 - Diamicton;
3 - Granules; 4 - Coarse sand; 5 - Medium and fine sand;
6 - Silt and clay; 7 - Stratification; 8 - Deformed
sediment; 9 - Faults; 10 - Rip-up clasts; 11 - Lithologic boundaries, i) Unconformity, ii) Well defined,
iii) Poorly defined.

and the silt. These early fossiliferous deposits ('early
marine') are truncated by an erosion surface with a lag, above
which is the third stratigraphic unit, a medium sand with
prominent shell beds of *Hiatella arctica* appearing nearer the
top. These deposits represent 'later marine' sediments. The
top of the section is truncated by recent excavation.

The similarity between the unfossiliferous deposits and
the early marine sediments overlying them suggests that the
first marine fauna colonised a sea bottom which had been
derived locally, largely by slumping off the ridge. Although
we do not favour an ice re-advance (Richard, 1975), the ice
front need not have been far removed from the locality.
Proximity of the ice front is consistent with the findings of
Cronin (1976) and accords well with observations by Lewis
et al (1977, 503-504), among others.

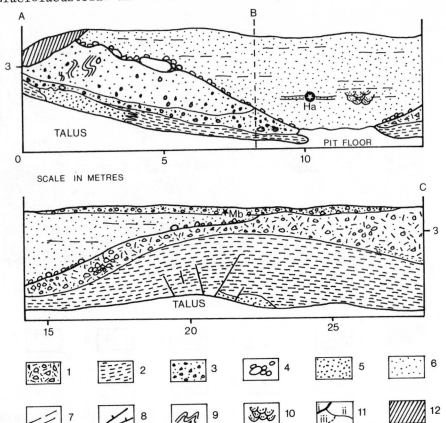

Figure 5. Section 2 in Trail Road pit at Twin Elm, July 1978. Aspect of exposure A-B is 310° and B-C is 255°. Fossil information as in Table 2. Key: 1 - Diamicton; 2 - Silt and clay; 3 - Sandy gravel; 4 - Boulders and cobbles; 5 - Coarse sand; 6 - Medium sand; 7 - Stratification; 8 - Faults; 9 - Deformed sediment; 10 - Small scale trough cross-stratification; 11 - Lithologic boundaries, i) Unconformity, ii) Well defined, iii) Poorly defined; 12 - Overburden.

Section 2 (Figure 5) is located approximately 100 m southeast of the previous exposure and is closest to the centre of the Twin Elm ridge. Two major stratigraphic units are visible in this section. The first is unfossiliferous and characterised by an abundance of argillaceous material. A large faulted body of silt is overlain by a diamicton which in places is overlain by laterally variable, unstratified coarse sand, and deformed coarse sand. The silts may be a distal facies of esker fan or subaqueous outwash, whereas the diamicton is open to a wider range of interpretations. Probably, the latter was deposited in a submarine environment prior to the establishment of any macrofaunal communities.

Ice rafting together with subaqueous slumping of ablation till are the most likely processes. The second major unit fills a depression on the surface of the earlier deposits, and comprises horizontally stratified medium sand containing articulated *Hiatalla arctica* valves. These deposits may represent a channel cut and filled in the nearshore zone or, since the exposure was not three-dimensional, be simply a long, troughlike hollow formed from the melt-out of a buried ice block. As such, the deposits may be of a marine kettle-fill nature, the origin and nature of which are described elsewhere (Hayward and French, 1980; Cheel and Rust, 1980a). The fossiliferous sands bear no textural relationship to the underlying sediments, but are similar to the 'later marine' sands in section 1. Both appear to indicate substantial nearshore sand movement. Although most of the surface has been stripped, a sandy gravel is present overlying the stratified sands. This unit comprises the local equivalent of the 'Stittsville lag' (Rust and Romanelli, 1975, 181; Cheel, 1980, p 30 *et seq.*) and is interpreted as a beach deposit. There is an unconformable boundary with underlying deposits and, in contrast to the medium sands with a biocoenose of *Hiatella arctica,* yields single valves of *Macoma balthica.* According to Cronin (1977), *Macoma balthica* was the species most able to survive the 'rigorous littoral environment' of the Champlain Sea.

Section 3 (Figure 6) is located approximately 100 m to the north of section 1 and is furthest from the ridge crest. In contrast to the two previous sections described, this section does not show the contact between the marine and premarine sediments, and instead, displays a different type of marine deposit. The majority of the section (Figure 6) comprises fine to medium sand with small scale trough cross-stratification. Such sediments are common in the middle shoreface zone (Reinson, 1979). Assemblages of *Hiatella arctica* are found in life position. Four sets of paleocurrent determinations, constructed from measurements of cross-stratification at various positions along the section, all show a definite northwesterly mode (Figure 7), a direction which is parallel to the long axis of the ridge. Coastal currents are suggested therefore, and the sands which are extensively exposed in this section are thought to be part of the 'later marine' sub-littoral facies of the Champlain Sea. Overlying the cross-stratified sands are coarser sediments which contain a variable proportion of gravel. Owing to disturbance by tree roots and excavation, no interpretation is offered beyond that they probably represent a littoral deposit, as suggested by the coarser texture and presence of *Macoma balthica.*

The lateral relationship between the three sections, and their position relative to the ridge crest, suggest that the sediments in section 3 are stratigraphically above, although topographically below, those in sections 1 and 2, as would be expected in an offlap sequence. By combining these three sections, therefore, a schematic type-section of Champlain Sea nearshore sedimentation can be deduced (Figure 8). Reworking and marine sediment transport appear to have been important at this locality.

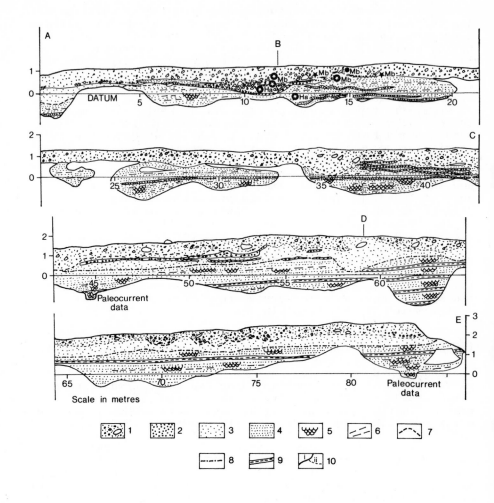

Figure 6.   Section 3 in Trail Road pit at Twin Elm, July 1978
Datum - 102 m a.s.l.   Aspect of exposure A-B is
125°, B-C is 235°, C-D is 220° and D-E is 310°.
Fossil information as in Table 2.   Key: 1- Sandy
gravel with boulders; 2- Granules and coarse sand,
3- Medium sand, unstratified; 4- Medium sand,
stratified; 5- Cross-stratification; 6- Stratification; 7- Lower limit of root churning; 8- Depth
to which bedding has been obliterated; 9- Parallel
laminations; 10- Lithologic boundaries, i) Well
defined, ii) Poorly defined.

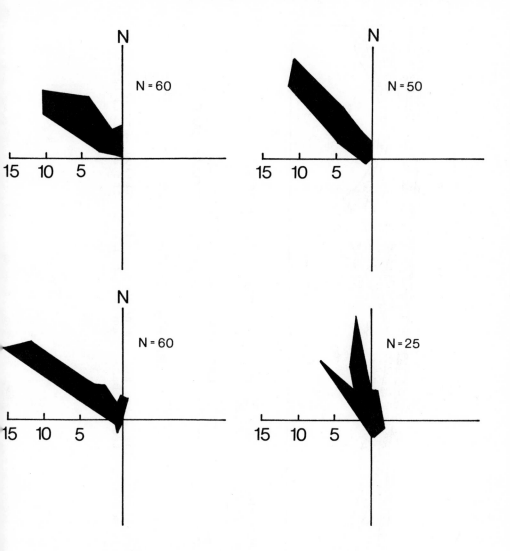

Figure 7. Paleocurrent data from trough cross-stratified
sands in Section 3 at Trail Road pit, Twin Elm.

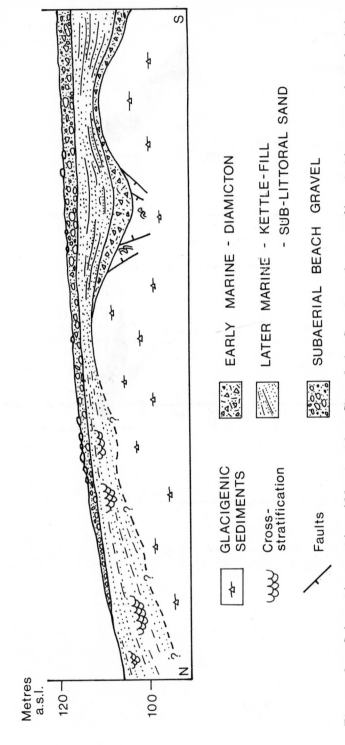

Figure 8. Schematic section illustrating Champlain Sea nearshore sedimentation associated with glacigenic ridges south of Ottawa. Based upon Sections 1, 2, and 3 at Twin Elm (See Figures 4, 5, and 6).

EARLY MARINE - DIAMICTON

LATER MARINE - KETTLE-FILL
             - SUB-LITTORAL SAND

SUBAERIAL BEACH GRAVEL

GLACIGENIC
SEDIMENTS

Cross-
stratification

Faults

Metres
a.s.l.

120

100

S

N

B. Herbert Corners

The relative importance of littoral and sub-littoral deposits
in the Ottawa area can be discussed within the context of
several large sections exposed in a ridge of sand and gravel
which runs southward from Greely to near Osgoode (Figure 1).
This ridge is referred to as the Herbert Corners ridge. It
is a relatively broad and gentle feature which rises some
15-20 m above the surrounding terrain. To the east occurs an
undulating lowland of limestone bedrock and drumlinised
glacial till, with depressions infilled with organic deposits
on the former and Champlain Sea lutite on the latter. To the
west of the ridge is a second area of drumlinised till.

In their inventory of southern Ontario eskers, Chapman
and Putnam (1966, 82-85) refer to the ridge as an esker which
has been so severely wave-washed that its original form is
barely recognisable. Although not studied by Rust and Romanelli (1975), they suggest that this ridge also is of subaqueous origin. Richard (1976) and Richard *et al* (1977)
however, map the entire ridge as 'Champlain Sea: littoral
facies', thereby making its relationship to the other ridges
unclear. Harrison (1977) cites the mapping by Richard *et al*
(1977) as evidence that the ridge is a former recurved spit
dating from the latter stages of the Champlain Sea. The
ridge is interpreted here as having been built by sediment
transported by currents resulting from the refraction of
waves off the southeast end of the South Gloucester ridge
(the 'Bowesville moraine'; see Gadd, 1961, 1962). This would
be consistent with the presence of a considerable stretch of
open water (perhaps 150 km) to the northeast in Champlain Sea
times.

A number of commercial workings are active along the
Herbert Corners ridge. Some expose glacigenic sediments but
two, described here, reveal substantial marine deposits and
provide insight into the problems mentioned above.

A large section examined in Tierney's pit (grid: 553070)
in July 1978 revealed three major stratigraphic units (Figure
9). The lowest comprises unfossiliferous silty fine sands
with minor faulting and deformation. Overlying these are
fossiliferous sands exhibiting a strong depositional slope
(true dip - 35°) with microdelta stratification near the top.
The third stratigraphic unit comprises silty granular coarse
sand disposed in a gentle basin form. Single valves of *Hiatella
arctica*, convex upward, and separate plates of *Balanus hameri*,
with a preferred orientation, are present in these deposits.

The unfossiliferous faulted and deformed sands probably
were laid down in close association with ice. The lower
marine unit, also a silty fine sand, is thought to have been
derived locally from subaqueous outwash sediment and deposited
in a kettle hole. This unit represents the local equivalent
of the 'early marine' sediments while the 'later marine'
sediments are represented by the overlying stratified coarse
sand. The latter would reflect either a different source of
debris, or a lowering of wave base, or both. The microdelta

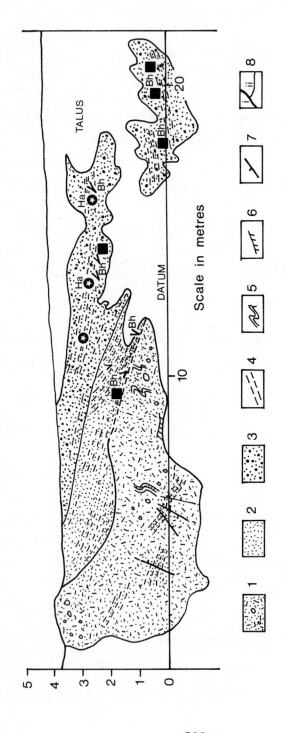

Figure 9. Section in Tierney's pit, Herbert Corners, July 1978. Datum – 88 m a.s.l.
Aspect of exposure – 80°. Fossil information as in Table 2. Key: 1– Silty
fine sand with gravel; 2– Medium sand; 3– Coarse sand; 4– Stratification;
5– Deformed sediment; 6– Planar cross beds; 7– Faults; 8– Litholologic boundaries,
i) Well defined, ii) Poorly defined.

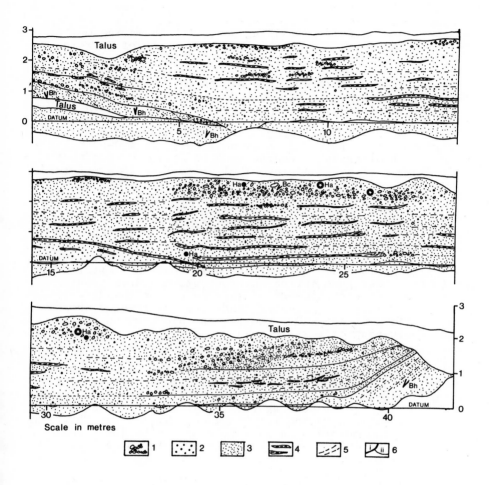

Figure 10.   Section in Pyper's pit, Herbert Corners,
July 1978.   Datum - 92 m a.s.l.   Aspect
of exposure - 88°.   Fossil information as
in Table 2.   Key: 1- Gravel; 2- Granules;
3- Coarse sand; 4- Clay; 5- Stratification;
6- Lithologic boundaries,   i) Well defined,
ii) Poorly defined.

structure present in the second stratigraphic unit indicates unidirectional filling of the kettle, as may the disposition of the barnacle fragments. This observation needs verification however, through experiments on the orientation of *Balanus hameri* plates in running water. Both marine members are referable to the 'kettle-fill' environment of Hayward and French (1980).

A second large exposure containing marine sediments was examined at Pyper's pit (grid: 560088), approximately 1 km to the north of Tierney's pit. Only part of the drawn section is illustrated in Figure 10. The section shows medium to coarse sand with infrequent and dislocated specimens of *Balanus hameri* overlain unconformably (e.g. at m 0-5) by an accumulation of granular coarse sand of variable stoniness with a number of beds and lenses of silt. Fossils are rare, but *Balanus crenatus,* including some still attached to pebbles and *Hiatella arctica* are present. These observations suggest that two phases of marine sedimentation are represented. The 'later marine' deposits possess the divergent stratification characteristic of kettle-fill (see Hayward and French, 1980) although this may not be an infilled kettle, and the margin of the hollow is formed by a slope on the remanié surface of the 'early marine' deposits. It appears that the latter were partially eroded in a marine environment, and this erosion may reflect the encroachment of wave base upon the former sea bottom. The extensive granular sands are interpreted therefore, as littoral and sub-littoral, an inference supported by the coarsening of texture towards the top (e.g. see m 20-25, Figure 10).

A corollary of this interpretation is the possibility that the 'later marine' sediments are intertidal, possessing as they do intercalated lenses and beds of argillaceous sediments similar to lenticular bedding (e.g. Reineck and Singh, 1973). However, stronger evidence for tidal activity in the Champlain Sea is required before such an inference can be justified. For example, no instances of herringbone cross-stratification have been recorded.

Finally, the local physiography associated with the Herbert Corners ridge should be considered. The bedrock to the east would have formed an extensive shoal at the close of the period of marine submergence. As well as reducing wave action on the Herbert Corners ridge and affecting faunal colonisation by creating a lagoon complex of low salinity, the presence of such a feature is a further barrier to the acceptance of a spit hypothesis.

In summary, the marine sediments exposed during the summer of 1978 along the Herbert Corners ridge all show important local reworking of the ridge but provide no direct support for the spit hypothesis. The marine sediments themselves, moreover, comprise only a small proportion of the ridge. The comment of Chapman and Putnam (1966) was therefore sound. Extensive exposures in the Osgoode Sand and Gravel pits, not described in this paper, reveal a substantial core of sub-aqueous outwash sediment. It follows that the larger 'barbs'

on the 'spit' (cf. Harrison, 1977) are probably branches of
the same esker/subaqueous outwash system, a large and important feature which can be traced from beyond Ottawa International Airport to Kemptville, a distance of 45 km (e.g. see
Richard *et al*, 1977). Such a feature is commensurate with
the scale of the Wisconsin ice sheet, unlike the supposed
spit in the context of the Champlain Sea. Finally, with
respect to the relative importance of littoral and sub-littoral
sediments, the absence of significant lag deposits points to
the greater significance of nearshore redeposition at this
locality.

CONCLUSIONS

The marine reworking of glacigenic deposits complicates the
mapping of both glacial and marine sediments in the Ottawa
region. The majority of reworking appears to have taken
place in the nearshore zone under the influence of wave
attack, with localised redistribution into kettle holes, as
sand sheets and occasional longshore accumulations. Littoral
sediments appear restricted to lag deposits, such as the
Stittsville lag and its local equivalents. The formation of
boulder beaches and beach ridges suggests a relatively high
energy environment in places in the latter stages of the
Champlain Sea. Geomorphological, stratigraphic and sedimentological evidence indicates that marine deposition along
the Greely-Osgoode ridge was mostly the result of the local
reworking of pre-marine sediments rather than the longshore
transport of sediment.

ACKNOWLEDGEMENTS

M. Hayward wishes to acknowledge financial support provided
by a graduate assistantship in the Department of Geography,
University of Ottawa, 1977-1979. Research was supported in
part by NSERC grant A-8367 (H.M.French) and a grant from the
Research Committee of the Graduate School, University of
Ottawa. We would like also to thank the various pit operators
who allowed us access to the exposures on many occasions
during 1977 and 1978. Discussions and companionship, both
in the field and office, were provided by P. Worsley (University of Reading, England, and Visiting Professor, University of Ottawa, 1977-78) and R. J. Cheel, University of
Ottawa. B. R. Rust (University of Ottawa) provided additional
stimulating discussion, and kindly read, and commented upon,
the final manuscript.

REFERENCES

Chapman, L.J. and D.F.Putnam, 1966, *The Physiography of Southern Ontario,* (University of Toronto Press, Toronto) 386 pp.

Cheel, R. J. 1980, *Late Quaternary glacio-marine deposits of the Stittsville area, near Ottawa, Canada. M.Sc. Thesis,* (Department of Geology, University of Ottawa), 154 pp.

Cheel, R.J. and B.R.Rust, 1980a, A sequence of soft-sediment deformation structures in Late Quaternary subaqueous outwash near Ottawa, Ontario. *Geological Association of Canada, Program with Abstracts,* 5, 45, Halifax.

Cheel, R.J. and B.R. Rust, 1980b, Coarse grained facies of glacio-marine deposits near Ottawa, Ontario, in *Research in glacial, glacio-fluvial, and glacio-lacustrine systems.* (Sixth Guelph Symposium on Geomorphology, May 1980).

Cronin, T. M. 1976, An arctic foraminiferal fauna from Champlain Sea deposits in Ontario. *Canadian Journal of Earth Sciences,* 13, 1678-1682.

Cronin, T. M. 1977, Late Wisconsin marine environments of the Champlain Valley (New York, Quebec). *Quaternary Research,* 7, 238-253.

Gadd, N. R. 1961, Surficial geology of the Ottawa map area. *Geological Survey of Canada, Paper,* 61-19.

Gadd, N. R. 1962, Surficial geology of the Ottawa map area. *Geological Survey of Canada, Memoir,* 63-16.

Gadd, N. R. 1971, Pleistocene geology of the central St Lawrence lowlands. *Geological Survey of Canada, Memoir,* 359, 153 pp.

Gadd, N. R. 1978, Mass flow deposits in a Quaternary succession near Ottawa, Canada: diagnostic criteria for subaqueous outwash: Discussion. *Canadian Journal of Earth Sciences,* 15, 327-328.

Harrison, J. E. 1977, Coastal studies in the Ottawa area. *Geological Survey of Canada, Paper,* 77-1A, 59-60.

Hayward, M. 1979, *Aspects of Champlain Sea sedimentation associated with glacial ridges in the south Ottawa region. M.A. Thesis,* (Department of Geography, University of Ottawa), 122 pp.

Hayward, M. and H.M.French, 1980, Pleistocene marine kettle-fill deposits near Ottawa, Canada. *Canadian Journal of Earth Sciences,* 17, 1236-1245.

Lewis, C.F.M., Blasco, S.M., Bornhold, B.D., Hunter, J.A.M., Judge, A.S., Kerr, J.W., Mclaren, P. and B.R.Pelletier, 1977, Marine geology and geophysical activities in Lancaster Sound and adjacent fiords. *Geological Survey of Canada, Paper,* 77-1A, 495-506.

Reineck, H.-E. and I.B.Singh, 1973, *Depositional Sedimentary Environments,* (Springer, New York), 439 pp.

Reinson, G.E. 1979, Facies models 6.Barrier island systems, in *Facies Models. Geoscience Canada Reprint Series, 1, Toronto,* ed R.G.Walker, (Geological Association of Canada), 57-74.

Richard, S.H. 1975, Surficial geology mapping, Ottawa valley lowland (Parts of 31 G,B, and F). *Geological Survey of Canada, Paper,* 75-1B, 113-117.

Richard, S.H. 1976, Surficial geology mapping: Valleyfield-Rigaud area, Quebec (31 G/I, 8, 9). *Geological Survey of Canada, Paper,* 76-1A, 205-208.

Richard, S.H. 1977, Surficial geology mapping: Valleyfield-Huntingdon area, Quebec. *Geological Survey of Canada, Paper,* 77-1A, 507-512.

Richard, S.H., Gadd, N.R., and J.-S. Vincent, 1977, Surficial materials and terrain features, Ottawa-Hull, Ontario-Quebec. *Geological Survey of Canada, Map,*1425A.

Rust, B.R. 1977, Mass flow deposits in a Quaternary succession near Ottawa, Canada: diagnostic criteria for subaqueous outwash. *Canadian Journal of Earth Sciences,* 14, 175-184.

Rust, B.R. 1978, Mass flow deposits in a Quaternary succession near Ottawa, Canada: diagnostic criteria for subaqueous outwash: reply. *Canadian Journal of Earth Sciences,* 15, 329-330.

Rust, B.R. and R. Romanelli, 1975, Late Quaternary subaqueous outwash deposits near Ottawa, Canada. in *Glaciofluvial and glaciolacustrine sedimentation,* ed A.V. Jopling and B.C.MacDonald, (Society of Economic Paleontologists and Mineralogists, Special Publication 23), 177-192.

Terasmae, J. 1965, Surficial geology of the Cornwall and St Lawrence Seaway Project areas, Ontario. *Geological Survey of Canada, Bulletin,* 121, 54 pp.

Appendix

Abstracts of Papers Not Submitted
For Publication

GLACIOFLUVIAL PROCESSES AND SEDIMENTATION IN THE CANADIAN HIGH ARCTIC

S.B. McCann,
Department of Geography,
McMaster University,
Hamilton, Canada.

ABSTRACT

Geomorphological and hydrological observations along the western margin of the Ellesmere Ice Cap, Ellesmere Island, between Makinson Inlet and Bay Fiord, provide a basis for evaluating the nature and present rates of glaciofluvial sedimentation in a high latitude setting. The discussion is in two parts: part one focusses on the hydrologic and sedimentary regimes, particularly the suspended sediment regime, of two unnamed rivers which flow from the ice cap into the head of Vendom Fiord, at latitude 78°N, and part two examines the morphology and sedimentology of their modern and relict Sandurs.

The two rivers drain an area of 1700 km^2, of which 74% is glacierized, and the basins contain 78 km of the ice margin. The seasonal flow pattern (mid-June to early September) was different in each of the three years of record (1973-75), but the hydrographs contain similar events - an early season snowmelt peak, a late season glacier melt peak, responses to precipitation, and jokulhlaup floods. Sediment transport rates associated with each type of event are presented and explained, at the basin scale, in terms of the sources of the water. The effects of diurnal fluctuations in stage on suspended sediment concentration at the ice margin and in small tributary streams are investigated.

A brief description of the complete suite of glaciofluvial landforms and sediments in the study area, is complemented by a detailed analysis of a small active sandur developed by the smaller river as it debouches as a single channel from a bedrock constriction on its lower course.

OBSERVATIONS ON GLACIAL AND SUBGLACIAL DRAINAGE CONDITIONS
IN THE VICINITY OF CASTLEGUARD MOUNTAIN, COLUMBIA ICEFIELD,
CANADA

D.C. Ford and C.C. Smart,
Department of Geography,
McMaster University,
Hamilton, Canada.

ABSTRACT

In the vicinity of Castleguard Mountain in the Rocky
Mountains very massive, resistant limestone and dolomite
formations are exposed as benchlands at altitudes of 1800-
2700 m asl and support highland ice caps and smaller glaciers
attaining thicknesses in excess of 280 m. Extensive bedrock
surfaces are freshly exposed by ice recession from Neoglacial
maximum positions. They display abundant evidence of two
distinct hydrological systems at the ice base i.e. an areal
regelation melt system and a channelled throughflow system
of glacier melt waters. Spatial and temporal variations of
the state of the basal melt system on both flat and inclined
bedrock surfaces are discussed.

Castleguard Cave is a relict groundwater conduit penetrating beneath the central mass of the Columbia Icefield.
Seepage waters collected in it permit analysis of basal
melt water types characteristic of the closed system condition prevailing at ice base. The Castleguard Big Springs
drain waters through inaccessible conduits beneath the
relict cave and appear to discharge much of the aggregate
melt of the central Icefield. The Springs hydrographs during
the melt season reveal features of the behaviour of the
throughflow drainage penetrating a central ice mass.